WITHDRAWN

The SUN GODDESS

Myth, Legend and History

This book is dedicated to: my husband
Simon, for his incredible patience and
refreshing lack of neuroses; Ron, Dakota and
the rest of the old group, who got me started;
and Steve, Ray and Sherri, for putting me
up (and putting up with me).
I never could have done it without them.

The SUN GODDESS

Myth, Legend and History

Sheena McGrath

BLANDFORD

A BLANDFORD BOOK

First published in the UK 1997 by Blandford

A Cassell Imprint

Cassell Plc, Wellington House,

125 Strand, London WC2R 0BB

Distributed in the United States by Sterling Publishing Co., Inc.,
387 Park Avenue South, New York, NY 10016-8810

**A Cataloguing-in-Publication Data entry for this title is available
from the British Library**

ISBN 0-7137-2662-8

Printed and bound in Great Britain by
Creative Print and Design (Wales), Ebbw Vale

Contents

Introduction

WHEN WE THINK OF THE SUN, most of us think of a male deity. The cover of a recent book, *The Ancient and Shining Ones* (Conway, 1993) is a good example. It shows a radiant god, with blond hair and a yellow mini-toga, holding a sunbeam in his hand. Modern pagan, mystical and Jungian imagery consistently portrays the sun as a male being. With such a load of predetermined imagery, it is not surprising that many are nonplussed by the idea of a female solar deity.

This book is about the woman in the sun, who was the man-in-the-moon's wife (notice that you never hear of her any more). To think of the sun as a woman, you have to reverse a whole set of ideas that mainstream western culture provides us with. The pattern goes something like this: masculine/feminine, bright/dark, day/night, active/passive, and so on. Anyone familiar with Lévi-Strauss's work will recognize the ideas.

My theory is that the Indo-Europeans, who were the ancestors of the Celts, Norse, Romans, Greeks and Hindus, believed in a sun goddess. Using comparative mythology, I tried to reconstruct the myths that surrounded this goddess, as well as the practices of her cult. This was an enjoyable experience, because the image of the Indo-Europeans is that of a people dominated by sky gods, with very few goddesses. To find out that the supposed sky and sun god was actually a goddess, and one with a rather interesting mythos, was a refreshing change. It wasn't patriarchy that changed the sun goddess to a god; it was poor scholarship.

One thing that most of us know about the Indo-Europeans is that they thought of fire and water as opposites. But, instead of the sort of Wiccan-style fire–male, water–female polarity, I found a fiery, active female and a passive, watery male. The fact of a god of the moon, connected to feminine things like menstruation and fertility, was a bit hard to take. However, he is only the stimulator, while the sun goddess actually experiences pregnancy or bleeding. This means that anyone who doesn't want to work with the moon god can simply relate to the sun. (An article called 'The path of the solar priestess' [Sunflower, 1990] is a useful guide in this.)

Anyway, I think it's time pagans and others explored some ideas that involve a change from the usual masculine–feminine round. Not every-one feels comfortable with the script that our society offers for gender roles, and I don't see why they shouldn't have some alternatives. In fact, it's always seemed rather odd to me that women who reject all 'manmade' culture are willing to define themselves according to a description of the feminine developed by men. Surely women can do better than that.

There are several reasons why people resist the idea of the sun goddess. The first is that the menstrual cycle is thought to coincide with the lunar cycle. The second is that the moon was female in the Greek myths, and this 'classical' mythology has become the pattern that others are judged against. Finally, the moon is seen as 'receptive', because it has no light of its own, but shines through reflection.

The moon connection is often defended on the basis that the lunar cycle is similar to the menstrual one, but in reality women's menstrual cycles are anywhere from 18 to 40 days long, and often do not coincide with the moon's phases. It has been suggested by romantic neo-primitivists that this is a modern disorder, and women once all menstruated together with the moon. It seems more likely that, in a culture where women were frequently pregnant or nursing, and often malnourished, it would be the absence rather than the presence of the period that would be the norm. This may be why they felt the need of a moon god who 'caused' menstruation and pregnancy by intercourse with mortal women.

The female sun is a goddess who 'bleeds' as well. During the three days when the moon is not seen, he is often together with his sister/spouse the sun, and like mortal women she menstruates after his visit. While this myth is a more unfamiliar one for most women, it shows that the moon-goddess myth of bleeding is not the only one. The identification of the sun and fire with menstrual blood in some mythologies (see especially page 108) bears out the idea that the sun goddess, who was a patron of women, bled just like they did.

The idea that the moon goddess is the norm, and the sun goddess the exception, is partly due to the way in which earlier writers did their research. When the Victorian folklorists were analysing myths, they frequently did so from the view that whatever was Greek was good. As a result, the moon and sun had to fit the mould of Helios and Selene, or Apollo and Artemis. It is common in early books on Norse myth to see a sort of apology for the 'reverse' gendering of the luminaries. The interest in solar mythology that was so fashionable then exacerbated this problem, because every hero was seen as a sun, and heroines or demi-goddesses were read as dawns or stars or the moon.

The moon goddess connection was defended by these writers on the basis that the moon was like the ideal Victorian woman, passive and receptive. However, this idea was being challenged by feminists even at the time it was being formulated. To say that women are 'naturally' receptive is to have a very functional view of women. Even this ideology's basis in sexual intercourse is questionable, according to Segal (1994). She points out that both partners in a sexual act are active and passive, and so the old idea that men 'take' women is just another sexist myth.

This book will look at femininity in the active, solar mode. The first part of the book presents various Indo-European cultures and their god-desses of the sun, and the second gives the reader some meditations and rituals to bring them into closer contact with the power of the female sun. Feel free to adapt any of these exercises, or research your own; I hope you find the sun goddess and her mythology as interesting as I do.

Throughout the text, an asterisk (*) before a word or phrase indicates that it is a reconstruction rather than a real word.

The Indo-Europeans

HE INDO-EUROPEANS are a coherent group, who probably came from a common homeland and spoke a common language or several dialects of one tongue; this allows for a tentative reconstruction of the sun goddess they would have worshipped. In this book I have tried to pull together all the evidence about a female sun in various cultures such as Greek, Celtic, Norse and Indian. Despite the many works on the mythology and religion of the Indo-Europeans, no one has ever really discussed the interesting problem of the sun deity. This is partially because explanations of all myths as natural phenomena are out of fashion, but also because Dumézil (see page 11) and his followers are unable to place the sun in their scheme. As Varenne (1991) says:

> [b]ut problems remain, starting with that of the sun god (and the correlated problem of the moon god): his preponderance in the Indo-European universe cannot be denied—Another problem involves female divinities.

The ideas that goddesses are scarce among the Indo-Europeans, and that the sun is male, are resolved if one sees the sun as a goddess. The main thrust of this book is that the 'problem' is a false one, since the sun goddess is an integral part of the pantheon, along with the sky god and earth goddess. This assumption is not odd, since many of the deities that scholars can trace back by both linguistics and mythology are indeed natural phenomena. Some of these are: dawn, day, sky, moon, sun, earth and wind. Just to give you an example of the method, this is how the sun god/goddess can be reconstructed (the female ones are underlined): Baltic <u>Saule</u>, German <u>Sól/Sunna</u>, English <u>Sun</u>, Slavic <u>Solntse</u>, Gaulish <u>Sul</u>, Roman Sol, Greek Helios, Iranian Hvare, Sanskrit Surya, which gives us a proposed original *<u>su/sawe</u> (Friedrich, 1978).

As well as the etymological fun, there are also the common characteristics that mark the sun deity. S/he usually drives a chariot, is either married to the moon or has him or her as a sibling, is all-seeing, and has a younger version of her/himself. The 'Overview' chapter (pages 145–9) discusses these common characteristics in more detail.

So who were these Indo-Europeans – people who apparently worshipped a sun goddess and took over so much of Eurasia? They apparently came out of a common homeland in waves of migrations, settling all across Eurasia. They are called Indo-Europeans because they eventually covered territory from Ireland and Scandinavia to India. Four of the largest language groups today descend from the once-common language scholars call Proto-Indo-European: Germanic, Romance, Slavic and Indic. Other languages related to these four include Baltic, Greek, Latin, Persian, Armenian and Celtic. Only isolated pockets of people speak the other languages (Ossetic, Albanian) or else the languages are extinct (Tocharian, Anatolian, Illyrian etc.).

Homeland

Where the Indo-Europeans came from remains a mystery, although there is no shortage of theories. Their homeland has been placed everywhere from Germany to India, on various grounds. These days the steppes between the Vogul river and Altic mountains are a favoured site. Their living area had the Dnieper and Volga rivers as approximate boundaries, as well as the Black Sea in the south. The invention of wheeled vehicles, which is believed to have happened no earlier than 3300–3100 BCE (Before the Common Era), helps date their dispersal from this area (Anthony, 1991). This, combined with linguistic evidence for Proto-Indo-European terms for wheeled vehicles, suggests that they were still together when chariots became common. With this new technology they migrated out of the steppes and across Europe and Asia. The emergence of Anatolian, Indo-Aryan and Greek as distinctive language groups by 1600 BCE indicates that the original group was well separated before 2000 BCE, as these languages must have had time to develop (Anthony, 1991).

Language and civilization

From reconstructions of their language, we know something of the original Proto-Indo-European civilization. They knew three seasons – winter, spring and summer – and had words for hot and cold. Plains and mountains surrounded them. They had a word for sea, but it seems to have been used for swamps and lakes. As for trees, they had words for birch, elm, ash, oak, willow and perhaps yew and pine. They buried their dead, as opposed to burning or exposing them. They seem to have had access to copper, although not bronze, and the dating of the Proto-Indo-Europeans means they didn't have iron. They had whetstones, and ground their grain. They farmed and raised animals (sheep, goats, pigs), and had a settled lifestyle. Wheeled vehicles and horses were known to them, and they used yoked animals to plough or for transport. Dogs had been domesticated and were common.

The discovery of the Indo-European language began when scholars gained access to the sacred texts of Iran and India; with the work on other languages going ahead simultaneously, they could compare the old forms of each language. Soon similarities revealed themselves. Words for plants and animals, various religious and social terms, words for military and agricultural pursuits could be traced back to a common origin.

For a while the *centum/sentum* language division was the basis of the family tree of Indo-European peoples. Originally, the division explained the difference between eastern and western languages. (*Centum* was the Latin word for a hundred, and *sentum* the Old Iranian form.) The languages that used the hard consonant 'c' were western ones like Celtic and Germanic, while the eastern languages such as Sanskrit used the softer 's' sound to begin words. This observation led to the belief that there was a discernible split between the eastern and western Indo-European languages. The discovery that the Hittites, occupying what is now Turkey, used a *centum* language disrupted the east–west division. Tocharian, a language spoken in the Chinese Turkestan region, was a *centum* language as well, and that made the division less useful in drawing up family trees for the various languages (Renfrew, 1987). Since then a variety of trees and models have been created to explain the diffusion of the Indo-European languages, but no one model has become accepted.

Comparative Mythology

The discovery that the Indo-Europeans were a distinct linguistic group led to a desire to see if they corresponded in other ways. The work of Georges Dumézil in comparative mythology renewed interest in the various deities and myths of the Indo-Europeans. Earlier scholars such as Max Müller relied on solar myths to the point where all heroes and gods were seen as sun deities, and this led to their downfall. The new comparativists avoided such sweeping theories in favour of a more sociological approach, which saw deities as performing various functions.

One productive area of comparative study was ritual, which filled in holes where myths had been lost to time. The Iranian Zoroastrians and the Hindus of India still preserve some of the ceremonies we would associate with the Indo-Europeans. Elements of their ceremonies – the domestic sacrifice to the fire, and the sacraments of marriage, birth and death – are four thousand years old. Christianity ended these practices in the west, while Islam did the same in parts of the east. However, the sacred texts and accounts by missionaries or historians can help to fill the gaps.

The presence of a priestly class among many of the Indo-Europeans (druids, brahmins) indicates that they took religion seriously. Sacrifice was an important part of that religion, and a class of priests tended to the propitiation of the gods. The priest invoked the deity to be honoured, asked for any favours that he wanted, and praised the deity. Then the food, vegetable or animal, was given to the deity. The food was either pre-cooked or burnt raw on the altar. The priest and worshippers actually ate most of the food, after giving some fat to the fire (Varenne, 1991). Giving a share of one's wealth to the gods was another kind of sacrifice. The Celtic habit of throwing gold in springs and lakes was of this kind.

Human sacrifice was not common among the Indo-European peoples, although they did practise it (Mallory, 1992). One common motif was the threefold death, where the victim was killed in a way that involved three different deaths. These often correspond to the three functions: king/magician; warrior; producer. The horse sacrifice was the major ritu-al, which mirrors its importance to society. (People and deities often had names related to words for horses.) The most elaborate horse ritual was the Indic *asvamedha*, which involved letting a horse run loose for a year with 400 warriors following it to keep it from mating or being interfered with. The Romans also had a sacrifice ceremony, called the E*quus*, and the Irish king of Ulster had to 'mate' with a horse and then eat it after it was boiled.

Another important ritual was the offering or drinking of *soma*. It was strictly limited to certain classes, and all aspects of it were hedged round by ritual. The making of the 'juice' was a sacred act. The *soma* was offered to the gods by burning it on an altar, or else drunk by the worshippers. Drinking the *soma* was an initiation ritual for young warriors, who then rampaged in bands through their cities or towns. It gave them a feeling of invincibility, which suggests that the actual plant was the hallucino-genic mushroom *Amanita muscaria*. Since it grows in the northern tem-perate zone, alcohol replaced it in the south, and later in the north as well. (Perhaps drug-induced ecstasy had become less popular.) Drinking festi-vals retained their religious nature for many of the northern peoples until Christianity ended them (Varenne, 1991).

Domestic rituals were the most important to the majority of people. They mainly consisted of worshipping the fire god/goddess each morn-ing by renewing the family hearth fire. One of the main things about the Indo-Europeans which impressed outside observers was their habit of guarding the fire. In India, Greece and Rome the domestic hearths were circular, and so were the main temples of the Roman hearth goddess Vesta and her Grecian counterpart Hestia. The Lithuanians kept sacred fires on mountain tops, and we know that the Germans and Celts wor-shipped fire.

Religious belief

The Indo-Europeans seem to share a threefold division of the cosmos, with the heavens above, earth in the middle and another world (the underworld) below. They believed in an afterlife, which took place not in a gloomy setting but in one where people feasted and were joyful. One journeyed from the dead body into another world, sometimes being tested along the way. If the soul passed, it went to Valhalla or the Elysian Fields, or the Iranian *para-daeza*. Burial rituals were important to the soul's safe conduct, as anyone who has read *Antigone* knows.

The sky was the most important of the three worlds, with the earth and underworld taking second place. The supreme sky gods always rule, never a god of earth. The sky gods as a group were called 'celestials' or 'shining ones', with names related to that of the sky-god root *dyew*. Among the sky gods we find the calm, law-giving god such as Mitra or Tyr, and the dark vengeful one such as Varuna or Odin, who punishes. To represent the warrior class, a god such as Thor or Mars appears among the celestials. The 'common people' have a representative in heaven too, although these often have to fight or otherwise win their way in (Asvins, Vanir).

Indo-European mythology has a structure that reflects the stratified society that created it. There is a basic division between sky and earth, and another one into classes of deities. This second division is a social one, among rulers and priests, warriors, and the farmers and artisans. This ideology was the basis for societies from Vedic India to Celtic Ireland, and once understood accounts for a great deal that would otherwise be obscure in their myths and customs. The goddesses of the Indo-Europeans are generally less prominent than the gods. However, in each pantheon there is at least one goddess who is 'transfunctional'; that is, she has a little of each function.

	India	Ireland	Iceland	Italy
First	Mitra	Nuada	Tyr	Jupiter
	Varuna	Lugh	Odin	Dius Fidus
Second	Indra	Ogma	Thor	Mars
Third	Asvins	Bres	Freyr	Quirinus
Goddess	Sarasvati	Macha	Freya	Juno

The gods of the first class (priests and kings) were the ruler gods. They are the day-sky god or his later replacement (such as Mitra instead of Dyaus) who is just and merciful, and his dark companion who punishes those who break oaths or do evil. While the light god protects oaths and the bonds of loyalty between people, the dark god is the enforcer of those oaths and bonds. The dark god is the ruler of magic, which makes him a little bit sinister, while the light god is more benevolent.

The warriors are the second type of gods. Thor, Mars and Indra are examples of this type. These gods reflect the values of the armies and fighters of old. When working for the social good, they defend the realm and aid the helpless. When they stray from this role they bring disaster, as when Thor slew the giant who built Asgard's walls and thus broke an oath. Indra's three 'sins' are another example. Unlike the first group, independence and group solidarity were the warrior values.

The gods of farmers and artisans are often in conflict with the first two groups. This may reflect a historic hostility between the classes. These gods ensure fertility, so even the tensions between them and the other functions couldn't keep them out of the pantheon. Often these gods are twins connected with a strong female figure (the Asvins and Sarasvati or the Dioscouroi and Helen). Another type is the phallic god, like Freyr and the Dagda, who is associated with sexuality and fertility.

As mentioned, the goddesses of the Indo-Europeans are not as well known as the gods. There are, however, many powerful goddesses such as Freya and Anahita among them. More broadly, there are several groups of goddesses who have important functions. Since society is split in three, the transfunctional goddess is most important. She has power in all parts of society. Anahita, whose titles were 'Moist, Heroic, Immaculate' is one such goddess. Her names and functions relate her to all three groups. Athena, with her owl of wisdom, spear and olive branch, is another such goddess. The tripartite goddess was similar, but threefold in appearance, instead of being one uniting figure. (The three Machas, who marry into the three classes, are typical.)

Other goddess types were the dawn goddess, sun maiden, earth goddess, hearth goddess and river goddess (Dexter-Robbins, 1980). The dawn goddess was associated with the red of morning, like Eos, Ushas and Œstre, and often had an erotic tinge. The sun maiden, such as Helen, Suryaa and Saules meita, was associated with twin gods of the third function, and the chapter 'Mazes' (pages 112–18) discusses them more fully. The earth goddess is a well-known type, although from the reconstructed *dhghom we only get Semele, Zemnya and Mati Syra Zemlja. The river goddess, from *don-u, is quite common, and gave her name to the Don, Dnieper and Dniester, as well as groups, such as the Tuatha de Danann and the Danaïds, and the goddesses Danu and Danaë. The hearth goddesses Hestia and Vesta have no linguistic parallels, but there are many other goddesses of fire among the Indo-Europeans.

Besides these goddesses, I am setting out to prove the existence of another goddess, a sun goddess. While it is true that not all Indo-European civilizations had a female sun, almost all of them can be shown to have had a goddess who filled that role, even if she was superseded by a god. She and the other deities who make up the actors in her cult are the focus of this book.

The Germans: Sól

THE MYTH ABOUT THE NORTHERN PEOPLE is that they were all ferocious Vikings. The truth, however, is that most of the Norse weren't Vikings, but farmers and craftspeople who lived relatively peaceful lives. They lived in a fairly civilized, stratified society that was one of the models for the feudal arrangements of the Middle Ages. Many of them were sailors, and their mythology shows their reliance on the sea. They lived in Scandinavia, which comprises Sweden, Norway and Denmark.

The people who later became the Germans share much of this mythology, since it was they who settled in Scandinavia and Iceland. The Germans lived between the Rhine and the Vistula rivers and eventually spread across the land to form the basis for modern Germany. Some of these German tribes later went to England, taking Woden/Odin and his companion gods with them.

Sturluson's *Edda* (1987) (sometimes called the *Prose* or *Younger Edda* to distinguish it from the *Poetic* or *Elder Edda* he uses as source material) synthesizes earlier poets into a coherent account of Norse poetry and myth. It is from the two *Eddas* that we have the story of the world's origin. In the beginning was the fire in the south, and the ice in the north. In the gap between them was the giant Ymir formed. Odin and his two brothers Villi and Vé were his sons, and they killed him, and made the nine worlds from his body. These are in three levels: gods on top, humans in the middle and the underworld below. The world of the sky gods, Asgard, is the topmost world. The great ash tree Yggdrasill is the *axis mundi*, the central pole that holds all the worlds together.

The sun and moon existed then, as sparks that flew out of Muspell (the world of fire), but had no path across the sky (Sturluson, 1987):

> *The sun did not know where her dwelling was. The moon did not know what power he had. The stars did not know where their places were.*

Odin and his brothers then put the sun and moon on their courses, so that they could travel the sky, and the sun could fertilize the earth with her rays. They did this by setting the sparks on courses, apparently in chariots, with two deities as drivers. One of Sturluson's older sources, *The Elder Edda* (Bray, 1908), states:

Sun shone from the south on the world's bare stones —
then was Earth o'ergrown with herb of green
Sun, Moon's companion, out of the south
her right hand flung round the rim of heaven.

Sól: Driver of the sun's chariot

The creation myth says that a woman named Sól, or 'Sun', drove the chariot of the sun through the sky. Her brother Mani drove the chariot of the moon. They did this because their father (a giant) named them after the sun and moon because of their beauty. This angered the gods, who put them to driving the chariots of the sparks of light to punish the giant for his presumption. Their father's name, Mundilfare, is sometimes translated as 'spinner of the world' (McCrickard, 1987), which may suggest an earlier, pre-Odinic origin for the sun and moon myth. Davidson (1969) connects this to a memorial stone found in Gotland, which shows a giant whirling disc, with two smaller discs beneath it. This, she says, represents Mundilfare and his world-mill. The world-tree is underneath the discs, and below that a serpent and then a boat. The boat is probably the ship the sun sails in at night. The two smaller discs are the courses of the sun and moon through the sky.

Every morning the sun rises from her home in the heavens and rides through the sky in her chariot pulled by two horses, Aarvak and Alsvidir ('Early-awake' and 'All-swift'). Attached to her chariot is a cooling bellows under the horses' withers to protect them from the heat, and the sun herself carries a shield called Svalin ('the Cooler') to keep from burning the earth. In the evening she returns to her palace in Hel, or the underworld, where she sleeps on a bed of gold. As the *Edda* (Sturluson, 1987) says:

God-blithe bedfellow of Glen steps to her divine sanctuary with brightness; then descends the good light of grey-clad moon.

(Glen is the sun's husband.) She then journeys through the underworld to arise from the gates in a mountain wall in the east. The crowing of Goldcomb greets her as she rises. (Goldcomb is the cockerel of the morning, who sits at the top of the world-tree, and wakes the hosts of warriors in Odin's halls.)

There are various titles of this goddess, including Alfrodull or 'Elf-beam' as the elves call her, or Glory-of-elves or She-who-shines-on-the-elves. (It is sometimes suggested that these titles mean the light elves were sun-worshippers [Davidson, 1987]). The dwarves and trolls know her as Dvalin's Doom, because she turns them to stone (Crossley-Holland,

1993). Other names for her are Everglow, Fagrahvel ('Fair Wheel') and All-shine. She is described as blithe, gracious, sweet, fair-faced and the bright maid of heaven.

Sturluson (1987) says that she is counted among the sky goddesses, who dwell in Asgard. (Germanic mythology distinguishes between the sky deities, called Ases, who live in Asgard, and the earth deities or Vanir, who have their own realm, Vanaheim.) He also quotes some more involved poetic kennings for the sun – 'fire of sky and air', and 'high wandering flame'. Conversely, fire is the 'sun of houses'. Poets also called the sun day-star, disc, lightning, light-bringer, sprinkler, sight, coverer, toy, ever-glow, all-bright seen, grace-shine, Dvalin's toy, elf-disc, doubt-disc and ruddy. The sun goddess was invoked for healing, even after the arrival of Christianity. A pine-wood stave (c. 1300) has been found with the following carved on it in runes: 'I pray, guard Earth and Heaven above; Sól and St Mary; and Himself the Lord God; that he grant me the hands to make whole, and words of remedy, to heal the Trembler, when treatment is necessary . . .' (Pennick, 1992). The Trembler is believed to have been malaria.

According to Sturluson (1987), Sól is married to Glen or Glaur, a rather mysterious character of whom all that is known is that his name means 'glow'. Rydberg (1889) says that she is married to Dag, the day god, by whom she has her daughter, a pattern which will be repeated with other sun goddesses. The German goddess Sunna is married to the moon, her brother. Glen could be either one of these, although he could also be a personification of the sun's rays or light.

Among her cult objects is the disc or wheel, and it is believed that the bronze chariot that archaeologists found in Iceland is a symbol of her. It is mounted on six wheels, carrying a disc standing on its edge and drawn by a bronze horse. Oddly, the horse stands on the first four wheels, per-haps to symbolize its swiftness, or maybe it was rolled as part of some ceremony (Davidson and Gelling, 1969). The disc was found often in Bronze Age artefacts, along with horses. Sometimes it is presented as if for adoration, held up by tiny people, or shown with hands and feet (Davidson, 1964). Green (1991) suggests that the little chariot was the focus for rites invoking the sun. Part of its cult significance lies in its dual aspect: it is gilded on one side and plain bronze on the other, which implies a day-side and a night-side. She suggests that worshippers would gather at noon to watch the chariot imitate the sun at its zenith travel-ling through the sky. The same action would be repeated at sunset with the plain face of the sun-disc facing the worshippers.

The sun's brother Mani also rides in a chariot across the sky, pulled by a horse called Alsvidir ('All-swift'). He needs no shield because of the coolness of the moon's light. (The Germans believed the moon was cold, in contrast to the sun, since it did not warm when it shone.) Two children called Hiuki and Bil accompanied him in his travels, a boy and girl he snatched from earth because their father forced them to carry water after dark. (This seems to be a cautionary tale.) They became, respectively, the waning and waxing moon, because both are smaller than the full moon.

When crime is rampant, and the end of the world approaching, Mani and Sól will grow pale, smile no more, and drive on trembling. The wolves who pursue them smile, but the gods will become fearful as the long winter, and their destruction, approaches. Then will come three winters with no summer in between when even the sun's light will not warm the earth. Great wickedness and misery will accompany this darkness. After this Ragnarok begins, and a giant wolf called Skoll ('Adherer') will finally catch the sun and devour it. Another called Hati ('Hater') will eat the moon. (The Swedes still call a perihelion a 'sun-wolf' [Grimm, 1880].) Then everything will be destroyed, including the gods. However, several of the sons and daughters of major gods will survive, including the daughter of the sun, who is born before the wolf swallows her mother. This girl, called Svanhild Gold-feather, will replace her mother, driving a new sun over a new and perfected world.

Che sun's daughter

The daughter of the sun is mainly famous from the verse of the *Gylfaginning* (Sturluson, 1987):

> *A daughter shall Alfrodul bear before Fenrir catches her. She shall ride when the powers die, the maiden, her mother's road.*

The sense of this verse is ambiguous. It sounds as if the sun might have the child just before the wolf eats her. This surely not be the case, since the child could hardly survive. Also, Baldr, Hödr and the rest of the survivors of the end of the world are all adults when the doom of the gods comes, so she should be also.

Another possible mention of the sun maiden is in the second Meresburg formula. It speaks of *Sinthgunt Sunna era suister*: 'Sunna and her sister Sindgunt'. Sindgunt ('companion') may very well be the sun maiden. Many Slavic folksongs also state that the sun and dawn are sisters, so there was probably a change over time from the original pattern (Grimm, 1880). Some think that she is the same person as Nanna Sintgunt, Mani's daughter. An alternative meaning of her name is 'the one moving into battle' (a planet) or 'heavenly body, star', so she may be the planet Venus, which accompanies the sun at dawn and sunset (Simek, 1993).

Her name is an interesting point in itself. She also appears in several genealogies under the names Sinthgunt, Svanfeather, Svanhild Gullfiödr (Gold-feather) and Hiltigunt. At least one saga states that she was the sun's daughter and names her various husbands (Rydberg, 1889). (The heroine Svanhild Gullfiödr is the daughter of Sól and the day god Dag, in one version.) There is also a suggestion that she may be a swan maiden, as one of her guises is a maiden named Swana, 'swan', who is a typical sun figure (Ward, 1968).

At any rate, the sun's daughter takes on many of her mother's characteristics. In one saga (Hollander, 1990), Gudrun, who replaces the sun as Svanhild's mother in later times, describes Svanhild as being:

of hue whiter   my walls within,
than bright sunbeams   were Svanhild's brows.

The Short Lay of Sigurth (Hollander, 1990) uses the same imagery to describe Svanhild:

Is a maid child born —   her mother she [Gudrun]
of hue whiter   than the very heavens
than the sun even,   Svanhild hight.

Even after she loses the divine parentage, she still retains her sunlike character.

A further survival in folklore are the maze-games in Germany and Scandinavia which feature a sun woman, and are usually described as remnants of Sól's worship. Comparison with Baltic, Vedic and Greek mythology suggests that it is the maiden who is rescued by the men who run the maze, so that it would seem it is Svanhild who is the focus here (see pages 112–18).

The sun and the elves

There is an interesting relationship between the sun and the elves. Her light killed the dark elves or dwarves, which is why she is called 'Dvalin's doom'. Dvalin was a dwarf who wished to marry Thor's daughter, so the god tricked him into staying up all night. The sunlight of dawn turned him to stone, so that Thor didn't have to give his daughter to a dwarf. The title Alfrodull suggests that the light elves get along better with the sun, and it is they who call the sun 'Fair Wheel' (Hollander, 1990).

The light elves are invited to Asgard to feast with the gods, and are sometimes mentioned along with the gods in ways that suggest that the two had an enduring relationship. Their women are supposed to be the most beautiful, and the Old English word ælfsciene ('elf-shining') was supposed to indicate this beauty. They lived in Alfheim, with the god Freyr as their ruler. He was the god of fertility, and had power over the barrows where the elves lived. There are stories of sacrifices offered to the elves at a barrow (MacCulloch, 1993).

The light elves were also worshipped in the way of fairy lore everywhere. In pagan times there was the Alfblot, or sacrifice to the elves, which was usually a small animal or a dish of milk and honey. People carved the elves into their doorposts, just as they did with some of the deities. In later folklore the elves became *Weiss Frauen* ('White Women'), beautiful blonde women in white gowns whom travellers met in the mountains during Easter season, and whose gifts should be kept because they would turn into gold when you reached home (McCrickard, 1990). They appear around Easter as flashes of white or women dressed in white. This seems to be a memory of the older sun cult.

Two of the dwarves, beings usually thought of as hostile to the gods, are also connected to the sun. Delling's 'door' is a kenning for dawn, and may be the same door as the one Sól rides through in the morning. His complement, Billing, guards the door of twilight, the west door in the mountains that the sun and moon ride through (Rydberg, 1889).

The sun goddess in the underworld

The sun visits the underworld every night in the *Edda*. Her castle is there. One interesting aspect of the sun's journey through the underworld is that the aspect of Hel seems to have taken on some of her radiance. Many descriptions of the realm of the death goddess Hel emphasize the light that permeates the place.

Since the sun seems to dip below the horizon and then disappear for part of the winter, the underworld may be lit by her during the dark season. Of course, in the traditions which state that the sun dies and is reborn, or that she is captive, it makes perfect sense that she is in the underworld. In the *Forspjallsljod* the gods send messengers to the underworld during a terrible winter (the Fimbulvinter, maybe?) to address Gjöll's Sunna. This character seems to be an underworld sun, perhaps the sun in winter, and Gjöll ('Echoing') is the river that runs through the underworld. They ask her about the mysteries of creation, but all she does is weep, which strengthens the suggestion that this is the doom of the gods (Rydberg, 1889).

The sun goddess in Germany

Since the Germans colonized Scandinavia, it is not surprising that the myths of the Teutonic tribes are very similar to those of the Norse. There are some variations, but the sun–moon myth is much the same.

The German sun goddess is called Sunna, and she is very similar to the Norse Sól. One interesting difference is that she sits down on a golden throne in the evening, which is the origin of the 'sun-set'. In the morning she just stands up again (McCrickard, 1990). Unlike in the Norse myths, there is no confusion as to whether it is she or a spark that is bright. Both the Swedish and German sun goddesses are spinsters. The sun was said to spin her sunbeams in the hour before sunrise, and a Hessian game commemorates this. It is a labyrinth hopscotch, with an accompanying chant:

Where does Auntie Rosie live?
– Up there, above.
What is she doing?
– Spinning silk.
How bright?
– As bright as her own hair.

In some versions the woman is identified as Frau Sonne (Wilkins, 1969). In Norway the sun is also a spinner, for flax and spinning wheels were offered to the sun on altars (by the Lapps, who probably took it from the Scandinavians [Holmberg, 1925]). This belief also operated as a taboo at Yule; no spinning, churning or turning of any kind, even of cartwheels, was allowed, as the sun was at a standstill (Gitlin-Emmer, 1993).

From Bavaria comes an interesting solar myth: the sun and moon were married, and she found him a disappointing husband. She was passionate but he preferred to sleep, so she bet him that whoever rose first in the morning would be able to shine by day. This ploy failed and the early-rising sun shines in the day, and the moon at night (Olcott, 1914). The basic incompatibility of the sun and moon is the basis of several European myths, and may have something to do with the Teutonic dichotomy of fire and ice, represented by the rival spouses, one hot and one cool. Another aspect of this dichotomy is the saying, 'east for sol, west for mane', which divides the heavens between them (Grimm, 1880).

The moon was also responsible for the kidnapping of a mortal girl, which roused the sun's jealousy, so she stole the girl's boyfriend. When the couple met again, they grieved at being so far apart, and the moon learned that the girl did not really love him. He wept from disappointment, his tears becoming the shooting stars (Olcott, 1914). The abductor moon who seduces mortal women and goddesses is a recurring theme, with the Baltic and Slavic moon gods seducing the sun's daughter.

Another folktale called 'The Forest Bride' describes the sun and moon. The sun mother lives in the forest in a house of glass, with a ruddy face too bright to look at, dressed in purple silk that gets darker towards the bottom, and black shoes. She sits spinning when the hero finds her. She sends him on to the moon, who is an old man in a similar glass house, with many silvery flies around him. He has silver-white hair and beard, a grey coat with silver buttons, and silver buckles on his grey shoes. His house is very cold (Vernaleken, 1889).

The sun goddess had strained relations with another god, the thunder and rain god. This is another Indo-European theme that runs throughout this book. An ancient rain-charm from northern Germany (Thorpe, 1832) hints at this tension:

> Patter, rain, patter!
> The king is gone to the bush
> Let the rain pass over,
> Let the sun come again.
> Dear sun come again
> With thy golden plumage
> With thy golden beams
> Illuminate us altogether.

The king is presumably the thunder god, who will be banished by the sun. This charm is very similar to some *dainas* sung by the Balts that oppose Saule and Perkunas.

According to Freya Aswynn, in Holland there was an ancient tradition of three main goddesses: Anbet as the earth, Wilbert as the moon and Barbet as the sun. This goddess probably laid the ground for the popularity of St Barbara in Christian times (Aswynn, 1990). (See also page 83.) This may explain why Slavic art often depicts St Barbara and St Catherine with solar haloes, which are usually reserved for important male saints (Singh, 1993). St Catherine took on solar symbolism as well; her feast on 25 November involved rolling burning wheels down hills, and in England it was a feast of spinning-girls. She was associated with lighthouses and beacons, and many of her churches were on hills. They tended to be lighthouses or overlook highways. Her symbol was the fiery wheel (Hole, 1965).

The sun goddess in England

The sun goddess continued into Old English tradition, courtesy of the invading Angles and Saxons. She rose in the east on her chariot, turning frost giants to stone, then drove across the sky with the wolf behind her. The wolf then swallowed her in the evening, and Dark drove his chariot across the sky, until Sun escaped. Then she and Day could ride across the sky again (Linsell, 1992). (Nott and Dag ['Night' and 'Day'] were sometimes thought of as a woman and her son who rode across the sky along with the luminaries, as the Germans had noticed that light and the appearance of the sun and moon didn't necessarily coincide.)

The Anglo-Saxons called her Sunna, like her German counterpart, and East Anglians worshipped her under the name Phoebe (Pennick, 1989). The word for 'sun' in Old English is also feminine: *sunne*. What forms her worship took is difficult to say, but King Canute forbade worship of the sun and moon. This suggests that there was some general worship of these luminaries. Traditionally, pointing at the sun or throwing sweepings towards it was insulting to the goddess, and thus unlucky. It was also unlucky to see the new moon through glass, presumably for the same reason.

More positive evidence of worship includes the charm for fertility of crops, sometimes called the *Æcerbot*, which mentions the sun among the deities who will make the crops grow. The second month in the Anglo-Saxon year was *Sólmonath*, or 'Sun month'. Cakes were made and offered in some way, although our source, the Venerable Bede, is silent on that point. Branston (1993) thinks that they may have been ploughed into the fields, as a way of transferring the power of the renewed sun into the soil. There may also have been a feast on the day of the sun, Sunday. In Old High German and Anglo-Saxon there are words for the eve of Sunday, incorporating the name Sunna, which suggests that her day was especially significant (Hastings, 1980). Since there is a tendency in both Germanic and Celtic tradition to count from the eve of a festival, it is logical that there should be a word for that occasion.

Freya: the mistress

Apart from Sól, there are some indications that other goddesses may have been seen as the sun in the past. Freya usually appeared among the earth gods (Vanir), but she did have some intriguing solar characteristics. She was principally a love and fertility goddess, who was known for her promiscuity and who favoured her brother Freyr as her partner.

Her strong connection to solar symbols such as gold and amber is one clue. A kenning for gold was 'Freya's tears', because she wept tears that turned to gold on the land and amber on the sea. Gold and amber are both connected with the sun in Indo-European tradition, along with quartz. The Norse also connected gold and Sól, so presumably they intended to draw a comparison between the two goddesses. This survived in folklore in a Swedish song called *Freya den väna solen* – 'Freya the beautiful sun' (Grimm, 1880). The name Freya simply meant 'lady', or 'mistress', and it has been suggested that this was just a title, not a name.

One instance of her weeping was when she lost her husband Od. She wandered all over searching for him, going under various names and weeping copiously. They were finally reunited when she went south and found him among the myrtle trees. *The Longbeards' Saga* (Guerber, 1994) recorded that when she returned north spring followed in her wake, and women began to long for their husbands' return. This seems like a typical sun-maiden myth, Freya bringing spring and fertility in her wake as she returns to the cold north.

Connected to this myth is the story of Freya's magical necklace, Brisingamen. The name may come from the Old Norse *brisingr*, fire. It was a circle of gold that she obtained by sleeping with the four dwarves who made it, one each night until they finished it. (Another name for it, 'wave-stone', suggests that it may be made of or contain amber [Gundarsson, 1993]. This story might also be part of her other myth of wandering, and suggests some sort of seasonal myth involving Freya's travels and progress through the stations of the year, since Gitlin-Emmer (1993) connects those four dwarves with the four who hold up the four corners of the earth, which would correspond to her search in all directions for her husband, and the travels of the sun over the sky.

Another association of Freya with the sun was her title of Syr ('Sow'), which persists to this day in Germany in the expression 'The golden sow is shining', as a way of saying that it's sunny (Gundarsson, 1993). The *Eddas* (Hollander, 1990) say that she rode a boar called Hildisvíni ('Battle-swine'), whom she described in one poem:

> *my boar gleameth,   golden-bristled,*
> *Hildisvíni,   by smiths twain fashioned*
> *of dwarfish kin   Dáin and Nabbi.*

In a manuscript of the *Hervarar Saga* it says that a king sacrificed a boar to Freya at Yule because he worshipped her especially (Gundarsson, 1993). A late memory of this occurs in the almond cakes showing a sow with piglets which the Swedish serve at Yule (Gitlin-Emmer, 1993). (It may be that her other boar was her husband, and her riding of him a fertility ritual of some sort. Worship of the Vanir did involve practices of a sexual nature [Davidson, 1964]). Among the petroglyphs of Scandinavia is a picture of a sword pointing to a pig's backside. Davidson and Gelling (1969) suggest that this represents the cult of Freyr, but I think that it represents the mating of sun goddess and a sword-wielding deity. The animal is interpreted as a boar by Davidson and Gelling, but it could just as easily be Freya's sow. Both are sun symbols, and there is nothing about the image to suggest its gender.

By substituting the part for the whole, folklore preserved some of Freya's solar and fertile nature in cat symbolism. (Two cats drew her chariot as she travelled about.) One instance is a Danish festival involving breaking a barrel decorated with flowers, called 'knocking the cat out of the barrel'. This takes place on the Monday before Ash Wednesday, and is probably connected to the sun's return. Another instance is the cakes handed out on St Lucia's day, which are sometimes called 'Lucy-cats' (*Lussekatten*) or 'Golden Carriages' (Gitlin-Emmer, 1993). The timing of these festivals is important, because both are celebrations of returning light. The game 'cat's cradle' was a ritual to keep the sun in the sky in northern countries, and it may well represent a memory of when Freya was the sun.

Lucia: the goddess of returning light

An interesting offshoot of the worship of the sun goddess is the modern festival of St Lucia. She was originally an Italian saint who was known for having plucked her eyes out when a pagan suitor admired them, and who appears holding a plate with two eyes on it in pictures and statues. Sometimes she holds a lamp or burning horn as a pun on her name, which means 'light'. It may be that she is an old goddess in imported disguise, but at any rate the popularity of the festival in the north suggests a pagan background.

It is a Swedish festival, held on 13 December, called 'Little Yule'. In preparation for the festival, everyone cleans the house, finishes the threshing, spinning and weaving, and makes candles. Much baking is done, as this event is seen as the beginning of the Yule celebrations. On the day, the youngest daughter of the house gets up before dawn, puts on a white dress and crown of nine candles, and wakes the family with coffee and *Lussekatter* (cakes baked in the form of sun-wheels seasoned with cardamom or saffron). On this day, despite the early morning, all the lights of the house are on, and all the candles burn.

The girl is called the *Lussibruden* ('Lucia bride' or 'queen'), and serves as the representative of the goddess, bringing the blessings of light and food. Since the girl represented the reborn sun, it was always the youngest daughter who performed the ritual. In some places a girl would dress in a white dress with a red sash, and the crown of candles, and ride a horse around town. She was accompanied by 'star boys'. Mummers dressed as demons and trolls followed her (monsters whose winter licence ended with the sun's return), and everyone celebrated the return of the sun, singing songs (Cooper, 1979) like:

> Now St Lucia's day is come
> Darkness cannot linger
> Cold, soon banished by the Sun,
> Lifts his icy finger.

The Lucia queen had to visit every home in the area with gifts of coffee and food, as well as the stables and cow byres. It was extremely unlucky if the procession did not stop at your door (Hole, 1965). In the Tyrol she brought presents to girls, as St Nicholas did for boys (Miles, 1912).

One myth of Lucia has it that she comes at dawn across the iced-over lakes crowned with light, bringing food to the poor. (In this she resembles the Russian Kolyada.) A similar figure in Alsace was the 'Christchild', represented by a girl. Her face was floured, and a gold paper crown placed on her head. With a silver bell in one hand and a basket of sweetmeats in the other, she went around the community giving treats and restraining her companion, a sort of wild man dressed in bearskin (Miles, 1912). However, some Swedes called Lucia a goblin and said she led the Wild Hunt, which seems more appropriate to the winter hag, Holle or Skadi. This seems to reflect an ambivalence about this chancy time of the year, and anyone connected to it. It may also reflect a pattern that recurs with the Celtic goddess Brigit – the transformation of the hag into the light-bearing goddess of spring.

In fact, a whole set of seasonal rituals revolves around the overcoming of the winter hag by the returning sun. The hag is first propitiated, as with Mother Holle to whom the Germans offered braided bread at Christmas. In Bavaria, Perchta and her children are said to be at large through the twelve days of Christmas. However, on 6 January everyone dons masks and drives them away with whips. In other places the hag is offered bread around the spring equinox, when the days and nights are equal in length and people can feel confident that the sun is back. Germans burned effigies of the winter witch on Shrove Tuesday, or at midsummer eve. Then they sang songs of the conquest of darkness and the triumph of Dame Sun (Gitlin-Emmer, 1993).

Œstre: goddess of the spring sun

The Saxon goddess Œstre, who gave the Easter festival its name, may be another sun maiden. She represents the return of spring and fertility, and for this reason some see her as a version of Sól's daughter. Part of the reason she may be a solar deity is that her name is similar to that of the Baltic Auszrine, daughter of the sun, and many other sun maidens and dawn goddesses. If so, she may be a German counterpart to Svanhild Gold-feather and other versions of the sun's daughter.

Her festival was often celebrated at the beginning of the year, in the spring (Hastings, 1980). This is because a connection was made between the dawn of the day and the start of the year, which was expressed in the goddess of new beginnings. Her festival was carried to England and became the Christian Easter there. (An interesting aside to this is that the English year once began on 25 March.) This adds to the idea that she is the sun maiden, since the rescue of the maiden often occurred in March (Ward, 1968). Her name is related to the word east, and on the spring equinox the sun rises due east (Forlong, 1906).

Another word derived from Œstre's name is oestrus, which is the technical term for 'heat' in animals. Obviously her festival celebrates the spring sexual receptivity in animals, which helps repopulate animal stocks after deaths in the winter and the slaughtering in autumn. In earlier times her festival was marked at the spring equinox by decorating stone altars with flowers and dancing around them, as well as lighting bonfires (Guerber, 1994).

The giving of eggs at her festival shows a double connotation of fertility and solar symbolism: two of the egg's meanings (Monaghan, 1994). The fertility symbolism is appropriate, since in spring hens are fertilized and begin to lay eggs again. The decorated eggs were often hung on branches outside the house, or else on egg-trees or maypoles. Christians justified all this by saying that the egg symbolized the risen sun of righteousness, so it would seem that there was a sun connection all along (West, 1975). The egg is particularly connected to the sun maiden so it seems appropriate to Œstre.

The SuN iN the RuNes

The sun being such an integral part of the culture of these northern peoples, it is not surprising that it makes an appearance in their symbolic alphabet, the runes. In the Elder Futhark (so-called because it is the older version), the rune for 's' is called the sun, sigel. In shape it resembles a lightning flash, or an 's' with angles instead of curves, an alternative form. Pennick (1992) gives its meaning as 'sun, brightness, victory'. There is also another form of the Sól rune, a circle with a ray coming out from the bottom (Pennick, 1992). The Anglo-Saxon rune-poem (Linsell) says:

Sun ever proves a joy to seamen
when they cross the fish-bath-sea,
till the brine-steed brings them to land.

The connection of sea and sun might seem odd, but it is certain that sailors like fair weather. In Sweden petroglyphs have been found showing ships and sun-wheels, suggesting an established link between the two (Davidson, 1964). In rune-magic there are surf-runes, which control the weather, and sigel was probably one of these. One of Freya's names, Mardoll, means 'beauty of light on water' and suggests the glittering of the sun on the sea, so it may have a poetic resonance as well.

Another sort of link between the sun and the sea is the labyrinths of Scandinavia, where spring rituals to free the maiden sun took place. They were often near the sea, and sailors would run them during the year before setting out on a voyage, either to secure a good catch, or else to get good weather (Kraft, 1982). Since the sun gives good weather, and is linked to the sea in the runes, the running of the labyrinth may have been freeing the sun to shine on the sailor, as well as averting bad luck in the labyrinth's windings.

A later version of the Futhark, the Swedish-Norse, calls the same rune Sól, meaning the goddess Sól, sun. It has the same meaning as the other two. The Old Norse rune-poem (Fries, 1993) says:

*Sól is the light of the world.
I bow to the divine decree.*

The Old Icelandic poem (Fries, 1993) also refers to the sun goddess:

*Sól is the shield of the clouds
and shining ray
and destroyer of ice.*

This expresses the basic Norse polarity of fire and ice, which is the basis of their creation myth. The sun's return brings with it fair weather and warmth.

Bronze Age

The rock carvings (petroglyphs) of Sweden and eastern Europe are a fascinating record of belief and ritual in prehistoric times. Combined with other evidence such as archaeological finds and later mythology, one can try to reconstruct the early sun-goddess cult. Many of the pictures offer fascinating additions to the later record of sagas and poems.

One image of the sun is the feet found in some petroglyphs. (The foot pattern also turns up on a pot alternating with sun-discs as a border [Davidson and Gelling, 1969].) An associated pattern is the 'sandal' which resembles the later sun-wheel, which Davidson and Gelling think shows a connection between them. The feet presumably are the footprints of the sun as she moves across the land during the day. They may also relate to the sun's dance, which would burn footprints into the earth as it was on the horizon, so it would seem that it danced on the earth.

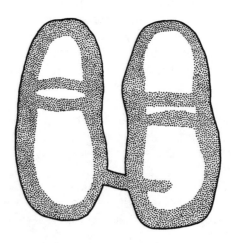

Petroglyph from Scania showing the usual footprints pattern.

There is no question that the disc is a solar symbol. However, the gender of the sun in the petroglyphs is open to question. Some read the little men (if one interprets the little 'tails' that end their bodies as penises [see page 150]) who hold sun-discs like shields and the disc-with-axe motif as images of a sun god. There are other explanations, however. The sun and axe may represent a mating scene, since the axe represents the thunder god, a deity unlikely to also rule the sun. The weapon often stands in for the god, as in the sword and sun scenes. As for the little men, they may be carrying the sun in some sort of ceremony. It is not even certain that they are men, since often the tails stick out at an angle more appropriate to swords, or sometimes capes. Kühn (1966) suggests that they may be a sign of vestments worn by priests. Sometimes these figures carry the solar disc on a pole, which perhaps is the forerunner of the carrying of fires on poles at midsummer so common across Europe.

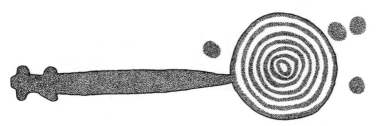

PETROGLYPHS SHOWING THE SACRED MARRIAGE OF SÓL/FREYA.

The sword and sun-disc picture (above) suggests a mating of sky and sun deities (Davidson and Gelling, 1969). The sword points towards the centre of the disc, and probably represents the mating of the sky god, whom the sword represents, and the sun goddess. This implies a sacred marriage of a sword god and the sun, which seems to have been lost. Sól has a husband in the *Edda*, named Glen, of whom little is known; perhaps he was the sword's owner. The image discussed earlier of a boar or sow with a sword pointing to its backside is another example; it can easily be read as a sacred marriage of Freya in sow form and sword-wielding god.

The sun-disc also appears mounted on a ship, which represents the journey of the sun at night, across the water to the east. This myth was common to places where the sun appeared to set into the water, and so had to get back to the east by sailing. Like the famous bronze chariot, the sun-disc would have been stood on end in the boat. Perhaps the suns shown mounted on ships were carried to a ship and set afloat or sailed somewhere.

This record in stone shows that the solar goddess was worshipped in earliest times. Whether as Sól, Freya or Lucina, she persisted through medieval times, and with the help of folklore she has remained for us to discover today.

THE SUN IN HER BOAT, PROBABLY SAILING BACK TO THE EAST AT NIGHT.

The Balts: Saule

THE LATVIANS, LITHUANIANS AND PRUSSIANS have lived around the Baltic Sea in northeast Europe for about four thousand years. They are mostly farming people, and their festivals are based on an agricultural calendar. Many of their folk customs reveal a pagan past, and the folksongs are very informative about the beliefs of the older religion.

The Baltic languages are famous for their closeness to the original Indo-European. Apparently Balts can read Sanskrit with little difficulty. As a result of this archaic nature of their languages, Indo-European scholars use them as a control when reconstructing words. The same applies to their mythology. Compared to the rest of Europe the Balts remained pagan for a long time. The Latvians worshipped the thunder god Perun until 1750, and Lithuania was not Christianized until the fifteenth century (Balys, 1975). Under the circumstances they seem like an ideal forum for investigation of early Indo-European mythology.

The fact that the Balts worship a sun goddess, who is a central part of the pantheon, suggests that the gender of the sun may have originally been female among the Indo-Europeans. This chapter pays careful attention to her and her cult, especially since it will be used for comparisons in later chapters. Many of the characteristics of the sun and her relations with her fellow deities are entirely typical of a solar goddess.

In Baltic cosmology, all the sky gods live together on the hill of the sky, where they have houses and farms. Besides them, another group of gods live on earth. Earth herself is the sun's daughter and the chief sky god's wife (Zemnya). The sun goddess is married to the moon, and has a daughter whose marital adventures make up part of the mythology. The gods all turn out for these weddings, which are occasions of great rejoicing in heaven.

Saule: dear little sun

The sun goddess is Saule, which means 'sun'. She is an important goddess, so much so that one version of the world's creation is that she formed the world out of an egg-shaped mass after warming it for many years (Newall, 1971). The sun goddess is central to the understanding that the Balts have of their cosmos: the world is divided into two parts – *vi saule* and *vina saule*. *Vi saule* is the ordinary world around us, where the sun (Saule) shines every day. The part of the world known as *vina saule* is where

31

the sun goes at night, the underworld or realm of the dead, which is either under the sky-hill or in the west (Biezais).

Sometimes the Balts call Saule the 'sun virgin' and sometimes the 'sun mother'. She can take on two forms – a mother with many daughters; or one with a single daughter who is dawn to her mother's sun. A folktale says that a young man used to see two suns in the sky at morning and evening, but just one during the day. He went off to seek the second sun, which would be the sun maiden (Jouet, 1989).

The Latvians see Saule as a more autonomous figure; while, according to the Lithuanians, the divine smith Teliavelis placed her and the moon in the heavens. Despite this, the two luminaries are very anthropomorphic. They are married, and seem much like their Latvian counterparts, engaging in very human behaviour such as quarrelling (Lurker, 1994). They both wander the earth as well. She appears in the guise of a beautiful maiden with golden hair, and the moon as a fair young prince. He sometimes seduces women and takes them to the moon. As Saule is protector of orphans, her missions are a little more benign (Balys, 1975). In her most celestial aspect, she is described by the Balts in terms of metals, to give an idea of her shining. She spins gold, silver and bronze, and she dresses in dazzling silk clothing embroidered in silver and gold. She dances in silver shoes on midsummer morning.

Saule played an important role in agriculture, and farmers addressed prayers to her at sunrise and sunset. All the Baltic deities seem sympathetic to farmers, since they have their own farms, which they tend. She comes down to inspect farmers' fields, hitching up her skirts and walking about with them (Katzenelenbogen, 1935):

St John's mother has roamed over the rye
Lifting up her velvet skirt.
When she dropped her velvet skirt
The ears of rye bent.

The sun's care for the crops was acknowledged in rituals. During rye harvesting women would stop at sunset, place a sheaf in front of them, plant their sickles in their sheaves and sing a song to the setting sun, thanking her for a good day (Velius, 1989).

She also rules all things feminine, including weaving, spinning, laundering and music. All prayers to Saule had to be made with the head uncovered, an ancient sign of respect (Gimbutas, 1963). (Even now men take their hats off in church, and in front of royalty, to show deference in the presence of the sacred or powerful.) She has a moral aspect; she helps the unfortunate and punishes evil-doers, and with the fate goddess Laima she looks after women in childbirth and orphans. People pray to them both for health as well (Katzenelenbogen, 1935):

Little sun, so white,
Give me your whiteness.
Little Laime, so healthful,
Give me your health.

The moral side of Saule is common to almost all the sun goddesses in this book. Many legends about the sun say that it will not shine if there is too much evil about, or else that sin darkens it. The dyad of daughter and mother, her travels through the sky, and her connection to fertility are typical of Indo-European myth.

The sun's husbands

Saule has three different husbands: the moon god, the storm god and the sky god. Her first husband was the moon god, Menuo, and their children were the stars and the earth. Apparently they once lived together, but there are several stories that explain why this is no longer the case. One is that the sun and moon lived in a small house, and so begat the earth, their daughter. But they fell out of love, and wished to divorce. God sent Perkunas the thunder god to decide who got the daughter. He either had them race, and gave the sun day-custody when she won, or else arrived at this solution in a Solomonic fashion (Balys, 1975).

The other explanation for the end of this paradisiacal season is that the moon seduced Saule's daughter Auszrine, whom she had promised to the sky god's sons. She was furious and cut him about the face with a sword. This caused the marks you see on the face of the moon (Monaghan, 1990). The moon god's reputation as a seducer probably stems from this incident. In other versions it is the storm god Perkunas who cuts him in half (Hastings, 1980):

It happened in the spring-time
That the sun and moon did wed
But the sun rose up early
And from her the moon fled
The morning star was loved then
By the lone wandering moon
Who with a sword was smitten
In deep wrath by Perkun.

Perkunas is another husband, and in one Latvian version it is she who is the adulterer, leaving Menuo for the storm god (the dawn goddess is then his daughter, while the other stars are the moon's children [Machal, 1925]). The moon then rejects her and rides the sky at night, shrinking from shame and anger, which causes its phases (McCrickard, 1990).

Perkunas is the thunder and storm god, who whips evil sprits with his lightning bolts, and rides a chariot, pulled by two goats, the wheels of which make thunder. He is just, but impatient and irascible. Perkunas is a very typical Indo-European thunder god, and, like many of them, his function as rain god makes for some tension with the sun. He has nine sons, of whom three shatter, three thunder and three lighten (Machal, 1925). It may be one of these who forges a golden chair for Saule that sticks her fast when she sits in it, in retaliation for her banishing Auszrine from heaven (Coxwell Fillingham, 1925).

As for her third husband, the sky god, Dievas, Gimbutas (1963) says:

> [h]is homestead and his sons, Latvian Dieva deli, Lithuanian Dievo suneliai, were particularly closely associated with Saule, the sun, and her daughters...

He and his sons are responsible for freeing the sun and her daughters in one myth (Lurker, 1994). One of the folksongs or *dainas* describes him riding across the sky-hill with the rest of the heavenly deities, to his wedding to the sun (Biezais), and others tell of his sons' courtship of the sun's daughter(s). His sons often appear as twins, and represent the morning and evening stars, or the constellation Gemini. Their name, Dieva deli, means 'God's sons'. (They have their counterparts in Greek and Indic myth, confirming their Indo-European origins.)

Dievas was literally the sky, the hill of heaven (God = sky = light [Gimbutas, 1958]). He follows the common pattern of the kindly god of the day sky, who is sometimes mistaken for the sun by writers. The Balts saw him as a farmer with a family, whose enclosure was on the hill of heaven. His main function was to fertilize the earth, Zemes-meita, and specifically to make the corn grow. With the fate goddess Laima, he allots human fates. He allots the fates of men, and she determines the women's. He creates order in the world, and guards moral law on earth. He leaves the sky-farm and visits farmers, and is part of agricultural festivals throughout the year (Biezais).

He seems to have had some connection to the moon, for there is a myth in which the devil takes advantage of Dievas's habit of sleeping to make an imitation sun. He sets this opposite the other one, but Dievas awakes just in time, and pours water over it. However, it flares, and once a month he has to douse it again. This doused sun becomes the moon, and it is interesting that Indo-European myth links the moon and water, as opposed to the fire of the sun (Coxwell Fillingham, 1925). In the songs, his sons and Saule's daughters quarrel over the girls breaking the boys' swords, or the boys stealing the girls' rings. (Girls wear a ring on their left hand until they are married, as a symbol of virginity [Katzenelenbogen, 1935]; this is why its loss is serious.) This causes the sun and sky to become estranged, and Dievas disappears for three days (Biezais). This habit of disappearing connects him to Menuo, who ages and dies each month, reappearing after three days.

THE SUN'S JOURNEY

She lives with her daughters in a castle either at the far end of the sea or else beyond the hill of the sky. (The idea of the sky as a hill explains why the sun is high in the sky at noon, and lower in the morning and evening.) Like many other sun deities throughout the world she rides across the sky in a chariot, which in Baltic mythology has copper wheels. Fiery horses that never tire draw it across the sky. At twilight she stops and washes her horses in the sea and then drives to her apple orchard in the west. All the Baltic deities have farms on their lands on the sky-hill which they tend. The setting sun is a red apple that falls from the orchard, as one of the *dainas* has it (Hastings, 1980):

> The Sun in the golden garden
> Weeps bitterly,
> The golden apple hath fallen
> From the apple tree.

The goddess's tears at its fall make red berries on the hillside, which explains the red sky of sunset.

Another version is that the sun is a jug or spoon into which light is poured, and which Saule's daughters wash in the sea at sunset (Savill, 1977). (Her daughters are the morning and evening stars, who attend her at the beginning and end of her journey.) At night, she travels back to the east side of the sky-hill, sometimes diving into the sea, or travelling under the earth. (In Baltic cosmology the earth floats in the ocean which surrounds it, so these two ideas aren't contradictory.) She then swims or sails back in a golden boat with sunbeams for oars or drawn by swans while the moon rides overhead. As one of the songs (Jouet, 1989) says:

> Saule the white in resting
> Lies in a golden boat.
> In the morning, in waking,
> She dresses herself in silver.

Sometimes at night she dances on a stone in the middle of the sea, especially on midsummer eve. (This stone may be the same as the hill of the sky.)

Saule herself is described as 'dear little white sun' or 'dear little red sun'. Her colours are red, white, gold and silver. Among her symbols are the rosette, ring, wheel, floriated cross and rayed circle. The daisy is one of her flowers (Gimbutas, 1963). Anything that is round and rayed suggests the sun, hence her symbols of daisy and rose. The *dainas* call her the rolling sun, since, by a sort of substitution of part for whole, the sun is thought of as a wheel rolling through the sky. The Balts also described her as a rosy apple, golden crown, precious belt/necklace, golden goblet, or a ring fresh from forging, as a way of explaining what it is about her that shines (Gimbutas, 1963). These metaphors for the sun explain songs like the one above, which describes the sun as a golden apple that falls in the sea. A common description of Saule is *balta saulele*, dear white sun; while her daughter is *skaisti*, red (Balys, 1975). The colour white comes with a range of secondary meanings, such as good, honest, as well as being more accurate for the noonday sun, while the rising and setting sun is redder.

The poetic comparison of the sun's golden light at the edge of mountains and treetops to a dowry is apt since Saule ruled spring and summer, when she marries the moon (Jouet, 1989). When the heavenly twins courted her daughter, the *dainas* say that she wept for the loss of her daughter, and over the chest laden with silver and gold. She seems to have a connection with marriage generally, as in the following song (Jouet, 1989):

> *Saule was weaving her crown*
> *Seated in the sun,*
> *Weave, Saule, give me one,*
> *I must go to the house of the suitor.*

Festivals of the sun

Saule's main festivals are midsummer and a spring festival roughly equivalent to the Celtic Beltane. On midsummer eve people stayed up all night, in the hopes of seeing the sun's dance as she came over the horizon. They assembled on a high hill and raised a bonfire on a pole, and danced and sang around it. The songs offered thanks for the sun's favour and prayed to her for various benefits in the future. Everyone shared a meal of cheese and mead. People would bathe in the holy waters, rivers and streams that flowed east towards the rising sun, for health or to get married (Gimbutas, 1963).

The sun appeared dressed in apple blossom with a wreath of red-fern blossom, and danced on the silver hill of the sky in silver shoes. Her dance gives the festival its name, Ligo, 'swaying', since the songs described Saule as rolling, swaying and hopping (Gimbutas, 1963). Gimbutas suggests that the movement of the sun is an important theme: the dynamism of life and life-giving things is a vital contrast to the stillness of death and winter. However, the sun declines from that day. One *daina* says that 'Little John' breaks Saule's jug, the summer solstice 'breaks' the solar orb (Machal, 1925). (The summer solstice is now celebrated on St John's Day, 24 June. This has led to the day being deified as well, into a sort of Janus figure [Katzenelenbogen, 1935].)

Ligo was also a festival of sexual licence, and some songs suggest that

Saule raised her skirts at dawn (McCrickard, 1990). She did this as a ritual gesture towards fertility and perhaps also as a sort of blessing, since she was a nurturer of life on earth. This may also be the meaning of the reference earlier to her raising her skirts in farmers' fields. It was also the festival of the marriage of the sun and moon. The Lithuanians say that Saule goes forth at dawn in a chariot drawn by three horses, one of gold, one of silver and one of diamond, to meet her husband the moon. On her way she dances and emits fiery sparks (Ralston, 1872). Women, both married and unmarried, decked themselves in wreaths of oak leaves, although normally only maidens wore them, as part of the general licence of the day.

The spring holiday was a celebration of the return of the sun, and the renewal of nature. A festival for the beginning of Lent involves sleigh-riding with much whip-snapping and shouting; Gimbutas says that the movement and noise are intended as sympathetic magic to increase the dynamism of the sun and the forces of fertility. This is the season for singing rounds and circle–dancing, once again to celebrate vitality and encourage the sun. The people extinguished their winter hearths and lit new fires outdoors (Crowley, 1994). Easter was a festival of the dawn goddess Auszrine (Jouet, 1989). People decorated trees with ribbons and bits of cloth at this time of the year, possibly for Auszrine's wedding, as *dainas* refer to the Dieva deli or Saule decking the trees before the event (West, 1975).

At winter solstice a goat was sacrificed to Perkunas, whom the Balts believed smote the winter spirits with his axe. The shepherds would gather about a bonfire, and sing songs, after which the priest brought a goat to the fire and killed it (Ralston, 1872). People lit bonfires as well to help the sun as she recovered from the winter darkness (McCrickard, 1990). The Balts explained the hammer worship that scandalized Jerome of Prague with the myth of the sun's imprisonment. A king stole her and locked her up in a high tower, but the 'stars of the zodiac' freed her with a giant hammer. For the stars of the zodiac, one can read the twin sons of Dievas, and the giant hammer belongs to the smith god Kalvatis. (Their use of the hammer earns them the nickname of 'the workmen of Perkun', since some *dainas* portray him as a smith [Hastings, 1980].)

These days there are two winter solstice festivals. The first honours the ancestors and is called Kucios. Families lay out a feast for the ancestors consisting of twelve or thirteen types of food, one for each month of the year. They also offer grain to the fire at the end of the feast, and burn a log representing the old year. This is to remove any lingering traces of the old year. The second festival is called Kaledos and celebrates the rebirth of Saule Motule, 'Mother Sun'. The people carried her image through towns and fields, and the worshippers wished everyone prosperity. (St Lucia's Day in Sweden is similar.) It is also the festival of the Old Man of Kaleda, a sort of Santa Claus (Crowley, 1994).

The hearth fire

Another feature of the midsummer festival was that the hearth fire was allowed to go out. It was relit with much ceremony, but otherwise the hearth fire was never to be extinguished. This custom continues from the days when the Baltic tribes had official sanctuaries on high hills and river banks with perpetual fires. The fire was made by rubbing together a stick of oak (male) and one of softer linden (female) (Hastings, 1980).

There is a goddess who represents the actual hearth, whose name is Aspelenie ('the one behind the hearth'), probably much like the Roman Vesta, who was given offerings. The mother of the family carefully banked the fire every night as a sign of respect for the gift of fire and the goddess of the hearth. McCrickard (1990) says this goddess was another of Saule's daughters, which may be a poetic way of saying that the original fire was the sun. The swallow brought the first fire to earth, which is how it got its red face and dark tail (see page 52). (There is still a swallow dance in Lithuania.) The Latvians call the actual flames *uguns mate* ('mother of fire') and the Lithuanians Gabija (*gaubti*, 'to cover').

The sun maiden also visited families' hearths six times a year, when her mother Saule drove her out of her home for loving Menuo or Perkunas's son. On some summer nights she could be seen as a small flame beside birch trees (St Elmo's Fire). This gave rise to a myth of the origin of fire. A young girl walking from one village to another saw a flame by a tree. On looking more closely, she saw a beautiful young woman wearing a crown in it. The woman spoke to her, saying that her lover, Perkunas's son, had been driven from heaven, and her mother had exiled her as well. Now she would live among humans in the fire, so the girl took a spark home, which she never allowed to go out. The connection of daughters and the hearth appears in the custom that, when a daughter left her fam-

A LITHUANIAN DISTAFF SHOWING SOLAR MOTIFS, INCLUDING THE SNAKE.

ily on her wedding day, she said to the fire, 'Thou holy fire, who will guard thee?'

Another connection between Saule and the hearth was that Baltic families kept a snake called a *zaltys* in their homes (the Latvians called it *zalktis*). The snake lived in a bed of straw by the hearth, and the family fed it milk and cared for it. To have your *zaltys* die was extremely unlucky. In folksongs Saule wept when a snake died and punished anyone who mistreated one. It was called 'the envoy to the gods', and it was involved in prophecy (Lurker, 1994). According to McCrickard (1990), the common grass snake is the species kept by the Balts.

AUSZRINE: STAR GODDESS, SUN MAIDEN

Saule's daughter has several names: Auszrine, Barbelina, Wakerine and Saules meita (Monaghan, 1990). As Auszrine she is the morning star, and appears with her mother at dawn. (Gimbutas [1963] says that the name Auszrine is related to that of the Vedic Ushas, another dawn goddess.) The Balts considered her the type of all that was desirable, as an expression from Lithuania shows: 'he wouldn't even be satisfied with the Daughter of the Sun' (West, 1975). Sometimes she has the evening star Wakerine for a sister. They look after Saule's house and accompany her through the underworld at night. Sometimes Saule is thought to have drowned in the sea at sunset and her daughters rescue her by persuading the earth goddess to let them get their mother from the realm of the dead. When they obtain the key, Saule is resurrected and begins her ride across the sky (McCrickard, 1990).

When she is called Saules meita ('Saule's daughter') she is the sun maiden who represents the sun of spring. Alternatively, she may represent the red sky before the sunrise. There is a consistent tradition of dawn goddesses being worshipped as the spring sun, since both represent beginnings (Hastings, 1980). In this form the twin Dieva deli court her, or else they are her brothers. They save her when she drops her golden ring into a well or is otherwise in danger of drowning. This rescue may be the vestige of a myth in which they rescue the sun from winter or darkness (Monaghan, 1990). Ward (1967) quotes:

> The Sun Maiden was wading in the sea;
> Only her crown was visible.
> Row your boat, O Sons of God,
> Rescue the Sun's soul [or life].

The myth of the seduction by the moon connects to this because many of the songs suggest that her mother originally promised her to the twins.

Then the moon steps in, or Saule hands her over to him instead. Although the moon gets punished for abducting her, the sun maiden doesn't escape entirely from the thunder god's wrath. One *daina* (MacCulloch, 1925) goes:

> When the morning star was wedded
> Perkunas rode through the doorway
> And the green oak was shattered.
>
> Then forth the oak's blood spurted
> Besprinkling all my garments,
> Besprinkling, too, my crownlet.

The song is slightly vague, but the breaking-in and the blood suggest that the maiden's encounter with the moon and thunder gods involves the loss of her virginity, a usual moon-god theme since the moon is often the 'real' husband of women.

In Latvia there is a star god, Auseklis, who takes the place of Saule's daughter as the morning star. He courts the sun maiden, though, which leads to a dispute as the moon seduces his betrothed, which ends in Perkunas cleaving the moon in bits (McCrickard, 1990). This incident seems to have led to a sort of rivalry between them (Jouet, 1989):

> Menesis counts the stars,
> If they are all there, tonight.
> All are indeed there,
> Auseklis wasn't there,
> Auseklis was saved
> To choose among Saule's Daughters.

Perhaps because of this courtship, Auseklis then becomes part of all heavenly bridal processions as a sort of protector god (Lurker, 1994). He combines aspects of the dawn goddess and the heavenly twins in an interesting way. (His presence at birth is like that of other dawn goddesses who lead the baby to its first light.)

Dieva deli: heavenly twins

The twin gods are the sons of the sky god Dievas, and *dainas* describe them as the morning and evening stars (Hastings, 1980):

> Hither rode the dear sons of God
> With steeds dripping with sweat
> Folks say the moon has no steeds of his own
> The morning star and the evening star
> They are the sons of the moon.

(Among their other functions they draw the moon through the sky, or at least accompany him on his travels. The confusion in the song between Dievas and Menesis seems to hint that they were once more alike than they are now.) The Dieva deli in their horse form also pull the sun's chariot, as a *daina* (Ward, 1968) says:

> Both the Sun and Moon
> Ride one steed;
> Already the sun dismounted,
> The moon was ready to go.

This idea ties together the representation of the twins as horses and their accompanying the moon as evening and morning. Folk art also persists in portraying them as both men and horses: one example is a distaff topped with two horses' heads and below them two men's heads (Gimbutas, 1958).

The twins are yet another example of the very Indo-European nature of Baltic myth. (In Indo-European languages the words for twins are consistent, *émain* in Irish, *geminus* in Latin and *yama* in Sanskrit being cognate [O'Flaherty, 1980].) They correspond nicely to the Dioscouroi of Greek myth, and the Vedic Asvins. The twins of all three mythologies are rain-makers and share the same basic characteristics (Hastings, 1980). Among these are a connection to a sun maiden. This was discussed briefly above, and will be covered in detail in the Mazes chapter (see pages 112–18).

The horse: sun totem

One of the intriguing things about the Iron Age civilizations is the prominence given to the horse. Among the Balts it is the totem of Dievas and Saule. Horse and sun motifs found on ancient pots and belt tongues suggest that this connection is an ancient one. She is sometimes represented as a mare, and Dievas's twin sons as gold and silver stallions. They pull the sun's chariot through the sky, and often appear with her in folk art (Gimbutas, 1958). At other times she rides fiery, tireless horses, which she washes in the sea in the evening.

Horses are also very important to Dievas, and he drives one, two, three, five, nine or more at a time (Gimbutas, 1963). (In one song, Saule drives in nine chariots drawn by 100 horses!) The large number of horses corresponds to his rank as a sort of chieftain of the sky, just as it does for the sun. On late Bronze Age to early Iron Age face urns, motifs of sun-discs raised on stelae and accompanied by horses are very common, as well as humans in chariots pulled by horses, or riding horses. Horses' bones are common finds in hill-forts of this period, sometimes comprising over half of the domestic animal bones found. It seems that the horse was well loved; graveyards for horses persist into the twelfth century and Prussians used to be buried mounted on their horses. The Balts must have had a tradition of horse worship, which seems logical since horses were associated with two of their most prominent deities.

Swans of the sun

The songs suggest that Saule sails the sea in a golden boat in the evening, or sometimes has her chariot drawn by swans like Apollo. This is a more ancient myth than that of the wheeled chariot pulled by horses (which suggests the Iron Age). The swans or other water birds, who flew in the sky and could also dive under the waves, were appropriate for the sun goddess. Archaeologists have found models of chariots drawn by birds in eastern and central Europe, so the idea was probably widespread (Davidson, 1964).

The axis mundi

Gimbutas (1963) describes the following:

> A peculiar cosmogonical tree of the Baltic peoples was the wooden, roofed pole topped with symbols of sky deities – suns, moons, stars – and guarded by stallions and snakes.

Even in the twentieth century these poles, as well as crosses with a sun symbol around their arms, were found in front of homes, beside sacred springs and in the forests. People erected them for marriages and illnesses, and to ensure good crops.

The idea of a central pole of the universe is not unique to the Balts. The Norse tree Yggdrasill expresses the same notion of a link between the worlds, and the possibility of travel. Siberian shamans travel up and down a central tree or ladder that connects the cosmos and makes their spirit voyaging possible. The pattern also appears on Latvian Easter eggs as a 'Tree of the Dawn' (Newall, 1971). This pole is related to the tree that Saule sits in at night in some *dainas*. This tree or iron post is beyond the hill of the sky, next to a grey stone. Two horses stand by the post, probably Saule's. When the axis is a tree, it is usually an oak or birch. This tree has silver leaves, copper branches and iron roots (note the white/red/black colour scheme).

Alternatively, it is a linden or apple tree. Saule rests in it, hanging her belt up and sleeping in the crown. At dawn, when she rises, the belt turns red. The Balts consider the apple tree to be feminine, and it is closely linked to Saule, who has an apple orchard, from which tumbles a red apple that is the red sun of twilight. Linden trees are also feminine (Gimbutas, 1963). Jouet (1989) quotes:

Touffu pushed the linden
At the edge of Saule's path
It's there that Saule hangs her belt,
Each night, in going to bed.

If Saule does sit in the world-tree, it is by virtue of her centrality to Baltic mythology. She and her daughter are important descendants of the Indo-European sun goddess; a dyad concerned with the welfare of the people in all its aspects. By her marriages to the chief gods she united various aspects of human affairs, and with her daughter governs the seasons.

The Slavs: Sointse

THE SUN GODDESS is harder to find among the Russians and the rest of the Slavs (Balkans, Poles, Scythians, Thracians) than among the Balts and Germans. While she can be found in folklore and songs, she does not appear in the official accounts from which we get most of our information about Slavic paganism. Medieval sources state that the Slavs worshipped the sun and moon, but are not forthcoming about the deities' gender. There is little information about paganism from that period generally, which makes things more difficult.

The Slavic people are also descendants of the Indo-European group, although they split off quite early. They lived nomadically on the steppes and were famed as warriors. The early split-off, along with eastern influences, explains the difference in language from the rest of Europe. They originally spoke one language (Proto-Slavic) and lived in the Ukraine or central Europe, although in the ninth century CE they spread across an area extending from the Urals to the Oder and into the Balkans (Hinnells, 1984).

The few Slavic deities we know of are mostly male. A temple outside Kiev in the ninth century featured the following deities: Perunu, Khursu, Stribogu, Simariglu, Mokosi. Perunu is a thunder god, Khursu probably is a sun deity, Stribogu a wealth-giver or wind god, Simariglu a protector deity (Hubbs, 1993). Mokosi is the only female of the group, a water-related fertility goddess (her name means 'Moist'). Other gods included Svarog (sky), his sons Dazbog (sun/day) and Svaroghits (fire), and Volos/Veles (crops and flocks).

The sun seems to have been male at least part of the time, judged on this evidence. Khursu's identification with the sun is rather tentative, but one chronicler equates Dazbog and Helios. Svarog is sometimes said to be a sun god, but this reflects the common mistaken assumption that sky gods are sun gods. (It seems likely that he was a sky god since his name can be interpreted as meaning 'bright' or 'clear'. One of his functions was to cause rain in summer, which suggests that he was much like Dievas.)

However, when scholars began collecting songs, riddles and other information about the beliefs of peasants, a female sun appeared. She is similar to the Baltic Saule: married to the moon, with the dawn and twilight as daughters, and the thunder goddess for a mother. Since she occurs most often among the western Slavs, especially the Ukrainians, the one probably influenced the other. A typical song (quoted in McCrickard, 1990) is:

> Beyond the high mountains
> Beyond the swift-moving clouds
> Into the arbour where sits
> The fair maiden Bright Sun.

The solar goddess is always a bride or a young maiden, unlike the moon, who ages each month.

Another influence that might account for the sun goddess is the Scythians, another Indo-European group who came across the steppes into Russia. Their cult of the Great Goddess was combined with the pre-existing solar worship to produce a powerful deity who appropriated to herself the solar symbols of cock, firebird and horse (Rice, 1957). This same goddess appears in women's embroidery patterns later, holding fruit or flowers, or the reins of her attendants' horses. The cloths with these patterns were significant parts of women's rites, and will be discussed in more detail later in this chapter.

Solntse: the red sun

When we turn to the language, we find that the Russian word for 'sun' is solntse, which is a neuter word ('e' ending), but according to linguists it is a diminutive of an earlier feminine word. Also, verbs relating to the sun are usually inflected feminine (Encyclopaedia Britannica). The word solntse is cognate with the rest of the sun-goddess names in Europe: Saule, Sól, Sul. The modern word for moon is the feminine luna ('a' ending), which suggests a borrowed word, since the moon in folksongs is a man. (Russian is liberally peppered with loan-words.)

The concept of redness is closely linked to the female sun. The word for red, kras, is linked to the word for beautiful, and both are used to describe beautiful maidens or women associated with the sun (Hubbs, 1993). One folksong (Ralston, 1872) says:

> Warm, warm, O red Sun!
> Shine, shine, O bright Moon!

and another one describes 'The red sun with its rays . . .' (Ralston, 1872). This redness is often set against the whiteness of the moon god in Indo-European mythology, so we may have a remnant of ancient ideas here.

At home with the sun: husband and daughters

In folklore the sun comes complete with a family. In one song she is a maiden playing in the meadow of the sky. A character called Ivan calls her his mother, the moon his father, twilight his sister and the grey falcon (morning star?) his brother (Mueller, 1879). Ivan turns up again in songs from eastern Czechoslovakia as dawn's brother, with the sun as their mother (Ralston, 1872). (He is probably an Auseklis type of morning-star god, replacing the divine twins.) The relationship of the various deities changes with the country: the Serbians make the morning star Solntse's sister, among the Russians it is dawn, and the Slovaks think that there are two Zoryas, dawn and twilight, who harness the sun's horses along with the morning star (Mueller, 1879).

Solntse lives in a palace with gates in the east and west. She lives there with the moon, and their arguments cause earthquakes, which suggests a subterranean home. The stars in the sky are their children. Solntse is said to plough the sky, harrow it or sow seed, which recalls the Baltic sky-farms (Mueller, 1879). On midsummer day the sun and moon are married, and their dancing lights up the sky with dazzling rays. Once the day is over, they go their separate ways across the sky until spring, when they meet to talk about their adventures. If they are getting along when they meet, the day will be fine, but if Myesyats (the moon god) is proud, as he tends to be, there will be words and bad weather (Warner, 1985).

Human families are often compared to the celestial household (Ralston, 1872):

> In the midst of the court there are three rooms:
> In the first room is the bright Moon
> In the second room is the red Sun
> In the third room is the many Stars.

The song goes on to compare the master of the house to the moon, his wife to the sun, and their children to the stars. (This is a common theme of the songs sung at Christmas time.)

The goddess Peperuna, twin to the thunder god Perun, also lives in the sun's home. She bathes Solntse when she returns each evening from travelling the sky. In a folktale, a man visits the home of the sun, at the edge of the world. The sun's mother makes him hide himself, and in the evening a young girl enters the cottage. She takes off her dazzling dress and hangs it up, and her mother bathes her and puts her to bed. In the morning the mother serves breakfast to her daughter and dresses her again, which causes the room to fill with light. The mother says that it is time for the sun to leave, and she flies off into the sky (Warner, 1985). The mother of the sun is probably Peperuna, since they perform the same function.

Dawn and twilight

The sun's daughters are Zvezda Dennitsa and Vechernyaya Zvezda, the morning and evening stars, who tend to Solntse's horses. There are also the two Zoryas, Zorya Utrenyaya, and Zorya Vechernyaya, who open the east and west gates for Solntse (*utro* means 'morning' and *vecher* 'evening'). In Serbia, one of these, the sun's sister, is married to the morning star, like Saules meita and Auseklis. In some myths there are three Zoryas, evening, midnight and morning, who watch a dog tied to the Little Bear (Ursa Minor). When the dog escapes the world will end (Grimal, 1965).

Serbian folksongs describe the morning star as a woman who watches over humans, and quarrels with the moon (Mugge, 1916). She supplanted the sun as Myesyats's wife in some songs and tales, as the feminine sun was forgotten, and they are often said to meet at dawn to discuss humans' activities (Cohane, 1973). Slavs greet her in the morning as 'the brightest maiden, the most sublime, the most honourable' (Eliade, 1987).

As the goddess of the dawn and spring sun, Zorya was invoked to cause love and longing in young men. Many of the songs of spring invoke its goddess to bring about love, and also are sung under the windows of young married couples. Zorya was given a part in the arranging of marriages (Ralston, 1872):

> Where do I intend to live? Why, at Pan Ivan's,
> At Pan Ivan's in his Court,
> In his Court, and in his dwelling,
> And in his dwelling are two pleasures:
> The first pleasure – to get his son married;
> The second pleasure – to give his daughter in marriage.

The dawn goddess was also invoked by lovers, who encouraged her to linger, so the day wouldn't come and part them.

Cult of the dead

Both Solntse and her daughter are closely connected to the cult of the dead. Burials used to be done at sunset so that the souls could make the journey to the afterworld in the company of the goddess. Otherwise the soul would wander about in the dark. Some Croatians would open the coffin before the interment so that the sun would shine on the body, to warm it and take the soul with her (Ralston, 1872). The ancient Slavs were buried with their heads to the east, or their eyes or face oriented eastward, presumably for the same reason (Gimbutas, 1971). The moon was the abode of souls, and they crossed the bridge of the Milky Way to reach it (Warner, 1985). (They went to the moon for rebirth; this is a common element of many cultures. It is one reason why the moon god is the 'real' husband of women, since he is the one who impregnates them.)

The afterworld of the Slavs corresponds with this solar orientation. It is located in the east, shines with an everlasting light, and is the pleasant abode of the dead. This paradise had many names, among them Rai, Iry or Vuirei, and was thought to be where the sun rested in the evening, coming over from the west so it could rise in the morning. This place was always summery and the trees grew golden fruit (Ralston, 1872). (It is very similar to other Indo-European conceptions of a pleasant abode for the dead.)

One version of this paradise is called Bouyan (connected to words meaning burning, ardent, vernal, fruitful), and was ruled by Zaryá, a sun maiden who is probably the same as the goddesses Zorya Utrenyaya and Zorya Vechernyaya, who personified dawn and twilight. She sits under a dripping oak on the 'fiery stone' Alatuir, which was made of amber. There she sews with red-gold thread, an idea that turns up in many spells. She was asked to sew up wounds, since a healing river flowed from under her seat (Ralston, 1872). This sitting suggests the German sun goddess, and perhaps Zarya has taken over her mother's role here as well. The healing water empowered by the sun is another common motif in female solar mythology.

Solstice goddesses

The Russians had a tendency to personify abstractions, and the seasons were included in this group. The festivals of the winter and summer solstices had their own deities. These goddesses show interesting solar motifs, and perhaps were sun goddesses in their own right.

The goddess of the winter solstice was called Kolyada, a word related to the word for 'wheel'. She was a figure similar to Lucia in Sweden, and probably also a solar figure. At the solstice she was said to dress in her best and turn her sledge onto the summer track, in celebration of the new season (Ralston, 1872). Her name connects her to the Norse sun goddess, who was represented as a wheel. (Saule is also sometimes shown as a wheel, and described as rolling through the sky).

As part of the Christmas festivities there would be a procession with a girl dressed all in white, leading a procession around town followed by people with torches singing songs about her and the returning of light. The songs also are meaningful, since they describe her as being born on Christmas Eve, beyond the river that marks the boundary of the underworld and this one (Hastings, 1980). Presumably this is the same river as the one that flows from under Zaryá's stone Alatuir (McCrickard, 1990). Another song describes how she was lost on the eve of Christmas and the people search for her all through the town, which probably reflects old beliefs about the winter solstice (Ralston, 1872). After losing the sun in the darkest day of the year, it returns and is honoured by a procession and the offering of gifts to its representative.

Kolyada also took on the function of midwife sometimes, as in one song that said she came 'to feed the wife so that she gives birth to children' (Hubbs, 1993). She presumably represented the first light the child sees, like the midwife goddess Juno Lucina ('light'). Her festival also involved spinning, which was a form of sympathetic magic, since often the sun goddess was a spinster and sewer. Women kept logs burning to encourage the sun and bring its strength into the house. Another game played at this time has solar motifs: women dropped golden jewellery in a bowl of water, and drew items out to tell their fortunes (Hubbs, 1993). The mingling of sun and water is of course a common image of union, which would stimulate fertility.

The goddess Iarila's festival was the summer solstice, celebrated with fire and water. Her name means 'ardent sun' and she was a fertility deity (Ann and Imel, 1993). Effigies of her and her brother were burned together, and sometimes they were said to have mated incestuously. Iarilo is incarnated in the sun-wheel, and is described as a youth in white riding a horse. His twin sister is both a maiden and a mother, who in Belorussia appears in white carrying flowers, riding a horse. Girls sang and danced round her, while she carried a sheaf of grain and a human mask. Like other sun goddesses, she also had a connection to death (Hubbs, 1993).

There were many similar goddesses, whose names varied with the place: Lado and Lada, Kupalo and Kupal'nitsa (only a pair in southern Russia), and Kostromo and Kostroma. They were Christianized as Ivan and Maria (John and Mary) probably because of St John's Day. They bathe together in sexual union on this day, a sun-goddess myth the Slavs share with the Armenians. This association of sun and water also appears in Ukrainian lore, where the female sun is called 'Mother Hot Sun' and 'Mother Holy Water'.

At the solstice the god Kupalo and his consort were worshipped by girls who were dressed as brides and led to a nearby river. There they jumped and worshipped the goddess. The water from the river was sprinkled on their houses to sanctify them. Later the whole village lit bonfires and jumped them. The sun-goddess motifs should be clear. The sun was said to dance and jump as she went out to meet her husband the moon. The water and bonfire rites are similar to Baltic practices, and suggest the solar nature of the festival. The fact that the goddess of this type had a twin brother and the festival included sexual games reminds one of the Germanic Freya and her brother Freyr.

The embroidery goddess

An important piece of a bride's trousseau among the Slavs is the traditional red-embroidered towel or handkerchief kept by women. One typical piece shows a woman with lines radiating from her head holding the reins of two horses with their riders facing forwards (Gostelow, 1977). Often the riders had birch branches twined in their hair and hold offerings, or else are priests. (This represents the twin horse gods who pull the sun's chariot through the sky [McCrickard, 1990].) The goddess usually holds the reins of the horses, and the background is filled in with horses, cocks, firebirds and other solar symbols (Rice, 1957). Another popular embroidery pattern shows a woman with rays coming from her head holding two fat hens, and a smaller woman next to her with the rays on her head and two flowers in each hand (Gostelow, 1977). This could be a sun mother–daughter duo, probably Solntse and Zarya.

THE SLAVIC EMBROIDERY GODDESS WITH THE TWIN HORSE GODS

The goddess who figures in these pieces is a descendant of the Scythian Great Goddess mentioned earlier. The solar symbols that came to be associated with this figure show her relationship with Solntse (Rice, 1957):

> The towel's designs closely followed early prototypes, with the goddess invariably forming its main motif. She often appears in the same pose as that in Scythian metal-work...

Both the Slavic and Scythian goddesses share the typical Indo-European themes of the dual sun and her connection the divine twins with their horsy attributes.

This piece of embroidery was passed down from mother to daughter and was also used in many ceremonies. They were placed on the bride's head at weddings, on the bones of ancestors to win their help, wrapped around bread offered on the family altar, and draped from birches to celebrate the returning sun. The cloth was hung high in a birch tree, and a ring dance was performed around the tree. If no tree could be found, the participants had a young woman standing in the centre with branches twined in her hair, and the embroidered cloth was hung on a bough. The dancers imitated the horses of the sun by stamping (Gostelow, 1977).

There were also choral songs sung, by the circle, with one woman standing in the middle holding a round loaf and an egg dyed red. She faced east, and sang songs celebrating spring. This was followed by the destruction of an effigy of winter or death, which was either a male figure of straw and rags, or a woman in white holding a broom (winter storms) and a sickle (harvest) (Ralston, 1872). In spring, dolls were burned, drowned or buried to symbolize the end of winter. This was celebrated in songs (Reeder, 1975):

O little sun [solnce], fine weather,
Come out, pretty one,
From behind the mountain!
Come out little sun,
It's springtime!
Oh, fine weather, have you seen
The beautiful spring?

Oh, little sun, have you seen . . .
The witch-winter?
And so cruel, she ran away
From spring...

Other solar customs

Several other holidays celebrated by the Slavs also show the influence of the sun-goddess cult. The Easter season was called Svyetlaya, 'bright', and was probably once the festival of the Slavic version of Œstre, who is connected to the east and brightness just as Zaryá is (Ralston, 1872). The famous Ukrainian Easter eggs are often decorated with sun patterns. The star or star-flower, the wheel, and a pattern of spokes radiating from a centre are all thought to be solar symbols, as well as the swastika and the reel (Newall, 1971). The sun was believed to dance at Easter, and also to walk the earth (Ralston, 1872).

The summer solstice honoured the sun goddess by lighting fires, sprinkling water and foretelling the future. The Bulgarians said that on this day the sun danced and whirled swords about. It lost its way as it came up, and had to be led by the dawn maiden. Thoughts of mortality caused this hesitation, which the Serbians said made the sun stop three times on St John's Day, overcome by fear of winter (Ralston, 1872). On St John's Eve in Poland the sun is believed to bathe in the river, and dance and play in the sky. Girls dance 'after the sun' (clockwise), singing, 'Play, sun, play, here are your little suns!'

On 1 September, the Russians extinguished their hearth fire in the evening, and rekindled it at dawn the next morning. On this day the swallows were believed to hide themselves in wells (Ralston, 1872). The birds were believed to have brought fire from the sun to those on earth, but were burnt in the process, which is how they got the red markings on their heads and tails (Armstrong, 1958). It is significant that the bird that brought fire from the sun or heaven disappears around the time of the autumn equinox, when the sun's power is waning. That they go into wells is equally interesting, considering the sun-immersion imagery of the Celts, Balts and Germans.

'Fiery Mary': the thunder mother

Folklore assigned to the Virgin Mary many of the roles played by pagan goddesses, including the contradictory roles of thunder and sun goddess. However, these roles can be reconciled if Mary is seen as an all-powerful goddess, the mistress of all the planets and the heavens.

As the goddess of the sun, she takes over in part from Zarya. She also sits on the stone and sews in Buyan. Alternatively, she sits on a golden stool, sewing golden thread with a golden needle. In this role she is associated with swans, and one prayer says that she drops a swan feather on the supplicant from a bird she holds in her lap. Sometimes she is called 'Mary the Swan'. The prayer to the Holy Icon (Hubbs, 1993) calls her:

> Light of All / Highest of all creation . . . / Holy Star / Bright Moon / Beautiful Sun / Blessed in miracles / Life comes from your flesh / Even in your icon / There is astonishing power / Sun comes from your rays / Your radiance fills the stars.

Like Lucina, she is invoked by women in labour, to bring her golden keys and let the child into the light (Hubbs, 1993). (The sun goddess Lada was also called Mary, which fits oddly with the erotic nature of her festival.)

The goddess Peperuna, who bathes the sun each night, was also Christianized as Mary. In Russian Orthodox tradition she is called *Presvyataya Mariya Gromnitsa*, the 'Very Holy Mary the Thunderer'. Her especial festival is 2 February, Our Lady of the Candles, when tapers are lit in church. These tapers are brought home and lit before the icons when thunder threatens. In Poland they were taken home lit (it was very bad luck if they went out) and used to mark a cross on the ceiling, which guarded against lightning (Benet, 1951). From Peperuna she inherited her title of *Oynyena Maria* ('Fiery Mary'). Mary became the sister of Elijah the thunder saint, who replaced Perun. She is said to hold the golden keys of lightning, and appear in a column of flame just as Perun did (Hubbs, 1993).

This continuity of folklore and myth seems to indicate that the sun goddess is not such an evanescent figure after all. Despite the seeming hegemony of the male suns, the tradition of the solar female has been there all along.

The Celts: Grian

THE CELTS ARE PERHAPS the most written-about people in this book, except the Greeks. This is partly because of the many strong goddesses in their pantheons, which attract feminists, and partly because of the romantic aura that hangs over the Celtic Fringe. It is difficult to summarize the religion and myths of the Celts, since they were nomadic tribes who had no centralized worship. However, out of what seems like chaos there emerge among the Gauls, Britons and Irish striking similarities of functions, and sometimes also names, in their deities. By keeping these patterns in mind, one can sort through the many deities, both local and pan-national, and see the connections between them.

Much of what is known about the Celtic deities comes from folklore and literature recorded by monks, so that it is difficult to know whom the ancient Celts regarded as solar. The monks tended to treat the stories as a series of tales about extraordinary people rather than gods and goddesses. This sometimes obscures the actual nature of the deity in question. Often, however, one can make educated guesses based on things like imagery related to the god/goddess and customs surrounding his or her worship.

Despite this, once you start looking it is surprising how many goddesses there are with a connection to the sun. There are of course gods with these connotations as well, the Irish gods Lugh and Ogma being perfect examples. It is significant, however, that in both Welsh and Irish the words for 'sun' are feminine (*huan, grian*; Farrar, 1987), and that in Irish an exemplary woman is referred to as a 'sun' (McCrickard, 1990). Another feminine word for the sun in Irish is Mór, a personalized name, as in Mór *dhuit*, 'May the Sun bless you' (Farrar, 1991) and *ta Mór 'na surde*, 'the sun is up' (Dineen, 1927). Traces of sun goddesses appear throughout the Celtic realm; in Gaul (now France), Britain and Ireland. Some of them have a still-living tradition as proof of popularity; others have become completely obscure. For some there is only a name, and what scholars can guess through comparison with similar deities or from statuary and inscriptions.

The sun goddesses of the Celts tend to fall into three types. There is the light-bearing goddess connected to eternal flame and wells, named Minerva by the Romans. The second type is the solar horse goddess, who takes mortal lovers and is a symbol of the fire and speed of the sun. The third type is the goddess named after the sun, often a sun maiden alone or as one of a pair, who is sometimes rescued, fulfilling the classic Indo-European pattern.

Fire goddesses

The principal symbols of the first type are the eternal flame and the healing waters, along with the imagery of eyes and light. Both Sul of Bath and Brigit of Kildare are goddesses of this type. They both had perpetual fires in their temples, and both possessed the power to cure all illness (but especially those of the eyes). MacCrossan (1993) suggests that these may have originally all been one goddess called Sulis or Suleuia, whose epithets would have been Briganti, 'high one', or Belesama, 'most bright'.

Sul

Sul was the goddess of the hot springs at Bath in southwest England, a good example of the fire and water duality so common in Celtic thought. She ruled the thermal baths where heat and moisture mingled. The baths next to her temple were a healing centre where the naturally heated water evoked awe from visitors. The temple was in the centre of town, which probably grew up around it, since the baths were the most prestigious healing shrine in Britain (Webster, 1986). Her festivals were 2 February and 22 December (Farrar, 1987). Some think that the cakes known as Sally Lunns were offered at her altar.

Many writers think that Sul means 'sun' (Lurker, 1994; Monaghan, 1990; McCrickard, 1990), and it can also mean 'eye'. Her name is also close to words meaning 'burning' and 'shining', which suggest the solar fire (MacCulloch, 1911). Further, it is etymologically the same as the other names of sun goddesses in western Europe: Sól, Saule, Solntse etc. The cluster of images surrounding her clearly relate to her name, which seems almost like a pun, or at least a shorthand way of indicating the main outlines of her cult.

The Celts had created a shrine to the goddess around what they considered to be a sacred spring (they frequently worshipped such water sources). When the Romans arrived, they built the baths and a large sophisticated temple. They renamed the goddess Minerva Medica, just as they Romanized many other Celtic deities as they settled into the conquered areas. Her other name, Sul Minerva, shows the continuing power of the British goddess, as she is named first. Her statues showed her as a matronly woman in a bear hat with an owl under her foot, and a perpetual fire was kept burning in her temple (Monaghan, 1990). As a sort of tribute to Sul's solar and healing power, they put up statues of Apollo, to whom the Romans attributed the same functions. The temple they called Aquae Sulis, 'The waters of Sul'. It remained extremely popular with them, which helped to preserve it for archaeologists.

The perpetual fire kept in the shrines of the goddesses furnishes a hint of their solar nature. In Sul's case, an early traveller's guide (Condren, 1989, quoting Solinus) speaks of:

> hot baths, finely kept to the use of men, the sovereign of which baths is that the goddess Minerva [Sul], in whose chapel the fire burneth continually, and the coals do never turn to ashes, but as soon as the members are dead, it is turned into balls of stone.

The same idea occurs in stories of Brigit's fire at Kildare, which also burned without ash or waste (Gerald of Wales, 1982). This relates to the perpetual light of the sun, which also burns without waste or exhausting itself.

In R.J. Stewart's book *The Waters of the Gap* (1981), he suggests that:

> The steaming waters of Aquae Sulis would have been thought of as heated by the eternal fire, which renewed the Sun in Winter and the actual fire kept burning in the temple was a visible sign of this energy.

A hymn sung at Brigit's shrine shows that the goddess herself was the perpetual fire kept there (Monaghan, 1990):

> Brigid, excellent woman, sudden flame, may the bright fiery sun take us to the lasting kingdom.

This could be read as the saint, symbolized by the sun, carrying the soul to salvation through her intercession. Many of the prayers and stories of Brigit refer to her radiance or brightness. A prayer recited by monks, called 'Bride's genealogy', calls her a 'radiant flame of gold' (Carmichael, 1992). Fire is symbolically interpreted as solar in the Celtic tradition, a fact which could explain a great deal of the symbolism surrounding Brigit and Sul. Also, an obscure word for the sun, *tethin*, which is related to *teine*, fire, is of feminine gender (McCrickard, 1990). This brings together the sun, the fire and the goddess. The sacred fire could have been a way of making the sun-fire available to the worshipper.

Sul or the Suliviae (her triple form) was a goddess of healing and purifying, but also, oddly enough, a goddess of cursing. Tablets have been found in her springs with curses inscribed on them, in Latin mostly, which suggests that this was a Roman custom. If it was, the populace took it up with enthusiasm. It is still possible today to visit wells with cursing stones in them (Bord, 1976). (The Celts threw things into water sources to honour the spirits who lived in them, as is well attested by Roman accounts and archaeology.) There may be a connection here to the Norse sun goddess, who punished oath-breakers (McCrickard, 1990). As the all-seeing eye of the sun, she could administer punishment. It is interesting in this context that the cursing tablets often don't specify the person, but leave it up to the goddess to find the offender.

Sul's name is cognate to the Irish *suil*, which means 'eye', as in the eye of the heavens (Stewart, 1981). It may seem strange to connect eyes and springs, but there is a tradition of saints who plucked out their eyes and then either created a well, or used an existing one, to bathe their eye sockets and restore their vision (Saints Caolainn, Medana and Brigit). There is also a healing well at Ardagh in Ireland which was created when St Brigit dropped a coal she had been carrying in her bosom, which is another variant on the well-creation theme (Bord, 1976).

The idea seems to be that the goddess leaves a little of herself to give the water its power. The eye and the coal may be the same symbolically, a part of the sun goddess that transfers the heat and power of the goddess into the waters. There is also the similar shape of eyes and wells, which may have suggested the pun in Sul's name of eye/gap/sun, since all three share a rounded shape and either give or reflect light.

Further to that is the connection between eyes, sun and water that Green discusses in *The Sun-Gods of Europe* (1991): that sun and eyes were both seen as seeking truth and justice, and connected with light and power. Eye-power could equal sovereignty, and divine eyes reflected light as water and mirrors do. The warm water of the sun-shrines came from the heat and light of the sun, which in turn came from the sun goddess or her eyes. Models of eyes were left at Bath, and the saints' legends mentioned above make the connection between eyes and water. Several other Celtic goddesses of water had connection to eyes and light, including Sequaentia at Dijon, to whom the Celts left eyes and heads as offerings. The shrine to Apollo Vindonnus (Apollo being a Grecian god of the sun and especially its healing power) at Essavois is dedicated to clear vision and clear water, showing that the motif is a deeply rooted one.

Another connection between the sun goddess and the well or spring is the belief that the sun went into the sea at night, or down a hole or a well. This may have been how the Celts and Romans accounted for the warmth of the waters of Bath, which was an unusual phenomenon, and ensured its popularity through the ages. A Gaelic prayer to the sun at the beginning of this book says, 'you sink down into the perilous ocean without hurt'; this is an example of this tradition. The sun's visitation or gift of herself to the well gave it its healing power, and in the case of Bath its warmth. (The fire in the temple may have been a reminder of this presence.) Offerings of coins marked with phoenixes could well suggest the sun reborn from the waters (McCrickard, 1990).

Both Brigit and Sul are goddesses of healing waters, and people may have thought that the goddess's power to heal entered the water as she passed through it. Customs such as the Hogmanay (Scottish New Year) rite of dropping a live coal from the peat fire into a bowl of spring water and then sprinkling the house and family with the water for protection expressed this linkage of fire and water. (The story of the well formed by a coal dropped by Brigit is another example of this type of belief.) A variant was the use of quartz talismans to purify water and heal, since the Celts thought of quartz as a sunstone. (They may have seen quartz as solidified light, as the Hindus do [McCrickard, 1990].) One of these talismans was kept for dipping in the Bride's Well in Keppoch, Scotland. People went to the well for healing water and dipped the stone in it, while reciting a charm (McNeill, 1989). In many places people dropped quartz pebbles into holy wells as offerings.

The general governance of inspiration and handicrafts that was the province of Sul caused the Romans to assimilate her to their goddess Minerva. It is interesting that the Celtic goddesses so named have names that suggest the main themes of fire, light and power. From this description one can see the similarities with Brigit, both goddesses who taught the arts and crafts, and who were represented in their temples by an eternal flame. The prohibitions of St Eligius in the seventh century testified to the tradition of Brigit's patronage of women's arts: women were not to invoke Minerva (Brigit) while weaving, dyeing etc. (Beresford Ellis, 1992).

It is interesting that many deities associated with Minerva have names that relate to the sun or light. Belesama, or 'most bright', is the same as one translation given of Brigit. There was a grove dedicated to her at Vaucluse, in Gaul (Ross, 1992). Archaeologists have found around forty inscriptions mentioning the Suleviae in Europe, mostly in Rome or the Lower Rhine. These goddesses, whose name is plural for Sul or Sulevia, were patronesses of healing and called Minerva by Caesar (Beresford Ellis, 1992). The Suleviae appear on dedications as far east as Dacia, so they were popular goddesses.

Brigit

Brigit is one of the most popular goddesses of Ireland, and certainly the most enduring, representing as she did a beneficent force among the many war and death goddesses of the Celts. Various scholars have translated her name as 'fiery arrow', the 'bright one', or 'power' (Monaghan, 1990; Condren, 1989). Her sacred fire, kept first in her temple and later beside her church, was maintained faithfully until the Reformation.

In the genealogies of the Irish gods, she was either the wife or the mother of the chief male god, the Dagda. The main legends rarely mention her except in a capacity of wife or mother. However, statuary and inscriptions throughout the Celtic realms feature her name and image, which suggests that her cult was popular and widespread. The north of England was once known as Brigantia, as she was the tutelary deity of the tribes there. There she was a war goddess, along with the usual cultural aspects. Other features of her main holiday suggest that she was a fertility goddess as well, so that she was an extremely versatile deity, a quality much valued by the Celts. Because of her popularity, the Irish Christians adopted her as a saint, whose cult spread across Britain and Europe. Under the Christian dispensation, her cult of sacred wells continued, and pilgrimages to them became common. A group of nuns kept her sacred fire at Kildare, and her main festival on 2 February became her saint's day; thus many of the old customs surrounding her worship continued.

As both goddess and saint she rules poetry, smithcraft and healing, according to Cormac's Glossary, a ninth-century compendium (Condren, 1989). These three occupations are in the realm of culture and craft which Brigit, like Sul Minerva, oversaw. Both Sul and Brigit appear as triplicates. In the case of Brigit, this is because she governs three different functions, just as artists sometimes depicted another multi-talented god, Lugh, as three gods. Sul appears as the Suliviae probably for much the same reason, to show her threefold power over wisdom, healing and fire. In neither case do they represent the Wiccan three of maiden, mother and crone.

At Brigit's shrine in Kildare nineteen nuns kept a sacred fire, and no man could go past the hedge surrounding it. The nuns took their turns keeping the fire for nineteen nights, and Brigit herself tended it on the twentieth. (The fire was left to burn unattended until morning.) The sacred fire was of peat bricks, and it was reputed to burn without ash or waste. A door in the church led to the enclosure beside it, which suggests a happy combination of Christian and pagan belief. The women who tended the fire were called *Inghean an Dagha*, 'Daughter(s) of Fire'.

No one knows if her shrine existed before Christianity, but even so it was an unusual institution, being a residence for both nuns and monks, run by an abbess who had the powers of a bishop. The Archbishop of Dublin closed the shrine in the thirteenth century, because he felt that the sacred fire and its watchers were pagan. It reopened after his death but was finally outlawed during the Reformation (Howard, 1994). However, the popularity of the saint ensured that even now there are still many holy wells named for her, which pilgrims still visit.

Folklorists wrote down prayers invoking St Brigit at the beginning of the twentieth century, showing that the tradition of Brigit as a protective and fertilizing force was still alive then. The *Carmina Gadelica* by Alexander Carmichael (1992) recorded many of these prayers and songs. He worked in the Outer Hebrides, a remote area largely untouched by the forces of modernization. In these prayers and customs the tradition of Brigit's especially feminine presence continued with her protection of women and children. Despite her marriages to various deities and mortals in the legends, Brigit retains a strong flavour of women's mysteries. The enclosure around her sacred fire was forbidden to men, and dire punishment befell those reckless enough to trespass (Gerald of Wales, 1982). Women tended the hearth and their invocation of Brigit as they covered it at night shows that even the fire in the home shared in her sacred nature.

When one considers the solar nature of this intensely feminine deity, the first clue is her name, the 'bright one', or 'fiery arrow'. The fiery arrow could be a pun for the sun's rays. The other translation, bright one, also is suggestive of solar symbolism. Many other deities have been defined as solar with little more by way of evidence than a name (e.g. Belenos, 'shining', often thought to be a sun god). Other evidence includes the Bride's crosses made every 2 February in her honour, which are in the shape of quartered circles (sun-wheels) or a modified swastika, another ancient sun symbol. Both of these symbols appear throughout the Celtic realms and across northern Europe, and are generally agreed to have a solar connotation. The dandelion was her flower, an obvious sun emblem. People would go to wells dedicated to her to watch the sun dance at Easter.

One of the more obscure legends of the saint also reveals her solar nature. Brigit fell in a river at nightfall, and struck her head on a stone, and the blood from the cut stained the river red. This water then cures two dumb daughters of a nearby woman, and the stone becomes a sacred healing stone (McCrickard, 1987). The sun-goddess motifs are similar to those in the Baltic *dainas*: the goddess stains something red at sunset, and water she touches heals wounds. The sacred stone and two daughters correspond to other details of Saule's myths, but filtered through time and thus distorted.

Another such story is the *Life of St Brigit* (Gregory, 1985), which says that she was born at sunrise, at the threshold of the house, while her mother was going out with a pail of milk. As she stepped over the threshold, one foot inside and one out, she brought forth Brigit. This fulfilled a prophecy made by a druid that she would be born neither inside nor outside a house, nor during the day or the night. Later, the house that the saint was staying in flamed up to heaven, a fiery pillar rose from her head, she hung her cloak on sunbeams, and cow dung blazed before her (Condren, 1989).

All of these things point to her light-bearing nature, and emphasize the solar nature of her patronage of fire. Being born at sunrise corresponds with many solar traditions where the sun is reborn each day, and the fiery pillar could stand for light. (The sun goddess's head is often the source of her radiance, as in Germany.) Things burn around her, since she is identified with fire and the heat of the sun, and she controls the sunbeams. Attributes of the saint, such as the ability to multiply or improve food, and her connection to fertility, suggest the role that the sun played in agriculture, especially in extremely rainy Ireland. The northern sun goddesses brought fertility with their return, since the lengthening of the days indicates spring and vegetation, as well as the beginning of the farming season.

Her main festival (or saint's day) is 2 February, and is called Imbolc or Oimelc. This is when the snowdrops appear and the ewes bear their young and begin to lactate. The main theme of this festival is the return of light and spring after the dark and cold of winter, and many of its customs involve light and fire. A charm recited on that day (Stewart, 1981) echoes the light-bearing theme:

Hail reign a fair maiden with gold upon your toe,
Open up the West Gate and let the old year go;
Hail reign a fair maiden with gold upon your chin,
Open up the East Gate and let the New Year in;
Levideu sing Levideu the water and wine
The seven bright gold wires and the candles that do shine.

The reason for this seems to be to invoke the return of the sun and release the old year (represented by the Calliech or Hag of winter) to the west, which is the region of the land of the dead in Celtic mythology. Gold is the solar metal, and the linking of light and Brigit is well established (when the shrine at Kildare became Christian, the head of the monks had to be a goldsmith).

A significant part of the festival is the lighting of candles at midnight, which was once done on the eve of the festival, but is now done on 2 February. The symbolism of light reborn from the darkness could not be more obvious. A Christianized version of this idea has Brigit as Christ's foster-mother, distracting Herod's soldiers by either carrying two candles before them or else wearing a crown of candles and capering so that Mary and Jesus can escape (Matthews, 1989). (This is a tradition similar to that of the Swedish St Lucia, who also wears a crown of candles. Both represent the overcoming of darkness with light.) The Irish Church probably invented tradition to account for the blessing of candles on Bride's day.

The returning light is emphasized by a custom in some places in Co. Leitrim of affixing figures of the sun, moon and stars to a board and hanging them up with the Bride's cross (Durdin-Robertson, 1990). This ceremony also pertained to the increasing light and the return of the maiden sun from captivity. The returning sun brought warmth as well; Brigit was supposed to dip her finger in the waters to warm them on her feast day. She also carried a white hazel wand, which could stand for a sunbeam, especially since it too warmed the land as she passed (McCrickard, 1987).

Another Imbolc tradition is that of dressing a doll in white, with a pebble of clear quartz over the 'heart', and placing it in a basket (Ó Catháin, 1995). The inhabitants invited the doll into the house and performed various songs and chants. This custom from the Outer Hebrides connects to the solar aspect of Brigit because clear quartz (commonly called 'crystal') is connected in Celtic lore to the sun. The doll was laid in a bed and the hearth raked to catch the footprints of the goddess should she visit the household during the evening.

The Scots said that at Imbolc the winter goddess Bera released Brigit and spring after turning the world to ice with her silver hammer at Samhain (Toulson, 1981). A similar idea appears in a medieval Irish text called 'The Book of Linsmore', which tells of a game played by the boys of Rome where a gaming board is set up with a figure of a hag and a maiden on opposite sides. The hag let loose a dragon against the maiden, who countered it with a lamb, and then she released a lion, which the maiden defeated with a shower of hail. The book uses this game to explain Samhain (All Saint's Day), but it also relates to Imbolc as the time of the maiden's victory over the winter (Matthews, 1989). This symbolic conflict is a common sun-goddess motif, which occurs in other chapters.

Horse goddesses

The second type of Celtic sun goddess has the horse as her symbol. The horse is often an emblem of the sun in many European cultures, including that of the Celts. While it would be wrong to say that the horse and sun are always related, there are strong ties between them. Áine and Macha are two demonstrably solar goddesses who have the horse as an emblem.

Áine

Áine of Knockaine is a goddess noted among other things for her habit of taking mortal lovers. The hill of Cnoc Aine (in Co. Limerick) is her habitat, where she is still honoured although now referred to as a fairy. A charming legend about her is that she gave the meadowsweet its scent (Farrar and Farrar, 1987). She is the special patron of Co. Limerick, Ireland, and has two wells named after her in Derry and Tyrone. (there may be more under the pseudonym St Ann [MacCana, 1983].) One of them, Tobar-Na-h'Aine, is a life-restoring well (MacDonald and McSkimming, 1992).

Áine means 'brightness, heat, speed'. Her other title is *Lair Derg*, the red mare. (The word *ain* is cognate to the Latin *ignis*, 'fire'.) Another translation of her name is *ainne*, 'ring, a gold finger-ring' (O'Rahilly, 1984). MacCrossan (1993) suggests her name is similar to that of Aedh, an Irish fire god. Her festival is midsummer, and is marked by a torchlight procession about her hill, led by young women, and a bonfire-vigil. Manannan is often her husband or lover in the legends (Rees and Rees, 1991), and so she may be a counterpart of Rhiannon, another horse goddess, whose second husband is the Welsh equivalent of the sea god. Like Rhiannon, she had a son by a mortal man, although without the same subsequent tragedy (Rhiannon's son was stolen from her and she was accused of killing him after the frightened nurses framed her).

Her connection to the Welsh Rhiannon, her name and her title of 'red mare' establish her as a horse goddess. The derivation of her name from words connected to speed and heat suggests both an equine and a solar nature. These would symbolize the speed of the sun as it crosses the sky. Her solar nature relates to her connections to gold, fire and the colour red. Red is her main colour. That her festival is at midsummer, suggests sun worship. If her name does derive from 'gold ring', it is an interesting coincidence that some *dainas* described Saule as a gold ring. The Indo-Europeans persisted in seeing the sun as red, perhaps because of its association with fire. Gold was also connected with the sun, which seems more obvious. Of course, the red gold of the British Celts reconciles these two colour symbols.

The sun aspect makes for a tie with her sister Grian, whose centre of worship is seven miles away and whose name means 'sun'. Both have mounds named after them, presumably centres of sun worship, as hills often are. A less obvious tie between them is that Grian may also be a horse goddess. (Grian is often associated with Macha, who is definitely equine.) Áine and Macha have their similarities, both having relations with mortal men and sharing the horse as a totem.

Another goddess with connections to Áine, although not very strong ones, is Gráinne, through their relations with the hero Finn. Áine was smitten with him, but was under *geis* (taboo) not to sleep with a man with silver hair. Finn was young then, but the goddess's sister tempted him into a stream that would turn his hair grey, and so she got him for herself (Monaghan, 1990). Another story has it that she was his lover for seven years, and they had two children (Dames, 1992). It was at Cnoc Áine that Finn acquired otherworldly knowledge, by drinking from a well (Kennedy and Smyth, 1989).

Áine's festival is at the height of the sun's power, before it starts to wane into autumn and winter. To celebrate, farmers carried torches of straw and waved them over animals and fields for protection and fruit-fulness. This seems a way of carrying the sun's blessing of prosperity, through fire, which the Celts considered to be analogous to the sun's fire. It seems to validate MacCrossan's (1993) association of Áine with fire.

Macha

Macha tends to be remembered as a fierce war goddess of Northern Ireland who claimed the heads of the slain as her especial tribute. Condren's fascinating book *The Serpent and the Goddess* (1989) relates her earlier exploits as a queen and builder, which most books do not mention. From these stories one can trace the sun-motifs connected to her.

Macha's legend comes from several different sources; these may have even involved different characters who finally became one fearful triple goddess. She is first mentioned as the wife of Nemedh ('the sacred one'), who names the twelfth plain he clears after her. She dies of a broken heart after she has a vision of the destruction a war will wreak on that plain. The second mention is as the wife of the king Nuada whom Balor killed at the second battle of Magh Tuireadh, a battle between the new gods, led by Nuada, and the older ones (Beresford Ellis, 1992).

The next two stories are more detailed and suggestive. Both connect her with Ulster, and provide clues to her nature as a goddess. The first is the tale of 'The Debility of the Men of Ulster'. It begins with a widower whom a young woman visited one day. She did all the chores, always turning right, or sunwise. That night she slept with him, and all was well until he went to the annual assembly of the Ulstermen. She begged him not to go, and, when he refused her, not to mention her to anyone. Unfortunately, he broke his promise by bragging to the high king that his wife could outrun the king's horses. The king imprisoned him and sent men to get Macha to race his horses. They brought her, although she was ready to give birth, and made her race despite her pleas for mercy. To save her husband, she ran the race and won, collapsing at the finish line. Before she died, she gave birth to twins, and cursed the men of Ulster, so that in time of great need they would be as weak as a woman in childbirth for four days and five nights (Caldecott, 1988).

Another story is that of Mac Mong Ruadh, Macha of the Red Tresses, historically the sixty-seventh monarch of Ireland. She built Ard Macha (Armagh) and established Emain Macha (Navan) as the capital of Ulster. She gained her throne by a trick after she learned that she could not inherit it from her father. She beat the three who refused her in battle and she reigned seven years, after which she would not surrender the throne to them. She argued that none of the agreements about the kingship said anything about winning the throne in battle. She later tricked them into building her fort for her after she marked out the site with her brooch pin (Condren, 1989).

Thus two aspects of Macha the goddess appear: she is a goddess of sovereignty, and a horse goddess. Another account of how Ard Macha got its name suggests that there is a connection between her and the sun goddess Grian (Condren, 1989):

> And men say that she was Grian Banchure, 'the Sun of Womanfolk', daughter of Mider of Bri Leith. And after this when she died, and her tomb was raised on Ard Macha, and her lamentation was made, and her gravestone was planted. Whence Ard Machae, 'Macha's Height'.

One of her titles was 'bright Grian and pure Macha' (Condren, 1989). Both of these titles are early ones, from the stories of her queenship. Either she was the same goddess as Grian, or else they had common attributes.

Her horse form connects her to Áine, Grian's sister. Anne Ross connects the solar horse with healing, and Macha is said to have built the first hospital in Ireland. Some hints of Macha's solar nature carry over into her myths: her red tresses could be sunbeams, and she turns always sunwise in 'The Debility of the Men of Ulster'. While it is not certain that she actually is a sun goddess, she certainly shows the traces of the earlier horse and sun goddess that occurs across Europe.

Macha's brooch also is a significant point; the brass circle could be a sun symbol. One of the translations of Emain Macha is 'Macha's brooch' (Rolleston, 1994). There is a similarity here with Brigit, who was told she could have all the land her cloak could cover, and it expanded miraculously to cover many acres. In both cases an item of clothing symbolizes the goddess's sovereignty over her realm, and shows that like the sun's light they spread their influence over the land. Macha's red tresses, if they are sunbeams, can also fit in here, as the sun shines over the land, and rules it.

Another interpretation of Emain Macha is 'Macha's twins' from her children born at the end of her race. (The usual explanation of the twins is that they represent the two forts on Macha's plain.) McCrickard (1990) suggests that this connects her to the Baltic sun goddess Saule, who has the mare as a symbol, as well as an association with twin horse gods. (Epona, the Gaulish horse goddess, appeared with twin foals, and Rhiannon, the Welsh mare deity, has a son the same night as a foal is born [O'Flaherty, 1980].) This birth has its own significance. Some scholars think that this is part of an ancient Indo-European myth (O'Flaherty, 1980).

SUN WOMEN

The last category of sun goddesses is the ones whose name means 'sun'. These would seem to be the most obvious candidates for the role of solar deity, and it is a pity that for the most part their legends are so obscure.

GRIAN

Grian is an Irish goddess whose name means 'sun'. Some think she is Áine's twin. She is a very obscure goddess, who dwells on Cnoc Gréne, at Pailias Gréine in Co. Limerick, seven miles from Knockaine (Cnoc Aine). It was named after 'the Lady Grian of the bright cheeks', who fought off Conall's five sons by turning them into badgers, after they destroyed her *síde* (Logan, 1981). Both she and Áine are the daughters of Fer I, son of Eogbal. Grian is also sometimes the daughter of the legendary Finn or the alter ego of Macha (O'Rahilly, 1984). Other areas named after her include Loch Gréne, Tuaimm Gréne and the river Grian (Graney), all in the east of Co. Clare, as well as Greane Hill in Kilkenny (O'Rahilly, 1984). It is interesting that one of the three kings of the Tuatha de Danann was called MacGriéne because 'he chose Grian for his god' (Borlase, 1897). Of course, since the sun is a feminine word, she was his goddess.

An interesting sidelight on Grian comes from the *Rennes Dinesdenchas*, which records the stories of how places got their names. Two horses named Gáeth and Grian ('Wind' and 'Sun') were chased into the lake by a foal and drowned. Another version of the story is that the foal was a stallion called Serrach, who followed the horses looking for a mare to mate with, but instead frightened the horses into their watery death, hence the lake's name: Lake of Two Horses (Stokes, 1895). Macha and Áine were two other sun goddesses associated with horses, and Macha and Grian are sometimes said to be the same goddess. This story may record a legend about Grian's horse form.

Monaghan (1990) suggests that Grian represents the sun of winter. The old Scots idea of the 'big sun' of summer and the 'little sun' of winter could support that notion. (In their reckoning, summer would run from May Day to All Saints' in November, or Beltane to Samhain [Rees and Rees, 1991].) Grian's time would represent the period when women spent most of their time in the *grianán* doing the work and enjoying what little sun there was. There may have had a corresponding winter festival that has been lost, just as Áine's festival was celebrated in the summer. It would not be so unusual to have a dual goddess, one aspect of whom represents the stronger sun of summer and the other the weakened sun of winter.

A word related to the name of the goddess is *grianán*, which means 'abode of the sun'. It is a place apart, and the abode of women, sometimes just on top of a house or a special building of 'crystal' (clear quartz) which was the home of a fairy woman. In legend there was one at the top of the high king's dwelling at Tara. One such dwelling held Princess Sunbeam until the hero Conall passed the test of getting her out of it (Ralston, 1977). Quartz was the *grianchloichit* ('sunstone') which, as discussed earlier, was dipped in water to bring the healing power of the sun into it, and dropped in wells as an offering to the goddess who cured. Its very name proves the closeness of the connection between it and the sun. People dropped quartz into wells as an offering to the sun of the stone most precious to it, and perhaps to replace some of the virtue of the sun's power used in healing people, since they saw the stone as solidified light.

Grainne

It is difficult, because so many of the old stories were handed down as folktales, to distinguish who is and is not a god/goddess. One thing that is certain, however, is that the tale of Finn's pursuit of Grainne and Diarmuid has clear solar motifs. It may very well relate to mythologies about the sun and moon chasing each other through the sky.

Her story begins with her approaching marriage to Finn, the great Irish hero (Caldecott, 1988; Monaghan, 1990). She is unwilling to marry him, because he is now greying, but after he meets conditions she sets for him, their marriage seems inevitable. At the feast the night before the wedding, she sees Diarmuid, one of his men, and falls in love. (Diarmuid, whose grandfather is the Irish love god Aonghus mac Og, has a love spot that makes him irresistible to women who see it.) She passes around her golden cup of drugged mead, so that Finn and her father sleep, and then goes to Diarmuid and lays a *geis* (a form of taboo involving an obligation) on him to help her escape this marriage. He dithers a bit but cannot find a loophole, and so escapes with her.

Afterwards he can find no way to return, since he has provoked the wrath of Finn, and has promised Gráinne his protection. They travel the countryside, sleeping in a different cave every night. (Caves and dolmens in Ireland are named after them to this day.) At first Diarmuid won't sleep with her, but she puts another *geis* on him, and after he sleeps with her he falls in love with her, too. Finn chases them for a year and a day, then they make peace and the couple settles down for 16 years. At the end of that time Gráinne seeks peace with Finn by inviting him to stay. Finn visits them, secretly planning Diarmuid's death. A boar gores him and Finn refuses to use his curative powers to save him.

If Gráinne is indeed the sun, then Finn ('bright', 'white') would be the moon, chasing her across the Irish countryside. The refuge in caves explains where the sun goes at night. As we have seen, many caves and dolmens to this day are associated with the lovers. Dames (1992) thinks that the many dolmens associated with Gráinne were originally associated with Grian/Greine (the sun), which would make her a later form of the sun goddess (Beresford Ellis, 1992). Her story may be a later version of an ancient myth of a sun–moon chase.

The year and a day that Finn chases her is the year of folklore, which reconciles where the thirteen 'common-law' months of the lunar year (28 days each) and the twelve months of the solar year meet, just as Finn and Gráinne finally make up. (The lunar year only makes 364 days, and so the extra day is made up in the solar year of 365.) Finn's connection with boars, his silver hair and his ability to heal suggest the moon gods of northern Europe. (Local legend links him and Áine, saying that they lived together for seven years. Obviously sun goddesses have an attraction for him.) Advocates of this idea point to the fact that a word for moon in Irish is masculine (*luan*). It also refers to the nimbus of light around Irish heroes' heads when they enter their battle-frenzy (*luan láit*, literally 'warrior's moon' [Dineen, 1927]).

Gráinne's name is usually translated as 'Hateful' or 'Ugliness'. In that case she might represent, along with Macha, the more destructive aspects of the sun. Since both of them have somewhat ambiguous reputations, as opposed to the usual benign sun goddess, it may be that they represent some less popular aspects of the sun. If Gráinne is equivalent to Grian, she may represent the 'hateful' sun of winter that withholds warmth; this makes sense for northern countries. In the south it is the sun of high summer that is sometimes hateful, because of the terrible heat and drought it produces.

MacCana suggests that Gráinne is a form of the loathsome lady who is transformed by a kiss into a beautiful princess, which might help to explain Diarmuid's initial repugnance (this would be similar to the Calliech/Brigit form of sun goddess [MacCana, 1983]). If she represents the winter sun, it may be that her transformation through Diarmuid brings on the warm weather and her fair aspect. Many Celtic legends turn on such transformations, where the hero who overcomes his repugnance to the hag (usually described as surrealistically horrible) proves him to be worthy of her love.

In line with this is Dames's (1992) suggestion that their mating is that of the underworld god Donn and the sun goddess Grian/Griánne. Grain is a girl's name meaning 'beauty, brightness', which merges with *grainne* 'ugliness', as the goddess descends into the underworld. He also suggests that the legend of a golden sword that Diarmuid finds as he enters a cave with Gráinne on the night they lie together relates to the Swedish petro-glyph of a sword pointing to the middle of a sun-disc, especially since the Irish word *colg* means both 'sword' and 'penis'.

DÉR GRÉINE AND DIA GRÉINE

'The Expedition of Loegaire, Son of Crimthann' is an obvious sun-rescue myth. Loegaire is at an assembly with the men of Connacht, and a fairy king appears and appeals for aid. The king tells them that his wife has been kidnapped and he needs help to rescue her. He has fought seven battles for her already and needs to win this one to get her back. Loegaire and fifty men go beneath the waves with him and win the battle. They return with the king's wife, and Loegaire marries her daughter, Dér Gréine ('sun-tear') (Jackson, 1994).

It would not seem unreasonable to suggest that they may be a solar mother–daughter dyad. Fiachna (the king's wife) would be the sun mother, since solar females are paired so often. Dér Gréine's name is mys-terious, although it may mean that she is the rays or the glow around the sun, which would be a kenning. Other sun daughters symbolize the glow of the sun or the dawn. There is a similar myth in Scotland in which a fox and a young man named Brian rescue Dia Griéne from the Land of Big Women. Brian has to get her to bring a sword of light from the women, which he then cuts off the fox's head with, to reveal Dia Griéne's father, who was under a spell (Campbell, 1862). Her name translates as 'goddess of the sun', or 'sun-tear'. The story seems to have been a sun-rescue myth that became enfolded into a larger adventure.

Giolla Gréine and Aimend

Two more characters with more mysterious origins are Giolla Gréine and Aimend. Giolla Gréine was the daughter of a human father and a sun-beam, who was so upset at learning of her parentage that she leapt into Loch Gréine ('lake of the sun'), floated to Daire Gréine ('oak of the sun') and died at Tuam Gréine ('tomb of the sun') (Beresford Ellis, 1992). The *Dictionary of Celtic Mythology* (Beresford Ellis, 1992) lists Aimend as a sun goddess. She is probably the daughter of Dian Cecht, the Irish physician god who killed his son in a fit of jealousy. She watered his grave and 365 herbs grew out of it, one for each day of the year. This corresponds with the Celtic idea of the sun as a healing force, and with the observation that the sun makes plants grow.

Mór Mumain

Mór, as discussed earlier, is a name for the sun. It is also the name of a sovereignty goddess of Munster, who married many kings, and whose sons were all kings or at least bishops. It is not surprising that Munster should have a sun goddess as its progenitrix, since it is from this area that Grian and Áine hail. Her travels through Munster's thirds as she marries their kings form a just-so story of how each king in turn was sovereign of the province (Clarke, 1991). The fort where she died was named after her in the mythical geography of Ireland (Stokes, 1895). Another legend is that the kings of Ireland were seeking Mór, and the locals pointed out her 'House' on the western edge of Corco Duibne. They told the kings that when the sun shone Mór was on her throne (Rees and Rees, 1991). It may be a memory of her that survives in the proverbs of Mór the peasant woman and her servant (Dineen, 1927).

These sun women, along with Grian and Graínne, may be the basis for certain statues unearthed in France (Green, 1991). They are generally called 'Venuses' because of their form: a naked young woman. Archaeologists found them near springs in Burgundy, Vichy and Kent, and buried at Baden. They apparently came from manufacturing centres in Gaul and the Rhineland and were made of pipe-clay. The significant thing about them is that the manufacturers covered them with solar symbols. These are generally circles with six-sided stars or rayed or dotted rings.

The many kinds of goddess of the sun in the Celtic realm are a tribute to the diversity of the religious imagination. The goddess of inspiration in the eternal flame, the Indo-European horse goddess, and the goddess named after the sun itself are superficially dissimilar, yet all are fitting symbols of the fiery women of the Celts.

The Hittites: Arinitti

Until 1907, knowledge of the Hittites was limited to references to the 'Horites' in the Old Testament. But German archaeologists found the remnants of the Hittite capital in the city of Bogazköy, in Turkey, and this ancient empire began to be unearthed by modern scholars. One of the most revealing finds was a hoard of twenty-five thousand clay tablets in a variety of languages, which abound in details of law, rulership, religion and mythology. The finding of the buildings that the Hittites had lived, worked and worshipped in helped fill in the picture of this once power-ful civilization. One of the most significant discoveries was that Hittite was an Indo-European language, as discussed in the first chapter.

From their base in the Caucasus, the Hittites' empire had spread over most of Anatolia. They were polytheists who adopted the gods of every-one they conquered, and referred to them as the 'Thousand Gods of Hatti'. At the height of their power they controlled the central region of Anatolia, before collapsing in 1200 BCE, to leave a number of smaller civ-ilizations behind them. They borrowed some of their culture from the other peoples they encountered along their way, which makes them an interesting mix of Semitic and Indo-European ideas. These peoples included the Hattians, Hurrians, some Syrians and the Mesopotamians of the north (Güterbock, 1916).

The Hattians, as the conquerors called them, lived on the central plain of Anatolia, in an area bounded by the Kizil Irmak river. They had mostly female deities, including the sun goddess Wurusemu and her daughter Mezulla. Their myths and cults proved popular with the Hittites, who adopted them, although their scribes made the relationships between the deities more formal. Hattian myths have the common theme of a disap-pearing god.

The Hurrians were not native to the area, but are thought to have come from the northeast Caucasus, to judge by their language. They settled in northern Mesopotamia in the first millennium BCE, and their culture influ-enced the Assyrians, Ugarits and Hittites. They borrowed many gods from the Mesopotamians, but their weather god Teshub grew to prominence beside the sun goddess of Arinna (a Hurrian city) as the royal patrons.

Other cultures that the Hittites came into contact with during the expansion of their empire included the Luwian and Palaic peoples. The Luwian people also spoke an Indo-European language and lived in south-west Anatolia. They had many gods similar to those in the rest of the empire: weather god, moon god, and the goddess Kamrushepa, who rescues the moon, and later the fertility god Telipinu. After the Hittite empire collapsed, their language prevailed until their absorption by Greek colonies. The Palaic peoples lived in the north and were Indo-European as well. Archaeologists found tablets in Luwian and Palaic along with the Hittite ones mentioned above.

Two central deities of all the Anatolians were the god of the mountain and the goddess of the spring. The god was shown dressed as a warrior and riding a bull, while the goddess was shown as fecund and obviously feminine. Local cults abounded, although mostly they included the two main gods, and a sun god or goddess. The cult of the mountain expressed itself in state religion with a personalized mountain that the weather god stood on in pictures. Other gods included Telipinu, the disappearing god of fertility, who some see as a forerunner of Attis.

Sun Goddess

Among the deities that the Hittites adopted for their pantheon were several sun gods and goddesses. The most important of these was the sun goddess of Arinna who became a state patron deity. Inscriptions that mention her do so as $^{D}UTU^{URU}$ Arinna, which essentially means 'sun goddess of Arinna', which is a title; her actual name was lost. She was also known as 'one of Arinna', since that was her cult-centre (Leick, 1991), and also as Gasania, 'My Lady'. The Hattians called her Wurusemu, and worshipped her, although in a less formal fashion than the Hittites. However, the Hittites identified her with their main goddess, Hebat, and so she and the weather god became the royal patrons after 1400 BCE.

The divine couple had several children: two daughters called Hulla and Mezulla, and a son also called the weather god, who ruled either Nerik or Zippalanda. (The two daughters might have been like the Zoryas of Slavic myth, and the storm son of Teshub like Perkunas's sons, who were thunder and lightning.) They even have a granddaughter, Zinhuti ('granddaughter') (Güterbock, 1916). Zinhuti was often called on as an intermediary who would take the worshipper's prayers to her grandparents (Houwink ten Cate, 1969). The sun goddess's earlier incarnation among the Hattians, Wurusemu, was also married to the storm god, then called Taru, but their children's names didn't change from one culture to the other.

Queen of heaven and earth

The state cult centred on the city of Bogazköy, one day's ride from the city of Arinna. Not surprisingly, then, the cult of the sun goddess became a major state religion. She and her consort the weather god were the state patrons, called on to protect the king and queen and bestow their favour on all royal business. The sun goddess seems to have had precedence over her husband, and also was the main protector of state and king.

Her role in the state cult seems to have affected her functions as a goddess. In prayers and hymns she seems to perform as a queen (Lehmann, 1977):

Thou art mistress of the righteous judgement.
Over heaven and earth dost thou graciously wield royal authority.
Thou dost mark out the borders of the lands.
Thou dost hearken to complaints.

The same hymn also hints that she is chief priestess for the rest of the gods, just as the queen was her priestess:

For the gods dost thou, O Sun-goddess of Arinna, prepare the rites of sacrifice.

Many of these prayers refer to her as the 'mistress' of the rulers and land of the Hittites, and state that only under her patronage can they flourish. Even making allowances for flattery, it would seem that the Hittites saw the sun goddess as a powerful force.

Like many other sun deities, Arinitti gave judgement, as the all-seeing sun. One hymn to her states (Lehmann, 1977):

In the lands art thou an honoured deity.
Father and mother of every land art thou.
Blessed mistress of judgement art thou.
Thou art unwearying in the seat of judgement.

King Hattusilis and Queen Pudhepa prayed to her and the storm god to purify the country of sin, and to have mercy on the sinners. When anything went wrong they had to learn by oracle what had offended the gods and expiate the sin. Perhaps in such a legalistic system of morality it is hardly surprising that the merciful nature of Arinitti is heavily emphasized:

Thou, O Sun-goddess of Arinna, art a merciful deity.
Thou dost show mercy.
The blessed man is dear to thee, O Sun-goddess of Arinna.
To him dost thou, O Sun-goddess of Arinna, grant forgiveness.

Of course, a merciful nature is fairly typical of the sun goddesses covered in this book, such as Saule.

The prayers also give some idea of the Hittite cosmology and conception of the sun. The festivities surrounding Arinitti's cult involved sun-discs, and a prayer refers to her as 'torch of the Hittite country' (Houwick ten Cate, 1969). This may be a borrowing from the Babylonian sun god/goddess Shamash, who was often represented as a torch. Another idea that seems to have come from the Babylonians is that of heaven as a solid vault, with little openings and gates in it (Lehmann, 1977):

Thou dost open the doors of heaven.
And thou dost smite the gate of heaven and stride through.

This seems contrary to the Indo-European idea of the sky as an open space that the sun rides through, although the Iranians also thought of the sky as made of stone. There seems to be no mention of a chariot of the sun, or her horses, although the Hittites exported chariots and raced them. We know that she did live in the sky, because she is said to gaze down on the king and queen, and pass through the underworld at night (see below).

Goddess of war

Because Arinitti was identified with the rulers and the empire, the kings invoked her first in wartime and times of trouble, as the most powerful (and therefore useful) deity. The following came from the annals of the reign of Mursilis II (Gurney, 1990):

Sun-goddess of Arinna, my lady, the surrounding hostile countries which called me a child and made light of me and were constantly trying to seize thy territo-ries, O Sun-goddess of Arinna, my lady – come down, O Sun-goddess of Arinna, my lady, and smite these hostile countries for me.

It goes on to say that she did indeed smite the foe, and he expresses his thanks.

Sun of the earth

The sun in its underworld phase had another name: Lelwani, 'sun god-dess of earth' (Laroche, 1991a). This aspect was once an independent male deity, during the Old Hittite Empire. He was identified with the Mesopotamian goddess Erishkegal, and so became female. Queen Pudhepa invoked Lelwani as a goddess. Under Hattian influence Lelwani became associated with their sun goddess of Arinna, so the sun goddess took on chthonic characteristics. (Leick, 1991).

In this underworld capacity she was invoked at funerals, and given half the sacrifice, while the dead got the other part. (She must have been important to the dead, considering her part was an ox and nine sheep

[Gurney, 1990].) Offerings to the goddess in her chthonic aspect were made in pits. A royal grave found at Gávurkalesi has a relief on the wall facing the door of a goddess resembling Arinitti sitting on a throne with two male figures facing her, probably the weather god and his son (Deighton, 1982). Because of her role as the underworld goddess, the Hittites thought that Arinitti was powerful in magic and often invoked her in ritual (Leick, 1991).

Two goddesses associated with the sun are Istustaya and Papaya, who foretell the fate of the king at his coronation, with their spindles and bowls of water. Presumably they did this by measuring out his years of rule (like many fate goddesses) and seeking visions in the bowls of water. These two goddesses live in the underworld, and the sun goddess is often mentioned along with them, since all three goddesses are connected to the dead and the king. The two goddesses accompany the sun goddess as she travels through the underworld. The association with the sun goddess is intriguing because both spinning and reflective water are part of the sun cult. The Swedish sun goddess spins her sunbeams, and in Ireland at Easter people reflect the sun in bowls of water to bless the house. The Sumerian ideogram for Arinna was a spring, so water was probably part of her original cult, possibly centring around a sacred spring (Deighton, 1982).

Queen/priestess

The queen was also the chief priestess, and earthly representative, of the sun goddess, rather like the pharaohs in Egypt. Queens ruled until death, so until the Queen Mother died, the king's wife was powerless. Some derive from this a matriarchal or matrilineal system. The identification of queen and sun began with Queen Pudhepa (thirteenth century BCE) who was a priestess of Hebat, a sky goddess of the Hattians. Pudhepa combined Hebat and the Hittite sun goddess, and had seals made of herself in the embrace of the sun goddess of Arinna.

As the weather god was the sun goddess' consort, so the king was his representative on earth. The god was the real king of the Hittites, entrusting the throne to a mortal. Teshub, as the Hittites called him, had the bull as his symbol, both because of its roars that mimicked thunder and the fertility of its seed/rain. The king and queen enacted a yearly sacred marriage as the personified gods during the New Year festival, to further fertility of the earth (James, 1959). The king's function as chief priest of the sun goddess is in some texts a way of indicating his royalty.

The yearly procession

The rock-relief at Yazilikaya shows the celestial royal family, in a frieze of two processions of deities coming towards each other, with the sun goddess and weather god facing each other in the middle. The weather god is wearing a cap that rises to a point, a tunic and shoes with upturned points. He has a beard, and holds a sceptre in one hand. A bull is beside him, and he stands on two smaller gods, probably mountain gods. The sun goddess wears a tall cylindrical striped cap, a blouse with long puffy sleeves and a long pleated skirt. She too wears the upturned shoes, and stands on a lioness. Each stretches out a hand towards the other, and above the hands are the hieroglyphs of their names.

Behind the sun goddess is her son, carrying a double axe and a monkey, and then her two daughters. The son is probably the weather god of Nerik, and the two are Hulla and Mezulla, who wear the same clothes as their mother, and stand on a double-headed eagle. Like their mother, they stretch out one hand and appear to beckon with the other, which they curl back towards the chest. The annual 'sacred marriage', enacted by the king and queen in their roles as the deities' representatives on earth, is probably the basis of this frieze.

Temples

The city of Arinna had a temple complex dedicated to their patron goddess, but so far archaeologists have not found the city. It is said to be near the city of Bogazköy in modern Turkey, and was the religious centre of the Hittite empire of the north. There she would have been given daily offerings of cattle and sheep, bread, beer and wine. Her image would have a sleeping room in the temple, and temple assistants would dress and undress it each day as if it was a person (Otten, 1696).

The images of the deities in Hittite temples were generally kept in an inner room away from the mass of worshippers. The temple at Bogazköy had a central gate area with porters' lodges on either side, and an inner court with an area for purification by washing at the opposite end of the court. The actual temple, built of granite rather than the limestone of the rest of the temple area, stood behind this. Inside were the shrines to the various deities, in this case the sun goddess and storm god. Their images were made mainly of precious metals and carved in low relief. Once finished, they stood on low stone platforms. The festivals were celebrated inside the temple area, no doubt involving the images as well as sun- and moon-discs, bulls (storm god) and other animals made of pottery (MacQueen, 1986).

During one of the yearly festivals the queen sacrificed to eight images of the sun goddess of Arinna, provided mainly by earlier queens. Three of them were statues, and five sun-discs (Gurney, 1990). During these ceremonies they probably recited prayers like the following (Stone, 1979):

The Sun Goddess of Arinna is an honoured deity; Thy name is held high among names; Thy divinity is held high among the deities; Nay, among deities thou alone Sun Goddess art honoured. Great art Thou alone O Sun Goddess of Arinna; Nay compared to thee no other deity is as honoured or great... Thou controllest kingship in heaven and on earth.

These and other prayers show the power and majesty of the sun goddess. Like many Middle Eastern sun deities she has power both in this world and the world of the dead, striking down evil-doers and giving judgement wherever she is.

Hebat

A ritual text suggests that there was a special relation between Arinitti and the mountain goddess Hebat (Gurney, 1990). During the reign of Queen Pudhepa they were conflated, perhaps because they were the most popular deities of their territories. She appears in one of the surviving myths, which states that when the gods were fighting the giants she hid in the god's home and the giants tried to threaten her there. The Hittites saw Hebat as a mother goddess, and made Sarruma her son. She also had her own court, a group of goddesses and her vizier Tiyabenti. The goddesses included Kubaba (later Cybele), Ishtar (the Syrian goddess) and Isara (goddess of medicine) (Laroche, 1991b). Her cult animal was the lion. Her name survives in prayers like the following (Houwinke ten Cate, 1969):

O Sun-goddess of Arinna, my mistress, queen of all the countries, in Hatti-land you gave yourself the name 'Sun-goddess of Arinna', but furthermore in the land which you made into the cedar's land, you gave yourself the name 'Hebat'.

Estan

The Hittite cultus included a sun god called ^{D}Sius, who as the all-seeing eye was the god of justice. He developed from Ishtanu, who comes from the Hattian god/goddess Estan. Gurney (1990) thinks Estan was a sun goddess who lost her position to ^{D}Sius. (Ironically, the sun goddess of Arinna then replaced him and became the chief deity.) This seems to be a logical conclusion, since some of the texts refer to Estan in feminine terms, such as 'O sun-goddess, my queen' (Leick, 1991). It is difficult to say if Estan's solar aspect was independent or just an offshoot of Arinitti.

^{D}Sius was also the chief sky god, who apart from his solar connection was very much like the prototypical Indo-European lord of the sky. His name comes from the original word for sky, **dyeus*. ^{D}Sius rose from the sea every morning, which led to him being depicted with fish on his head, in a variant on the underworld aspect of the sun.

Kubaba/Cybele

If the land of Asia Minor produced a primordial sun goddess, one of her more enduring variants was the goddess Kubaba, who became the Roman Cybele. The British Museum has two statues of her. Both hold mirrors, which was part of the sun cult. More to the point, a winged sun-disc was carved into one image, floating above her head. This sign indicates a sun deity and was also associated with Wurusemu and Estan. Many Hittite images of goddesses show them enthroned, receiving worship, with the mirror in their hand and the sun-disc above (Persson, 1972). Another relief of Kubaba shows her in just this pose, facing the god Karhuhas, who wields a spear (MacQueen, 1959).

In the Hittite city of Kargamis, the goddess Kubaba was worshipped as queen of the city. She was paired with another deity called Adamma, who remains obscure. At Aleppo Kubaba-Adamma featured in the retinue of Hebat, who was the main goddess of the western empire. From there she spread across Cappodocia into the Anatolian plain. After the collapse of the Hittite empire her worship continued, with evidence appearing in Malatya and the Halys valley. In the sixth century BCE, a goddess Koubebe appears in the west of Asia Minor, at Sardis. The arrival of the Phrygians in the ninth century BCE changed her into an erotic goddess associated with Attis and ecstatic worship (Laroche, 1991c).

A relief from Carchemish shows Kubaba seated on a lion, an animal associated with the sun goddess of Arinna. This animal was later associated with the cult of Cybele, who travelled in a chariot drawn by lions. The evolution of Cybele may have been shaped by the cult of Telipinu's consort, Hatepuna, who had a harlot as her priestess and was represented as one. Her husband was a disappearing god of fertility, not so far from Attis. These elements, blended together, gave us the Great Mother with the dying consort known as Cybele.

Nikkal

The Hittites borrowed many Sumerian deities, and one was the moon god's wife, Nikkal. She has very little myth of her own, but some detect in her traces of a sun goddess. Her name means 'Great Queen' in Sumerian. The moon god Sin courted her by giving her lapis necklaces and making orchards in the deserts. Priestesses of Arinitti named themselves after her, which suggests that they saw her as a solar deity.

Perhaps it was their idea of a sun goddess that shaped their perceptions. The Hittites took up the ancient sun women of Anatolia, and syncretized them with their own version of the Indo-European sun goddess to produce the mighty sun goddess of Arinna.

The Armenians: Arevhat

THE PEOPLE WHO NOW LIVE IN ARMENIA AND GEORGIA are the last of a group who spoke an Indo-European language separate from the others. The Armenians themselves are thought to have migrated from the Balkans to Asia Minor. They were originally an Uartian and Hurrian people who mixed with a group of Indo-Aryans. Their nearest linguistic neighbours were the Phrygians, Thracians and Greeks, and eventually this proximity Hellenized their religion. The original inhabitants of Armenia, the Uartians in the kingdom of Van, contributed to religion and mythology as well. They were worshippers of the sun and moon, to whom they built a famous temple at Armavir.

Armenia

The Armenian origin myth says that the sky is frozen water, and the sun and moon float through the upper sky buoyed up by air. Their mother is the earth, although in Christian times she is sometimes identified with the Virgin Mary. The sun is a beautiful girl, who blushes with pleasure at sunset as she goes to embrace her mother. She walks by day, but she is shy, and so is armed with needles with which to transfix anyone who stares at her (Coxwell Fillingham, 1925). (This suggests that the sun cult forbade such disrespect.) The sun is really two suns. One is the visible sun (*aregakh*) that is female, and shines on the earth. It receives worship from humans. The other sun (*arew*) is the cosmic sun that makes day. Its gender seems more ambiguous, with some indications that it may have been masculine. This may be due to influence from the Iranian Zoroastrians and other astrologically inclined societies nearby (Mahé, 1992).

The moon (Amins) is the sun's brother, as in Germanic myth. Amins walks the night sky because it is more dangerous, and he wishes to protect his sister, whom he loves dearly. Early each month he is plump and happy after seeing her again, but then he fades as he begins to miss her again. Eclipses occur when the sun and moon meet, and more legends explain why this is so. One says that when they both meet the moon loses its head and becomes dark. He carries on his neck a bloody wineskin. Sometimes the moon puts the wineskin on the sun and she becomes dark

(Mahé, 1992). The moon's name may come from the root Men, the name of the Phrygian moon god. His name now is the word for 'month' (Ananikan, 1925).

The eighth month of the year, along with the first day of every month, was sacred to the sun. White horses were sacrificed to the sun, and altars featured images of the sun and moon (Hastings, 1980). In more modern times, sheep and calves were sacrificed to the sun. As well, twice a year (Charachidzé, 1968):

> . . . *men and women gathered in a dark pit to celebrate the cult there. They also held sacred, and used in their rituals, certain plants that 'turned towards the sun': the aspen, the lily, cotton, salsify, chamomile, and chicory. There is a little poem about this: 'Salsify, chamomile, chicory, amenable to the cult of Arevordi, grow in separate bunches, following the sun's course every day.'*

(The Arevordi mentioned in this charm were a group who called themselves the 'sons of the sun', and passed down an oral tradition begun by the magus Zradasht.)

Fire and water

The cult of fire and water is very strong in this part of the world, possibly because of Zoroastrian influence. One ancient site is dedicated to 'Sister Fire and Brother Spring', and the embers of the fire are always quenched by the spring, 'wiped with the brother's tears'. The Armenians believed that water that had doused sacred fire healed ills, and gave it to sick people to drink (Ananikan, 1925). This idea also appears in a story about a girl who was turned to stone and healed by the water in which the sun girl and moon boy had bathed (Coxwell Fillingham, 1925). This cult confirms the polarity of lunar water and solar fire common among the Indo-Europeans.

The familiar character of the mother of the sun appears in the story of the healing water, as the person who helps the man get the water. It is a saying that at sunset the sun is going to her mother, and they describe her as a brilliant woman with eyes that shine like the sun, dressed in gold, bestowing beauty on maidens at sunset. She lives in the sun's palace, bathing her when she returns home (Ananikan, 1925). (In myths where the sun is male, she nurses him as well. He starts as a child and ages through each day, so presumably he is born anew each night.) She has a lot in common with the Baltic and Slavic goddesses who bathe the sun. However, her description makes one wonder if she isn't the older sun goddess in disguise, especially since the actual sun is a girl.

Arevhat

There is a sun maiden, called Arevhat, who undergoes a number of adventures in Armenian folktales. (Her name comes from the word *arew*, 'sun'.) Her most famous exploit was her encounter with the dragon-prince, when she was lowered into the pit where a king's son in the shape of a dragon was kept. By speaking kindly to the dragon she broke the spell afflicting him, and he became a handsome young man.

She then related the misfortunes that brought her to him. Her evil stepmother turned her out each day to spin, and as she was sitting on a rock on a hillside, she dropped her bobbin in a hole. Looking down, she saw a crone who told her to run to the cave entrance and she would return the bobbin. Arevhat then did chores for the old woman, who turned her hair to gold in exchange for her good nature. When she went home, the stepmother tried to duplicate this with her own daughter, but the crone made her black and hideous.

After Arevhat married the dragon-prince, she returned to visit her family, which was foolish, since the stepmother threw her in a river. She floated a long way, and finally came ashore at a cottage. Inside a man was sleeping, but, since the sun was setting, she crouched in the doorway. The young hunter soon woke and told her that he was under enchantment for shooting arrows at the sun during three days when he was starving. He and Arevhat lived together, and had a child. Finally the hunter's mother journeyed to the sun's palace to get his forgiveness. The mother of the sun granted her wish, and gave her a healing formula. This formula brought many curious to see the restored hunter, among them the dragon-prince. Arevhat had to choose between them, so she gave the hunter their child and returned to the prince.

The motifs in this story are obviously solar, starting with our heroine's name. Her sojourns in the cave and with the dragon are myths of winter, when the sun disappears. She comes out each time better off than when she entered, once with new hair of gold, since the sun renews itself over the winter. (The crone bathes her hair, which suggests the mother of the sun.) The hunter she meets and dwells with is the moon, since he is at war with the sun, and only moves about at night. There are many myths where the moon is a hunter, and his three-day absence is explained by saying he is either hunting on earth or has wasted away because of his poor luck in getting game. (Note that although the actual sun deity is masculine in this myth, there are a profusion of feminine solar motifs in the story.)

Scythians and Sarmatians

The fierce nomadic tribes known as the Scythians and Sarmatians settled around the area now known as Armenia, bringing their culture into a rich mix of Persian, Phrygian and other Iranian influences. The Scythians arrived first, crossing northwest through the Caucasus to end finally in southern Russia. Some of them stayed behind and were assimilated into the local culture. Their empire finally collapsed in the sixth century BCE, partially due to the encroachments of their new rivals, the Sarmatians. These nomads came along behind them, looting and racing across the steppes in the same way as the Scythians themselves once had. The Scythians lingered on until the second century CE, when the Goths wiped them out. The Ossets, an Indo-European people living in the middle of the mountains of the Caucasus, are the descendants of the Scythians and Sarmatians, and retain some aspects of that culture, especially in religion.

Since Sarmatian women often fought alongside their men, they may have been the basis for the Greek descriptions of Amazons. They rode horses like men (not side-saddle) and used bows. No woman could marry until she had killed a man, although once she was married she put away her weapons. The Scythian women, on the other hand, led restricted lives, staying in the tents while the men fought (Rice, 1957). The Greeks knew both groups, and greatly feared them. Herodotus claimed that the Sarmatian women were the result of marriages between Amazons and Scythian men (Tyrell, 1984). As discussed in the Slavic chapter (pages 44–53), the Scythians worshipped the Great Goddess Tabiti, a goddess of fire and animals. The mirror seems to have been one of her attributes, and they buried people with mirrors (Rice, 1957). A plaque shows her seated, holding her mirror while a man drinks from a horn before her. The scene is reminiscent of Hittite depictions of the sun goddess. She influenced the development of Solntse, which would suggest that she also had some solar features. Greek and Roman writers called her Scythian Diana, and described her 'cruel' worship.

Whether she was Tabiti or not, the solar goddess survives in the Ossetic stories of the Narts, an epic cycle of three families of warriors. One of the most famous, Soslan, meets Atsyruhs, daughter of the sun, after he tries to kill her stag while hunting. He enters her cave, and is amazed at the splendour in which she lives. The giants who guard her bring her word of his arrival, and she immediately says that he is the one she is destined to marry. The seven giants set him tasks, which he must go to the land of the dead to fulfil. Soslan does so, and with the help of his mother and tutelary deities he wins his bride (Dumézil, 1965). Another myth features the sun's daughter (it is not clear if this is the same woman), who launches a blazing wheel at a hero when he angers her.

It is a pity that most of Ossetic mythology is known to us from heroic cycles; while it is better than nothing at all, it does concentrate on the heroes and gods. Perhaps more will be unearthed about the various goddesses and heroines of these people.

Georgia

The Georgians are another mixture of an aboriginal people and Indo-European invaders who crossed the Trans-Caucasus and Eurasian steppes around 1300 BCE. (The Georgian language, Kartevelian, apparently has similarities to Hittite, as well as the Semitic languages [Salia, 1983].) This wave of invaders changed the Bronze Age civilization of the natives drastically. The resultant mix of peoples developed a rich civilization, which underwent another upheaval when the Scythians and Cimmerians swept over Georgia in around 730 BCE. Whether Kartevelian is Indo-European or not is still a matter of some controversy, but the influence the Armenians, Hittites and northern invaders had on them makes it useful to include the Georgians in this survey.

The Georgians as such lived mainly in the regions of Colchis or Iberia, the former lying on the shore of the Black Sea, and Iberia in the interior. (This Iberia is different from the Spanish peninsula.) Colchis is also famous in Greek myth as the home of Helios and his family, and some of his sons and daughters were supposed to have ruled there. The city of Aea considered Aeëtes and his daughter Medea historical, according to Strabo. He suggested that the famous mines of Colchis were the real story behind the legend of the Golden Fleece. The connection between Helios' family and Georgia is a significant one for this book.

The Greek connection was strong enough that in the Hellenistic period the Georgians worshipped the sun and moon as Helios and Selene (Lang, 1966). Despite this, the common people preserved their own deities, for the grammatical gender of sun and moon is female and male respectively (Rustaveli, 1912). (Also, they may have adopted the names while ignoring the gender, as the Romans did with the god Men, whom they called Luna, while aware of his maleness.) Strabo says that the inhabitants of Colchis (Georgia) worshipped the goddess Leucotheia as a sun goddess (Burney and Lang, 1971). She had a rich temple with an oracle of Phrixus, where human sacrifice was forbidden. Later the Christians converted it into a church in honour of the Mother of God of Atskveri (Lang, 1966; Salia, 1983). Another goddess worshipped as the sun was a protective goddess of the city of Phasis, whom the Greeks compared to Rhea/Cybele. Her statue showed her holding a cymbal and with lions at her feet, which is why they seemed similar (Salia, 1983).

The people who lived on the plains were converted to Christianity early on, but the Georgians who dwelt in the mountains retained their shamanistic religion. Their priesthood has preserved the cult right into the present day. They believe in a tripartite cosmos: the sky where the gods live; the earth, where people live; and the underworld where demons live. There are two main bodies of water: a celestial lake and water under the earth. Fire also comes in different kinds: from the sky as lightning and from below as various seismic phenomena. The world is divided between the demonic and the divine, with all creation taking sides. An interesting feature of Georgian religion is its emphasis on the divine couple, siblings who behave like married couples (Charachidzé, 1991a).

SUN GODDESS

In the chief wine-growing area of Georgia they worshipped the sun under the name Mtsekale (the Georgian words for sun are *mze* and *mze tuali*), who made the vines grow. Elsewhere in the country the sun is known as Nana ('mother'), and asked in lullabies to make the children grow like the vines (McCrickard, 1990). The sun voyages between the celestial and lower worlds, from the water above to the water below. Georgians say that the otter is the only animal that can withstand the shock of the thrice-repeated light at twilight. Humans cannot look at it, but if one dips an otter skin in water just as the sun goes down, the skin will come out covered in gold. Her brother the moon god rises out of the water under the earth, according to the following order: the trout sees the first moon, the bear the second, and humans the third (Charachidzé, 1991a). The morning star controls dawn, and he also rules winter and summer.

The sun goddess had a powerful position in the Georgian pantheon, since it was a mainly agricultural society. The early Georgians respected women, which may explain the prominence of female deities. The old name for the sun was *dghe*, which survives in the word for 'day'. The worship of the Virgin or St Barbara replaced the worship of the sun (who is sometimes called Barbale [Arans and Shea, 1994]). However, the mountain Georgians still say the following prayer (Salia, 1983):

Glory be to the Divine Being, the day, the sun, and the angels who attend her.

The Svan-speaking Georgians still call the sun Barbale, a name related to words for wheel, circle and blaze of flame (Arans and Shea, 1994). She and the goddess Lamaria ('holy Mary' in her Christian guise) are worshipped solely by women, who practise their religion secretly and silently (Charachidzé, 1987).

Barbale and Lamaria are generally patrons of women, and especially milkmaids. In the town of Pari, when a cow was milked for the first time, the milkmaid took a ring of iron or a piece of stone of the same shape, and brought it and a cake of cheese to the old sanctuary of Barbale. There the offerings were given to the goddess, and the milkmaid pulled up some grass to put in the cow's ear. The rationale for this odd practice was that if she offered the grass to the cow, it might not eat it, or some might be lost, which would anger the goddess. Lamaria was the goddess of the home and worshipped by women, who knelt and asked her for help through her intermediary, the 'eye of the earth' (Charachidzé, 1968). (Perhaps the sun goddess was this eye?)

SUN WOMAN the MAGNIFICENT

The mountain-dwelling Georgians have a secret language used for giving oracles. The speaker delivers these prophecies while possessed by the deity. Gods usually possess males, while goddesses prefer women. (The thunder god is an exception to this rule, since he possesses women.) In the prophecies the sun plays an important part in the fate of the harvest. If the message is 'The sun woman has draped my sheaves of gold [the fields of the sanctuary]', then there will be a drought. If it is 'Sun woman the magnificent has sat on high, she has draped my sheaves of gold', this means that the heat will kill the harvest (Charachidzé, 1991a). (These oracles refer to the sun goddess as 'the sun woman', *mezkali*.) This secret language is of great interest to anthropologists because the Georgians call it 'the language of the Hat'i'. Some think that it may be a remnant of the Hattian language spoken by one of the Anatolian groups.

The GOLDEN huntress

The sun's daughter in the Caucasus was variously called Dal, Dali, Dala, Dala-lala or Dalila. She was the 'Lady of Rocks and Beasts', who gave hunters the choice of her love or luck in hunting. If they chose luck she immediately cursed them, but those who lay with her became extremely successful. When she tired of them, however, she turned them into animals or threw them from the highest rock of the forest, where she lived. Siren-like, she lured hunters to her by her loud voice, and was often washing her long, golden hair. The hair was the source of her strength, and its goldenness suggests sunbeams.

The MAN iN the PANTHER'S SKIN

The Georgian national epic is the twelfth-century *The Man in the Panther's Skin* by Shosta Rustaveli (1912). He wrote it in honour of the reigning queen Tamara, as a piece of courtly literature, but it grew quickly and has a great deal of aphorisms and side action. The main story involves Queen T' hinat' hin and her admirer Avtandil, who marry at the end, after many valorous deeds. Throughout the epic Rustaveli uses solar metaphors to describe women. The men also have sun characteristics sometimes, but overall the solar metaphor applies predominantly to women.

He likens her to the sun in passages such as the following:

Like a sun she blinded the eyes of onlookers by the sight of her light . . .
O sun, I compare thee to the cheeks of T' hinat' hin, thou art like her and she is like thee.

This last is interesting. He compares the queen's cheeks to the sun and sunlight several times, which seems odd, but the same motif occurs with the Irish Grian of the Bright Cheeks. As in the German folktale 'The Forest Bride', the goddess's head or face is the source of illumination.

Unfortunately, some writers find this hard to accept. In one translation I used for this book, the epic's translator 'corrected' the gender of the sun and moon for English, as she acknowledges in a footnote. I have returned them to Georgian usage, and the form Rustaveli intended:

> *When the moon is far from the sun, distance makes him bright; when she is near, her rays consume him — he is repelled, he cannot approach.*

In Georgian, the word 'sun' is feminine, the word 'moon' masculine, so changing them in English spoils the sense of the passage. Rustaveli constantly emphasizes how the queen is his sun, his source of illumination, so the metaphor relies on the feminine sun.

The myth-making nature of the epic appears to have rubbed off on the queen it was dedicated to; in folklore Tamara became or merged with a sun goddess. She rides a serpent with a golden saddle, bit and bridle (like Medea, another queen of Colchis). She holds Morning Star, the god of winter, captive as her slave. After her death, he escaped, but during her reign there was no winter. She subdued the sea, and burned up the crops and cattle when displeased with her worshippers, like the sun woman *mezkali*. A beam of light impregnated her while she was dwelling in her inaccessible palace, and she had her son in the woods to avoid shame (Charachidzé, 1991a).

This powerful queen is a descendant of the many other strong sun goddesses of this area. It is a pity that there are not more accessible studies of this part of the world, since they would contribute greatly to our knowledge of mythology.

The Greeks: Helia

THE Greeks were composed of two sets of peoples: an earlier group of Mycenaeans and the invading Indo-European tribes. The invading tribes were the Ionians, who had arrived in Greece by 1500BCE, followed by the Achaeans. This Greek-speaking warrior aristocracy ruled the mainland, and by 1200 BCE they had completed their movement into the area with the coming of the Dorians. The Cretan-Mycenaean period ended with their arrival. The next period is often known as the Geometric (1025–700 BCE), after the style of pottery made then. This was the time of Homer and Hesiod. Next came the Archaic (700–500 BCE), when the Greeks sent colonies to Italy. The glory period of the Greeks was the Classical (500–323 BCE), when they defeated the Persians and witnessed the flowering of their civilization. Finally, in the Hellenistic era (323–31 BCE), they were heavily involved in the Orient after Alexander's conquests. In 31 BCE the Romans conquered them, which ended their hegemony.

Greek mythology is a difficult subject for two reasons. First, everyone knows what 'the mythology' is all about, since it is the one most are likely to have read about. Second, it provides little for the scholar of Indo-European tradition, since the indigenous religion of the Mycenaeans fused with the Doric faith to a remarkable degree. To add to this, the Greeks borrowed much from the Near East, by way of their colonies there. From this fusion a tidied-up version of their gods and heroes was developed that owed as much to Hellenic creativity as to the matter they had to work with. Puhvel says in *Comparative Mythology* (1987) that the seeker for Indo-European deities among the Greeks will be left rather empty, and I agree with him.

He also points out that while most of us feel that we are familiar with Greek mythology, what we know is a tidied-up version that the Greeks developed, which was later transmitted to us through the medium of the Romans. Tribal variations and local deities got left in the dust. The official 'story' of the Greek gods is set out in Hesiod's *Theogony* (1966) and similar works. In the beginning there were the sky and earth, Ouranos and Gaea. They produced children, but Ouranos buried them in the earth, so Gaea finally rebelled and encouraged her son Cronos to castrate her husband. Cronos then became king of the gods along with his wife Rhea, another earth goddess. Cronos is mainly famous for his habit of devouring his children, but Rhea managed to deceive him and keep Zeus alive. When Zeus had grown up, he killed his father and rescued his siblings from Cronos's stomach. Thus the Olympians came to power.

Zeus and his band of gods dwelt on the top of Mount Olympus, which was both an actual mountain in Greece and an otherworld in the sky. Although there were many more deities and semi-divine heroes about, the main pantheon of the Greeks was eventually narrowed down to twelve deities. These were Zeus and his wife, Hera, the siblings Apollo and Artemis, Aphrodite the love goddess, Hephestios, her smith-god husband, Ares the warrior, Hestia the hearth goddess, Hermes, the god of commerce, the craftswoman Athena, Demeter the corn goddess, and the sea god Poseidon.

Apollo and Artemis

If you asked people who was the deity of the sun in Greek mythology, they would tell you it was Apollo. This is due to many authors attempting to simplify the deities for a mass audience by conflating the sun god Helios with Apollo. It is true that he is identified with the sun in later Greek myth, but this does not mean that anyone thought he rode across the sky each day as Helios does. Apollo is primarily the god of the lyre, accompanied by the Muses. His other function is healing, since both he and Artemis his sister can cause sickness by striking people down with their arrows, and so presumably can heal as well. He was imported from the Near East as a wolf god, who protected flocks of sheep, and obviously struck some chord in the Greek psyche, so that he became a sort of ideal type.

Apollo and his sister Artemis were imported into Greece by way of Cyprus, along with Aphrodite. Jean Markale (1986) states that Artemis was originally a sun goddess but Apollo usurped her function and became the sun himself. This is odd, because neither sibling was associated with a luminary to begin with, both being essentially functional deities. Also, there is no evidence that Artemis was ever a sun goddess, although the Scythians that Markale sees as her first worshippers did worship a sun goddess (see page 82).

Sun God?

It is from Greek mythology, as I said in the introduction, that some get the idea that the sun is always a male deity. Like this fallacious idea, the maleness of the Greek sun deity could use some re-examining. On the one hand it is undoubtedly true that Helios is a sun god, who was later subsumed by the god Apollo. Helios himself shares much with other Indo-European suns – the horses and chariot, the lunar sibling/spouse (Selene), a younger version of himself (Phaethon), and a castle from which he rises every morning. He sees and hears all, and is invoked when an oath is sworn, along with Zeus and Gaea. Like the German Sól, he punishes oath-breakers. He can cure the sightless, but also strike offenders blind. At night he sails back to the east while he sleeps in his boat/bed (rather like the sun-boats of rock pictures in northern Europe), or rows himself to the east in a golden goblet.

While he carries many of the traits of the Indo-European sun goddess, it is interesting that many of the women associated with him have names that relate to the sun. This may mean that once the Greeks, like many of the other Indo-European peoples, had a sun goddess. They may have later decided that any goddesses with solar names were likely to be related to the sun god they now recognized. This would have rationalized a lot of local cults not consonant with national ideology. Where Helios himself comes from would be hard to say. He has a lot in common with the sun goddesses of Europe, so he may be a gender-bending Indo-European deity.

The female sun

The 'other' sun can be found in the myth of the Heliades, one of whom was called Helia. Since this is but the feminine form of the word Helios, she must be a feminine side of the sun, later demoted to his daughter. This would be interesting in light of the existence of Helen of Troy, whom some think is a sun maiden. Helia and Helen would be a typical mother–daughter pairing of sun goddesses, very much within the tradition I have been tracing throughout this book (especially since both have the Hel- element in their names, which they share with Helios).

Another candidate for sun goddess is Perse, the wife of Helios. Kerényi (1991) identifies her with the Titan Theia, since Helios was often called after his father, Hyperion (Theia's husband). Kerényi says of Perse:

> The original receiver, Theia, need not however be a pre-Perse. The sun-receiver and the sun-bearer can always be the same person. The different names simply refer to different sides of her mysterious nature. And none of these as precisely suits that mysterious process through which she, as Pindar expresses it, bestows golden value [which means, most likely, giving the sun its solarity] as does the basically feminine solar name, Perse.

This Perse is a different one from the form of Hecate, who was the daughter of a god of light, Perses. Hecate was known as Perseis because he was her father. It is intriguing that while Perses is readily acknowledged as a god of light or the sun, a goddess with the same name (feminine form) is immediately assumed to be a moon goddess. Despite this, Perse ('lightbearer') is no less a goddess of the light and sun than Perses. While Theia gives light to her children, the sun, moon and dawn, Helia and Perse actually are the sun, no less than Helios.

She who shines far

Another female divinity of light, and possibly the sun, was Helios' mother Theia. She was a Titan identified with primal light, whose name meant 'the Divine'. Kerényi (1991) suggests she had the essence that made the deities what they are, which is fitting, since sky gods like the Olympians are usually seen as shining. As the goddess of illumination, Theia was the mother of Helios, Selene and Eos – sun, moon and dawn. Because she was the originator of light, one of Pindar's odes is addressed to her as if she were the sun (Sandys, 1915):

> Beam of the Sun! O thou that seest afar, what wilt thou be devising? O mother of mine eyes! O star supreme, reft from us in the daytime . . . swift divine driver of steeds… O queen…

The occasion was an eclipse at Thebes, which frightened the populace, since this was an extremely bad omen. Pindar seems to think that since Theia was the source of light she could restore it. The Homeric Hymn to Helios refers to Theia as Euryphaëssa, 'She-Who-Shines-Far', and emphasizes her eyes, which should be meaningful to anyone familiar with solar imagery (Boer, 1980).

Children of Helios

The Heliades are the daughters of Helios and the nymph Clymene. Their collective name means 'sun maidens'. They have various names, but are commonly called Helia (the female sun), Lampetia ('the illuminating'), Phaethousa ('the shining'), Aegle ('brightness, lustre, sunshine') etc. (Other Heliades have variously included Aetheria, Astres, Dioxippe, Merope and Phoebe.) Their brother is the ill-fated Phaethon who tried to drive his father's chariot and failed, falling from the sky after Zeus had to strike him down to save the earth. This sad event caused the sisters to turn into poplars and weep tears of amber, the solar gem. (Freya of the Germans weeps amber as well.) The sisters harnessed the horses of the sun for the philosopher Parmenides (Kerényi, 1991), just as they would do for the sun every morning.

Lampetia also was a figure of some consequence, whose name is the origin of the word lamp (Monaghan, 1990). She turns up in the Odyssey with her sister Phaethousa tending her father's sacred cattle. When Odysseus and his men washed up on their island, they ate some of the cattle, which angered the goddess and her father. Helios ensured that the blasphemers were shipwrecked. Only Odysseus survived, because he respected the taboo. Little snippets of myth like this are all that is left of what must have once been a vibrant sun-goddess cult.

Pasïphae

Among Helios's other children was Pasïphae, the daughter of Helios and the sun goddess Perse. She married the king of Crete, Minos, but mated with the Bull from the Sea to produce the Minotaur (also called Asterion, 'star'). Both he and his mother are connected with the maze, since it was built for the Minotaur, and one version has it that Pasïphae was put in it as well (Graves, 1955). (Ariadne the maze goddess was Pasïphae's daughter.) Pasïphae means 'she who shines for all', and this is read as being the name of a moon goddess, but she could be a solar deity.

The Bull from the Sea is her mate, and the lunar imagery is his, not hers. The white bull was sacred to the moon, and may well represent the moon himself in this instance. The bull's horns suggested the shape of the crescent moon to the Greeks and many other Near East civilizations. In one version of the Cretan cycle Minos himself is the product of Zeus's intercourse with Europa in the form of a bull and cow (Mercante, 1988). Add to this the fact that Minos means 'the moon's creature', and Minotaur 'Minos bull', and the identity of the bull becomes clearer. The moon-bull would also be connected with water, which would explain why they were sacred to Poseidon, who received both black and white bulls as sacrifices.

The mating of the lunar bull and the solar goddess/cow would have been a hierogamy (sacred marriage) similar to those of the moon and sun in Northern Europe. (After all, Theia was also called 'The Cow-Eyed' [Kerényi, 1951], and she is demonstrably solar.) The marriage of Minos and Pasïphae could be a typical moon–sun marriage, with the stars as children (since the Minotaur and Aridella are their offspring, and both are related to constellations). Another idea is that her mating with Minos/the bull was a ritual performed when the solar year and lunar year coincided, to express the harmony of the two principles (Faure, 1991).

In support of her solarity, a temple of the Laconian Pasïphae had a statue of her beside one of her father, and also a sweet spring (Willets, 1962) – typical sun-goddess motifs. She may have made a dyad with her father, since the sun maiden often mates with the moon. The spring or well is common to sun deities the world over. (Farnell, in his book *Cults of the Greek States* [1909], states that there are traces of sun worship among the Mycenaeans, 'dimly recalling the "Minoan" solar name Pasïphae'.) Like her sisters, she could and did use magic, cursing the unfaithful Minos, so that when he slept with other women he ejaculated scorpions and other poisonous creatures into them. This is typical of the uneasy relations between sun and moon, since his function requires his infidelity.

Circe

Circe, who was Pasïphae's sister, became queen of Colchis through her magic, but had to use Helios's rays to flee to the island of Aeaea when her subjects rebelled. Aeaea was said to lie beyond east and west, where Helios and Eos rose in the morning (Kerényi, 1991). (It was often said to be the island of Malta.) While she lived on her eastern island, she wove every morning and spun, which sounds like she was making sunbeams for her father. Her location suggests that she was a goddess of morning, a counterpart to the Hesperides, who were evening goddesses. Her name is the Greek word for circling birds of prey, especially the hawk (in Homer) and the association of hawk and sun is common. A fragment of Hesiod (1966: verse 390) says that she rode with the sun in his chariot (Goodison, 1989). Her attendants were goddesses of springs, groves and sacred rivers, which is significant because the Hellenic sun goddesses seem to be connected to water and trees. She and the Georgian sun goddess Dala have been linked through various motifs in the *Odyssey* such as hair-washing, siren singing and their solar connection (Arans and Shea, 1994).

Aega

Aega was another daughter of the sun, and dazzlingly beautiful. When the Titans attacked Olympus, Gaea hid her in a cave because her brilliance frightened them, which may be the remnant of a sun-goddess myth. (Saules metia being drowned in a spring and Arevhat falling into a cave are similar ideas; the sun is lost, and winter/darkness comes.) While she was in the Cretan cave she is supposed to have suckled the infant Zeus along with her sister Helice, and sometimes the goat Amelthea (Schmitz, 1884). A later story has it that she became a constellation when Zeus was told by an oracle to take her skin (*aegis*) so that he could defeat the Titans. Since the constellation Capella was said to bring storms, it would seem that this and the suckling story are an attempt to explain a goddess who had fallen from power. (The words for gale and goat are related to her name.)

Her stepsisters are Circe and Pasïphae, whom Monaghan (1990) suggests made up a threefold sun goddess. Circe would represent the morning goddess, Pasïphae the risen sun, since she was the one who shone out, and Aega could be the sun in the evening or winter, since she is hidden away.

All of Helios's daughters have certain things in common. Circe, Paspïhae and Medea (his granddaughter, discussed below) are accomplished sorceresses, all show signs of being more than human, and all of them are connected with their father's cult-centres, where the worship of the sun continued to flourish even after the rise of more 'sophisticated' cults. The people of Rhodes continued to adore the sun in both male and female guise until Christianity ended their worship.

The cunning ones

Another famous descendant of Helios was the sorceress Medea ('well counselled'). She was the daughter of his son Aeëtes, the king of Colchis, and his wife Eidya ('the knowing one'). She appears in the story of Jason and the Argonauts as the clever woman who helps him to get the Golden Fleece, then marries him. They sail back to Athens, eluding the pursuit of the Colchians, and settle down. Later Jason remarries, and Medea kills his new wife and her children by Jason before flying off in her serpent-drawn chariot, given to her by Helios.

To understand the solar nature of Medea, one must consider the Georgian origin of the goddess. The western side of Georgia was traditionally called Colchis, and this was the home of Medea. She left her traces there as the goddess Tamara, a queen who is identifiably solar and rides a serpent chariot. Georgians still call their daughters Medea, and believe that the original was a sun goddess (McCrickard, 1990).

An important incident in the myth is Medea's murder of her brother. She killed him and cut him up, casting the pieces overboard so that her family would have to pick up the pieces instead of chasing her and Jason. Behind this piece of folktale cleverness may lie a piece of sun-goddess cult. Monaghan (1994) suggests that this act is related to an ancient sun cult centring on the goddess Cybele and her consort Attis. Unlike Attis, Apsyrtos was cut into pieces, but the principle of dismemberment remained.

Presumably the same goddess that harmed could heal, a motif that turns up in the legend of Medea. She restored the vigour of Jason's father, and King Pelias asked her to do the same for him. She convinced him that she could restore his youth by killing and cutting up a ram, and boiling it in a cauldron with some herbs. It came out as a live lamb, and so his daughters cut him up for boiling. Medea withheld the herbs, and he stayed dead. Her power to kill and restore suggests the regeneration of the sun herself, nightly and annually reborn. Kerényi (1991) seems to think that she killed and restored Helios every night (his golden bowl becoming her cauldron) but perhaps she herself was the sun, the dark fourth aspect of the nocturnal and hidden solar power.

Another destructive sun goddess is the monster Medusa, who has a slight resemblance to Medea. Both names are derived from a root meaning 'wise'. They enter Greek myth through the stories of heroes: Medea aids Jason in the quest for the Golden Fleece, and Medusa is slain by Perseus as part of a set of tasks set by his stepfather. Medusa was said to be a form of the Anatolian sun goddess. Scholars have likened her appearance to the sun, since neither can be gazed on directly, and the crown of snaky hair suggests rays. (The sun and the snake have a longstanding relationship; see pages 38–9). She is often shown as just a head, which would fit with being an orb in the sky.

Her gaze turned men to stone, just as Sól's did with trolls and dwarves. The basilisk gaze was her most prominent characteristic, and probably was part of a ritual involving using mirrors to 'see' the goddess. Monaghan (1994) points out that Perseus would not have been able to use his shield to accurately attack Medusa, since its convex shape would distort her reflection. The polished bronze is probably a memory of an ancient ritual. (It may confirm her origin in Anatolia, since the Hittite sun goddess was worshipped with mirrors [Persson, 1972].) Once Apollo became the main sun deity, Medusa appeared beside him. Often commentators mistook an image of Apollo or Helios for one of Medusa, and vice versa. The Gorgon and the god appeared together on coins, alternated on temple pediments, and appeared in the same part of the zodiac (Monaghan, 1994). Her face decorated lamp handles, which connects her to Lucina, who often holds a lamp.

A SHIELD WITH GORGON WHOSE SNAKY HAIR RESEMBLES SUN-RAYS.

She was the lover of Poseidon, the god of the sea, which points to another aspect of the sun-goddess myth. The story was that she and the god were lovers, until they made love in a temple of Athena. The virgin goddess changed Medusa's beautiful hair to snakes, and later arranged her death at Perseus's hands. When the young hero cut her head off, the horse Pegasus and the hero Chrysador sprang from her neck (Poseidon was their father). Snakes grew from the drops of blood. In distorted form, this myth is reminiscent of other Indo-European goddesses who mate with a god and give birth to twins that are associated with horses. (Other goddesses who fit this myth pattern are Macha, Rhiannon and Saranyu.) Medusa herself was sometimes depicted as a horse, and so was Poseidon. The sun goddess as horse is a common Indo-European motif.

Nymphs of the setting sun

Another group of solar females was the Hesperides, three maidens who inhabited the western paradise where the golden apples of immortality grew (see page 35 for comparison). This was next to the Islands of the Blessed, a typical otherworld. Originally there were seven Hesperides, but this was reduced to three: Aegle ('brightness'), Erythraea ('the red one') and Hespera ('evening light'). Their job was to guard the apples, which Gaea gave Hera as a wedding gift. When the Argonauts approached them for the apples, Hespera turned herself into a poplar (obviously the tree of sun maidens). These goddesses were probably a trio who represented dawn, noon and evening, just as Saule and her daughters or Solntse and her Zoryas did. They gathered in the evening to sing sweetly, which led to comparisons with the Sirens. (Oddly, sometimes one of the Hesperides was called Medusa, perhaps a memory of her connection to the sun.)

Eos: rosy-fingered dawn

In contrast to the Hesperides there is the dawn goddess Eos (Aurora to the Romans). She was the daughter of the Titans Theia and Hyperion, a sun god, and her siblings are Helios and Selene. She was described in flatteringly poetic terms, just as Ushas of the Vedas was, as a winged goddess tilting an urn of dew over the earth; or mounted on Pegasus and carrying a torch; or saffron-robed and driving a purple chariot with two horses. Her colourfulness related to her name, which may mean 'red of morning' (Kerényi, 1951).

Another similarity with other dawn goddesses was her numerous love affairs. She fell in love with Orion, who had been blinded for mistreating his wife. He was supposed to bathe his eyes in her light, and when she saw him she took him for her own (after curing his blindness). Eventually Artemis killed Orion, after he offended her. Another affair was with Tithonus, for whom she requested eternal life. Unfortunately, she didn't realize that he was going to age for ever, and so he withered away until he was turned into a grasshopper out of compassion for his suffering.

In the early days of the Greeks she rode beside the sun all day, becoming Hemera at noon and Hesperide at sunset (Guirard, 1963). What with this and her ability to cure blindness one is tempted to see an old sun goddess behind Eos. It may be that she was split off into a dawn goddess and an evening goddess, the latter function falling to the Hesperides as the Greeks began organizing local cults into national myths. Her horses were named Lampos and Phaethon, emphasizing her connection with new light.

Some suggest that Aphrodite was originally a dawn goddess who developed into a goddess of love with the importation of Asian motifs from Ishtar and Astarte. The dawn goddesses and Aphrodite are famed for their beauty, are associated with the sky, and have mortal lovers. Aphrodite was born of the sea, but of the sky god's sperm, and one of her more popular titles was Urania ('of the sky'). Both she and Eos are strongly associated with the sun and light (Kinsley, 1989).

Like the dawn, she takes many mortal lovers. She kidnaps the son of Eos and Hyperion to be her lover, which Nagy suggests was an usurpation of Eos's role as the mother/lover. Phaethon is this son, and the name is also applied to one of Eos's horses. This, Nagy suggests, is paralleled in the Vedas, where Surya is the dawn's son and husband, and he is described as 'bright horse' (Nagy, 1979). This suggests that Eos and Aphrodite were originally one goddess, of dawn and love, with Phaethon as her son/lover.

Helen the sun maiden

Another goddess of dawn and spring was the sun maiden Helen. Disentangling this goddess from the Spartan lady who was taken or went to Troy and was rescued by the Greek army after a ten-year war is a complex business. A good place to begin is with her family, who are often deities. Her brothers were demigods, the Dioscouroi, sons of Zeus, born after the sky god mated with their mother Leda ('darkness') in the shape of a swan. They were 'born' all in one egg, or as two sets of twins, the Dioscouroi in one egg and Helen and her sister Clytemnestra in the other.

One of Helen's titles is Dendritus, which suggests she was a tree goddess. Lindsay (1974) suggests that she was goddess of the plane tree. Other ideas about her meaning have centred on her name, which has been read in various ways. Some say she is the moon, because her name can be read as 'shining' (although more things than the moon shine).

Another interpretation is 'torch', which suggests a heavenly luminary, possibly a dawn goddess. Others point out the similarity of her name to Helios's, along with the tradition that makes her his daughter, and say she is a sun maiden. (Puhvel [1987] derives it as Helene: PIE *Swelena, just as the name of the sun god can be derived as Helios: PIE *Saweliyos.) There are Spartan reliefs of her twin brothers with a star between them, which suggests a symbolic representation of her, so that she was seen as a star

(Cook, 1914). A hymn at the festival of Eos/Aos (dawn) makes especial mention of Helen (Lindsay, 1974):

> Beautiful, Lady Night, is the face that the rising Dawn [Aos] reveals, or the bright spring at winter's ending; and so among us did golden Helen shine.

She seems to have been a combination of Indo-European sun maiden and a native tree goddess, since she is both sunlike and connected with trees and baskets. After all, Puhvel (1987) says that the sun maiden and twins fulfil the third function of fertility, making the crops grow and the trees bear fruit (Cader, 1976).

As a sun maiden, like Suryaa of the Hindus (see pages 106–7) and Auszrine of the Balts, she is part of an extremely ancient myth, involving her being stolen and then rescued by her twin brothers. This happens several times to Helen, which suggests that a number of such myths accumulated around her since she was such a suitable figure. The first is her abduction by Theseus when she is a girl. She is placed in his mother's care, and her twin brothers find her and free her (Lindsay, 1974). Theseus also carried off one of the Hesperides (Lindsay, 1974), so that, like Finn of the Celts, he seems to have a preference for solar females.

She lived with her husband Menelaos in a palace that is described as bright, even sunlike. The Laconian cult emphasized the connection with Helios, whose daughter she sometimes is. (She is Zeus's daughter the rest of the time [Cader, 1976].) It has been suggested that, while the Dioscouroi don't rescue her in the *Iliad*, the Atreidai, the hero Agamemnon and his brother Menelaos, fill in for them. They fit the pattern since, like the twins, they are skilled in war and leadership, although since they are mortal and not demigods, only one of them can be married to Helen (only gods get to flout incest laws) (Cader, 1976). It would seem, however, that even then the pattern of the two men who rescue the sun maiden had not been forgotten.

One aspect of Helen's cult that corresponds to her sun-maiden nature is the decorating of trees in springtime. A similar custom was prevalent among the Balts, and in both cases it is to celebrate her return. The dolls hung in the trees or on maypoles and left for the summer across Europe may be a memory of the images of her hung in trees, which gave rise to an explanatory myth that she was hung from a tree herself. (This myth purports to explain why she was linked with trees.) A myth that she had been taken to Egypt by Paris and rescued from there by the Dioscouroi is similar to the idea that Helios went to Egypt or else Hyperborea in winter. This would fit nicely with the myth of the returning sun maiden bringing spring in her wake. Both she and Auszrine are married in the springtime, so the garlanding and tree-dressing were celebrating the joyous event (West, 1975).

St Lucy of Syracuse, the saint attached to solar female cults in Sicily and Scandinavia. Note the solar motif of the eyes.

Ukrainian Easter eggs decorated with solar and fertility patterns.

THIS RELIEF SHOWS THE HITTITE SUN GODDESS FACING HER CONSORT, THE STORM GOD. HER SON AND DAUGHTERS STAND BEHIND HER.

THE ROMANS OFTEN IDENTIFIED CELTIC SUN GODDESSES WITH MINERVA. THIS STATUE SHOWS A MINERVA WHOSE AEGIS IS VERY SUN-LIKE.

THE ANATOLIAN
GODDESS
KUBABA, WHO
BECAME THE
GRAECO-ROMAN
CYBELE. NOTE
THE MIRROR SHE
HOLDS.

MEDEA WAS THE GRANDDAUGHTER OF THE SUN GOD HELIOS AND, LIKE THE REST OF HIS FAMILY, SHARED HIS SOLAR CHARACTERISTICS.

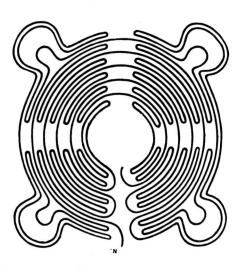

THE TURF MAZE AT SAFFRON
WALDEN, ESSEX, WHICH MAY HAVE
BEEN CONNECTED WITH A SUN-
MAIDEN RITUAL.

THE NORSE
MOON GOD
RIDING THROUGH
THE SKY WITH
HIS SISTER,
THE SUN.

A ROMANIZED STATUE OF MEN,
THE MOON GOD. HE HOLDS A
THRYSUS AND A PINE CONE, AND HAS
BEEN ASSOCIATED WITH ATTIS.

Phrygian saviour

A final point about the female element in the Grecian concept of the sun is the latent masculinity of the moon. While the main moon deity was the goddess Selene or Mene, Helios's sister, the Phrygian and Anatolian colonists had developed their own deity. The moon god Men is well attested throughout Asia Minor as a god of heaven and the underworld. He ruled heaven and the underworld, and made plants grow. A typical moon god, he drove a chariot with bulls or rode a horse, and ruled rain and rivers. His main epithet was 'Saviour', a name also associated with Hecate. He became extremely popular with the Anatolians, and the later Roman colonists as well.

Other evidence for the sun goddess and moon god reaches both backward and forward in time. Goodison (1992) points to the prevalence of solar imagery connected with female figures in prehistoric Crete, and McCrickard (1990) traces the sun and moon through Greek folklore into modern times.

Goodison (1992) notes that artefacts called 'frying pans' suggest a sun-cult, because of both their shape and the images on them. It would seem that the Cretans linked their female sun and the belly/womb.

McCrickard (1990) shows that after Christianity churches were called after Mary 'Beautiful-as-the-sun', an idea that persisted in stories of vain maidens who rivalled the sun in beauty. (One of these stories involves a maiden locked in crystal tower who must be rescued – obviously a sun maiden in disguise.) The sun designs painted on brides' faces are, she says, another indication of the sun's persistence. (I would also suggests that it may be a trace of an ancient sacred marriage, perhaps based on Pasïphae and Minos.)

With such evidence of a continuous tradition, no one can deny the role of the solar goddess in Greek myth and folklore. Obviously she and her lunar counterpart filled a need that Helios and Selene did not.

The Romans: Lucina

THE LATIN-SPEAKING ROMANS were once the minority on the Italian peninsula, and the history of the early Republic is one of near-conquest by the Etruscans. They were not even the only group jostling for room. The Umbrians and Oscans, who were also Indo-Europeans, were living comfortably in their own parts of Italy. The Latin-speakers, however, were successful in taking over the peninsula, thus ensuring the supremacy of their language. The Roman penchant for adopting foreign deities, beginning with the Greek pantheon and continuing through until the fall of Rome, makes it difficult to see the pattern of the Latin mythology. However, the work of many scholars has helped to clear away the encrustations and restore some of the religion of the Romans. While their mythology faded away, many of their rituals and heroic legends illuminated obscure areas of both Roman and other myths for Indo-European scholars. Unlike the Greeks, the gods of Rome are a fertile ground for comparisons with the other civilizations in this book.

Their gods do not seem to have been very personified, and were not worshipped with images (Jones and Pennick, 1995). Janus was the spirit of the door, Vesta of the hearth fire, the Lares of the household, but these were never seen as personifications, just powers. In the state religion the Capitoline triad of Jupiter, Juno and Minerva protected Rome. Mars the war god and Quirinus the god of peace were also important, along with the goddesses Diana (woods) and Venus (gardens). Saturn was the god of winter sowing. These were the basic gods of the Romans, along with many minor deities who ruled various aspects of life.

There is some question as to whether the Roman sun god Sol was a native deity. On the one hand, he was called Sol Indiges, which would seem to indicate an indigenous god. However, Dumézil disagrees with this in *Archaic Roman Religion* (1970), insisting that Sol is not one of the oldest gods. Whatever the case, Sol was certainly the Roman version of Helios, the Greek sun god, and he was the patron of charioteers, along with his sister Luna. A temple dedicated to him stood in the Circus Maximus to invoke his protection. He eventually got absorbed into the emperor cult of later Rome. However, since Roman religion is so unclear, it may help to look for females with attributes common to sun goddesses, since they may very well be earlier versions of the solar deity.

Goddess of returning light

Several of the civilizations in this book have a goddess who seems to embody primal light, such as the Greek Theia and the Hindu Aditi. The Roman goddess Lucina, whose name means light, seems to be one of those goddesses. Lucina had two aspects: Diana Lucina, the moon, and Juno Lucina, the sun. Juno Lucina was the midwife of the gods, bringing the light of day to the newborns. A temple to Juno Lucina, on the north side of the Esquiline, would not allow visitors that had knots in their clothing, as befitted a midwife goddess (Dumézil, 1970). (This is a form of sympathetic magic; no knots are permitted in the birth-room to ease the delivery.)

As Juno Lucina was the goddess who brought light to newborns, she seems to have picked up sunlike attributes along the way. Her festival was the winter solstice, which was celebrated as her birthday, a very solar motif! She seems to have been an obscure goddess, but her worship was the basis for the cult of St Lucy/Lucia in Christian times. St Lucy was supposedly a noble maiden who vowed virginity and pulled out her eyes when a pagan suitor admired them. She delivered them to him on a dish, and is often shown with the two eyes on a platter or else holding them like cherries. (Juno ruled eyebrows, as part of her role as the inhabiting spirit of women, just as Jupiter was in the forehead of men as their genius [Dumézil, 1970].) St Lucy's festival, on 13 December (originally on 21 December) became very popular in Scandinavia, probably because of their feminine solar tradition.

In Sicily, the tradition of St Lucia's Day also remains. On the eve of 13 December, all the men and boys in the town of Montedoro rush down from the nearby hill with blazing straw in their hands, shouting as they run. At the back of the procession someone carries a statue of the saint which depicts her carrying her eyes on a plate. When the revellers reach the plaza, they cast their straw on a huge pile of straw to make a bonfire, near which the saint's image is placed so she can watch (Miles, 1912). This festival of fire and light, to encourage the sun, seems appropriate to the goddess of returning light, the newborn sun. (Another Roman goddess, called Candelifera, carried the candles during confinement and delivery [Jayne, 1925; Ferguson, 1970]. This minor numen of the birth-chamber probably helped shape the character of St Lucy, who often carries candles or lamps.)

Diana

Juno's lunar counterpart, Diana, is a goddess whose name means 'light'. Her lunar associations seem to stem from her identification with the

Greek Artemis, which was a late idea. One theory about her significance is that she was the ruler of the open sky. (Her name derives from Divina = 'the shining one'[Lurker, 1994].) She may have been a female counterpart to the sky god, since their names derive from the same root, and she was probably equally important. (All Roman deities were couples, ruling the same things. The idea was to promote fecundity in all aspects of life.) Presumably her partner Dianus, god of the sky and woods, would have been a forerunner of Jupiter. Like the thunder god, Diana was worshipped under the open sky. McCrickard (1987) suggests that Diana originally ruled the sky, sun and moon, while the arrows from her bow were the lightning. (Many northern goddesses provide the lightning to their husband's thunder; for example, the Lapp goddess Rauni.)

Others think that she was the early sun goddess. If Sol was indeed a late god, then the wife of the sky god could have filled that role. As 'the shining one', she could be the sun. In her later form Diana, like Juno Lucina, was still involved in the rebirthing of light, only she returned it every morning. Cicero said, 'Diana is associated, it is thought, with the moon . . . she is called Diana because at night she makes the day' (quoted in Schilling, 1991). Even when she was called the moon, her connection with the light of day remained. Her main festival fell on the Ides of August, which was once midsummer, and women carried torches to her temple in Arcia, as if to stimulate her light-bringing by sympathetic magic (Schilling, 1991). (Some ancient coins and reliefs show Juno Lucina with a torch, just like many other dawn and sun goddesses [Boardman, 1981].) The timing of her festival suggests a pairing with Juno Lucina to ensure the continuity of light throughout the year.

The fire goddess

The Romans were not short of fire goddesses. Vesta ('torch, candle') was the Roman hearth goddess, whose fires were tended by the Vestal Virgins. She also received daily offerings from each family, at the hearth. The public hearth was the only round temple in Rome, and on 1 March the Vestals doused and relit the fire. On 9 June was the Vestalia, when barefoot Roman matrons offered food baked on their hearths, and the Vestals gave salt cakes baked on Vesta's fire. After eight days of offerings, the Vestals closed the temple, cleaned it thoroughly, dumped the garbage in the Tiber, and reopened. Like the virgin priestesses of Brigit, the Vestals were mediators in times of war.

If the fire went out, it had to be restarted by rubbing sticks of wood together, or else ignited using glass to concentrate the sun's rays. When needed, the fire was carried from one place to another in a bronze vessel. Both these things attest to the antiquity of her cult. She was honoured as a mother, and her fire was a symbol of the continuity of the family. As with the Balts and Slavs, a woman had to bring fire from her mother's hearth when she married. The goddess of fire celestial and earthly naturally suggests Agni, the god of fire, lightning and the sun: all forms of fire. The rounded temple echoed the form of the sun: the hearth as the earthly counterpart of the heavenly fire.

Solstices and goddesses

Mater Matuta was a goddess of the dawn and morning light, probably the same goddess as Aurora (the Roman version of the goddess of the reddening sky of dawn). She was an Old Italic goddess who became a goddess of women and childbirth. (She was later equated with the Greek goddess Ino and made patron of seafarers [Lurker, 1994]). The connection is suggestive in light of the Swedish rune poem, which links the sun and sailing.) Her festival was held on 11 June, and involved women leading a female servant to the sanctuary, then beating her with rods, driving her out; and then holding their sisters' children in their arms. This seems to relate to Vedic myths of Ushas, the dawn goddess, who is forced to cross the sky quickly so that day can come, and who nurses the sun god along with her sister night (Puhvel, 1987). Mater Matuta's festival is just before the summer solstice and probably relates to the last festivity of the dawn goddess (who is associated with spring) before summer and the elder (mother) sun deity takes over. Since the Roman dawn goddess has little myth of her own, this ritual and its explanation may help to fill the gap.

Diva Angerona had her festival on the shortest day of the year, 21 December. Her name itself may derive from the Indo-European word for narrowness (*augus*), relating to the constriction of the light (Puhvel, 1987). Her statue had its mouth bandaged and sealed, and she held a finger to her mouth. The solstice celebration must have involved silence on the part of the participants. Since the fate of the sun was so doubtful at the time of the solstice, she was also a reminder of that delicate situation. She was sometimes called a death goddess because of this (Monaghan, 1990).

The Etruscans

Apart from the Indo-European influence, the Etruscans had the most impact on Roman beliefs and practices. They ruled most of Italy at the beginning of Rome's history, and very nearly took over the city. This powerful and advanced civilization passed on much of its culture to the Romans, to the point where their city had an Etruscan name (along with its famous river, the Tiber). Who they were is not certain. It is not known if the Etruscans were native to the area or later arrivals. Their civilization is now mostly known for its elaborate funeral arrangements, and its status as a bridge between the Greeks and Romans.

Swift eye of the sun

The Etruscans are interesting to us because of evidence that they worshipped a possible sun goddess, Catha. Actually, Catha is a deity of slightly ambiguous gender. The *Liber Lintenus* (the wrapping on a mummy describing a series of ceremonies in honour of various deities) was photographed in infra-red light, revealing an inscription to *Ati Cath*, 'Mother Catha' (van der Meer, 1987). Despite this, s/he often appears on mirrors as a male figure rising from the water. Catha had an underworld aspect as well, since one inscription that is probably funerary says to 'pour out for Cautha every (?) year eighty times' (van der Meer, 1987). This may have to do with the time the sun spent underground each night. Cathesan (a compound of Catha and Thesan, Thesan being a dawn goddess) appears on a mirror riding his chariot out of the water, facing east, and at the top of the mirror he rides a boat, facing west (van der Meer, 1987). This is certainly the sun rising and then sailing west in the evening. Her nature becomes clearer when we learn that camomile was called sun's eye by the Romans, and *katham* by the Etruscans, while another Roman text tells us that she was 'Swiftness, daughter of the sun' (van der Meer, 1987). The emphasis on eyes and speed suggests that Catha was a sun goddess, perhaps in association with the other sun god, Usil. (Perhaps like the sun god of heaven and the sun goddess of Arinna, both were local deities who eventually became national, or else one was adapted to the Greek religious conception of Helios when the Etruscans began to import their ideas.)

Another goddess worth our attention is the dawn goddess Thesan, who appears on mirrors with Usil the sun god and Nethuns, the Etruscan Neptune. This is not surprising, since the sun is often shown rising from the waters. She seems to be the equivalent of Eos/Aurora. She was also the goddess of childbirth, who led the child to light like Juno Lucina.

The Bacchic moon god

The Etruscan moon god was called Tiv, and he was connected to the cult of Fufluns, the local version of Bacchus. A mirror shows Fufluns, Hercle and Vesuna, dressed as if for a Bacchic ritual. Vesuna wears a panther skin and radiate crown with a crescent mounted on it. Hercle also has a crescent on his head, while Fufluns only wears the radiate crown (van der Meer, 1987). It seems that Fufluns must have had a connection with the moon, since he also appears with Tiv on the Piacenza liver, a divinatory model of a liver divided into sections ruled by various deities. Fufluns often appears in name-pairs alongside Catha, probably as a sun–moon pair. Tiv himself is often paired with Usil, most notably on the liver model and in divination from thunder, where Tiv rules the left side of the sky and Usil the right.

These Etruscan deities seem to fit the sun-goddess pattern, while the

Romans, who are certainly Indo-European, seem to be indifferent to the sun and moon. However, the sun goddess Lucina comes from early Italic roots, and she and the solstice goddesses were probably from archaic Roman tradition.

The Indians: Suryaa

THE ARYANS were an Indo-European people who invaded southern India and settled in beside the established Dravidian culture. They probably arrived around 1500 BCE, and the Vedic civilization was in full swing by 1200–800 BCE. It is difficult to be sure about dates because there are no written histories from the period. The Vedas were passed down orally, just as the Irish lore was passed from druid to druid. The original Aryans were part of an Indo-Iranian group that moved into India, with later groups following into Iran, which means they form a distinct branch of the Indo-European group.

Being an Indo-European group, the Aryans were horse-riders, nomads and users of iron. The Dravidians were farmers and urban dwellers, who had a sophisticated and stratified society. The Rig Veda shows traces of the Dravidian religion, but it mostly reflects the values and beliefs of the Aryans. It consists of hymns to and about the deities, written in an allusive, sometimes enigmatic style. We can tell from these poems and other sources that fire was important to Vedic rituals, and the priesthood sacrificed and ingested the drug soma.

Hinduism is a polytheistic religion, so that (unlike Christianity) it preserves many of its ancient deities and forms of worship. It has survived at least three thousand years, without one centralized doctrine or leader. It is a very adaptable religion, which explains its success. Hinduism is a variety of cults, ranging from the worship of purely local gods to the great cults of Visnu and Siva. The Rig Veda is its earliest collection of literature, in this case hymns, which give a good idea of what the early religion was like. These and several other works form the basis of the Hindu religion.

Surya

Surya the sun god is very similar to Saule in his functions. He is a god who interests himself in the doing of humans, and punishes evil and looks after the unfortunate. His name comes from the root *svar*, 'to shine', and he is considered to be made of fire that consumes its own substance (rather like the fires of Sul and Brigit, the Celtic sun/fire goddesses) (Daniélou, 1963). Just like Perkunas and Saule, Indra the thunder god does not get along with Surya. He breaks the wheels of the sun chariot, and steals one to defeat a demon with. People pray to Surya for clear vision and a return to ruddy health, and to cure a cough, leprosy and jaundice (Jayne, 1925). He is sometimes called the swan of heaven, a common image for the sun deity (Pandey, 1989). He is all-seeing, the eye of heaven. Some of his titles are Vivasvat, 'owner of rays', Dina-kara, 'day-maker', and Karma-sakshi, 'witness of the deeds' (Knappert, 1991).

Iconography often colours him red, and shows him either dressed in the northern Indian style or else standing in his chariot with his seven horses. The seven rays stand for the planets (five plus the sun and moon) and the stars (Pandey, 1989). An ancient text describes an image of Surya that has the left side of the body female in appearance and coloured blue, which corresponds to the bisexuality of the sun in India (Pandey, 1989). (Unfortunately the image no longer exists.) His most famous temple at Konarak is now ruined, but one can still visit and get some idea of what it was like. Watts (1971) speculates that the builders intended the wheels on the sides and horses at the front to represent the sun's chariot.

Savitar

Another aspect of the sun god is Savitar, the 'stimulator'. He oversees the span of heaven, and, as his name suggests, encourages activity in humans and animals. He has yellow hair and a golden body, and he seems to have been a god of the setting sun, since it is said that he commands night to approach. He assisted Indra in his creation of the cosmos. One of the oldest mantras is addressed to him every dawn by worshippers (MacKenzie, 1994):

> Let us meditate on that excellent glory of the divine Vivifier,
> May he enlighten (or stimulate) our understandings.

This prayer is sometimes addressed to a female sun, who had a cult in the temple at Konarak in Orissa, built in the tenth century CE. 'In the Gayatri rite, every Hindu began his day with a prayer and hymn of praise to the sun (Suryaa) as the giver (feminine) of light, heat and fruitfulness' (New Catholic Encyclopedia, 1967).

Savitar also has a female aspect, a goddess called Savitri. She was a princess so beautiful that her dazzling eyes overawed potential suitors until finally the man who was worthy of her showed up (Parrinder, 1980). She married him, although he could only live one year more, and when he died she regained him by following the death god as he returned to his abode. As she walked with Yama, her wise conversation impressed him. For her great courage and wisdom, he granted her several boons, including the life of her husband (MacKenzie, 1994). That she is a sun goddess can be deduced from the solar motifs of dazzling eyes and underworld journey. (Another Savitri is the daughter of the sun god, who marries the supreme deity Brahma.)

Vivasvat

The third aspect of Surya is Vivasvat ('he who lights up'), the sunrise aspect of the sun. He married Saranyu ('knowledge'), the mare goddess, to produce the Asvins, as well as another set of twins. She left her servant in her place because she could no longer bear his brilliance, a woman named Shade, but he discovered the deception. He sought her in stallion guise, and in mare form she inhaled some of his semen and later gave birth to the twin Asvins. This story explains one of their names, Natsaya, which can be read as 'nose-born' (this story is of later origin than one that gives them Dyaus the sky god for a father [Lurker, 1994]). However, she still would not return until he became less bright. To win back his wife he went to the artificer god Tvastr and had some of his brilliance trimmed off on the lathe. Tvastr dripped honey nectar over his legs to take away some of his sunbeams, but Vivasvat would not let him take off any above his knees, and so his lower legs are covered in pictures (Pandey, 1989). (This story is also told of Surya, to account for this peculiarity of his images.)

Suryaa

The daughter of the god Surya is also called Suryaa (the longer 'a' makes it a feminine form). Since Savitar is an aspect of her father, Suryaa may be the same goddess as Savitri, mentioned earlier. Several Hindu texts use the word *savitri* to describe her. She is mostly known for being married to either Soma or the heavenly twins, and the form of weddings is based on the *Rig Veda* hymn about her marriage to the god of intoxication and the moon, Soma. As his wife she purifies him with her hair (rays?) and fetches him from the sky (probably for sacrifices). She rides in the Asvins' three-wheeled chariot, which got its third wheel when she joined them. Together they form the triad of sun maiden and twin gods also found in Greek and Baltic mythology (Griffith, 1991):

> When night was turning to the grey of morning, the Maiden, Surya's daughter, chose your splendour.

The twins won Suryaa in a contest with a group of poets by composing a thousand stanzas, and the losers begged them to set the poem down for them, as a consolation prize (Bhattacharji, 1970).

While there is no overt sun-rescue myth to attach to Suryaa, there is the myth of Suraj, who is stolen by a king who wishes to marry her, and is rescued when her father the sun (Suraj Deo) goes to the mortal to have her returned. However, this wily king then captures him in an iron pot. The result is an eclipse, and the now-frightened mortal lets the suns go (Elwin, 1942). Cader suggests that the original myth was that the Asvins would rescue the sun (their name Natsaya can mean 'the retrievers'). The evening star dived after it and the morning star led it back. Since the sun maiden rides in their chariot, it was probably her they were rescuing and returning. There is another myth that could relate to the rescue: in some of the hymns to the Asvins, there is a reference to a quail they saved from the wolf (Griffith, 1991):

The quail had invocated you, O Asvins, when from the wolf's devouring jaws ye freed her.

The myth is often interpreted as the Asvins saving Ushas, either from darkness or from the eclipse-demon. Since the dawn and the sun maiden are often the same, and Ushas is sometimes Surya's daughter, she and Suryaa may very well be the same goddess in this case.

AGNI

The fire god Agni was extremely important to the Vedic religion. He was the one who received offerings as an intermediary for the gods, when they were poured into the sacrificial flames. His seven tongues are flames which lick up the clarified butter given to him. His name is cognate to a group of words for fire: *ignis* (Latin), *ogni* (Old Slavic) and *ugnis* (Lithuanian) (Puhvel, 1987). Like Vesta, he is a household deity as well as one worshipped in large temples. He tends to be identified with the sun, and especially with the god Surya. Fire is the sun on earth, where it can be controlled (Dass, 1984).

He was born three times, in the sky from the sun, in the air from lightning, and on the earth from a stone or water, as fire. (The last may seem odd, but stones and water extinguish fire, so it was thought that the fire continued to live in the stone or water that put it out [Lurker, 1994]). Agni was in fact often perceived in the phenomena of lightning and sunlight, since both are forms of fire. He was thus related to Surya on the one hand and Indra on the other. He was also the vital spark in humans. According to another legend, his parents were Dyaus and Privithi, or heaven and earth. This version relates to the kindling of sacred fire, by rubbing a stick placed horizontally with one held vertically.

The main myth of Agni is that he disappeared and had to be found and convinced to return. He left because he feared that he would be used up in service to the gods as his three brothers had been. However, the gods tracked him to the waters, and promised him that he would not die when fires were put out, and that he could have the clarified butter and soma. After this, he returns to mediating between gods and humans (O'Flaherty, 1981). This myth includes a reference to the fire/water polarity. Another instance of this is Agni's hatred of fish (Puhvel, 1987). He is said to make the waters pregnant, a reference to the fire–water imagery of sex and fertility. He also appears in the Suryaa myth as the god who leads the bridal procession, and also possesses her before marriage (as he does with all brides) (O'Flaherty, 1981).

Tantra: fiery female

The basic premise of tantra is that the female is the active principle, energizing the passive male. It is not surprising that this lends itself to symbolism suggestive of the fiery/solar feminine. The association of fire with the female in tantra is proved by the following quote from the Upanishads: 'Whatever is moist, he created from semen, and from the mouth of the fire-hole (yoni) he created fire.' The semen is the moon fluid, for 'her skin is the press of the soma libation, the two lips of the vulva are the fire in the middle' (quoted in Parrinder, 1980). The man is the lunar, passive participant, and the woman the fiery, and so solar, participant.

In the Siva Samhita, a tantric dialogue between Siva and his wife Parvati, the sun and female emissions are said to be one (Ghosh, 1980):

> Know thee that the seminal fluid is the 'moon' and the ovarian fluid the 'sun'. It is necessary to coalesce the two within one's own body.

> In fact, I [Siva] am the seminal fluid and the ovarian fluid is Sakti. When the two are united in the body of the yogi, he attains a divine body.

It is also said that the moon in the head is the watery semen, while the devouring fire in the belly is the red female sun (menses).

In some tantric rituals the woman must be menstruating, because Agni the fire god was associated with the blood of women, presumably because of the colour. He is also identified with the sun while Soma is rain (Dass, 1984). (It is also interesting to note that in Jain symbolism the swastika symbolizes the sun's rays or a vagina [Parrinder, 1980].) The phallus is often symbolized by a white column (lingam) or a white thunderbolt, while the vagina is shown as a red lotus (O'Flaherty, 1981).

Soma, as lord of all things liquid, and the moon, is opposed to Agni. However, Agni is lord of the sacrifice, and so he loves soma, which is the main offering. Ions suggests that the marriage of Suryaa and Soma is a metaphor for this, a blending of fire and water. When the priests pressed the soma plant to express the juice, it was said that the god entered into the vat like a bull fertilizing a herd of cows (Ions, 1967). The polarity of water/fire and moon/sun works on many levels.

Marriage

The marriage of Soma and Suryaa was also the form for human marriages. Like the goddess, the bride was brought from her parental house in a cart that had two strings laid before it, one red and one blue. She then stepped over the threshold of her new home, and sat on the hide of a red bull. She was given to hold a child from a mother who had borne only sons. Then the bride and groom join hands, and they go around the fire three times, as the divine witness to the marriage, and make offerings to it. In one of the most important moments of the ceremony, she takes seven steps, led by her husband. She steps on a stone to impart firmness, or a fixed star is pointed out to her if the wedding takes place at night. In Hindu weddings the bride is given a mirror to 'dress her hair with' (New Catholic Encyclopedia,1967). During the ceremony, the priest would recite various scriptures, including the Surya-sakta, the 'wedding hymn of the goddess'.

The ceremony in total is very much like the hymn, from the leaving in the chariot to the circumambulations of the fire. This detail is a facet of Agni-worship, along with the offerings to the fire. The mirror would seem to be another archaic remnant, since the mirror is a frequent attribute of the sun goddess, and Suryaa is the prototypical bride.

Ushas

The beautiful goddess of dawn was such a popular deity that a whole book of the Vedas is dedicated to her. She is depicted in a crimson sari and golden veil, baring her breasts to banish night. This and her love affairs gave Hindu poets much scope for erotic description of her beauty. Her family relations are a bit confusing since she is the wife/sister/daughter of Surya. She rides with him in his chariot sometimes, and is said to have fled from it when Indra struck the wheel with his thunderbolt. Puhvel (1987) suggests that this was done because if dawn lingers the day won't begin. A hymn to Ushas suggests that she is welcome, but should not tarry. It may be that Indra throws a thunderbolt at her to hurry her along.

Another dawn goddess is the obscure Asva, who is represented as a mare. The mare is often assimilated to fire and even the sun, as with the mare that is buried in the ocean in Hindu myth. The fiery mare was put into the sea by Soma and Varuna, both watery gods, because it represented demonic fire. The association to the sun is that a ring round the sun during the rainy season is compared to the mare in the ocean (O'Flaherty, 1980). The fiery mare seems to have been associated with death, as was female sexual fire. (This may be because the penis seems to lose something and come out deflated from sex.) This seems to be the rationale behind the yogic practice of coitus reservatus, since semen is a sacred substance, and should not be destroyed. However, not withholding it is equal to the butter offerings given to Agni, since women's vulvas are fiery, and the semen is often likened to butter, which is offered to the fire by the priests.

Cows of light

The cows of Indra and Aditi were embodiments of light in its feminine form. The cows of Indra specifically represent the dawn rays of the sun. He rescues them from the cave they are penned up in, thus freeing the dawn light. The demons of darkness, Panis, had stolen them. Indra found the cows, and so, metaphorically, freed the dawn to light the world. The verses hint that this is an act from the beginning of time, another of Indra's heroic feats. If this is so, this could be another of the myths where the sun maiden is freed from darkness or winter. In line with this inter-pretation, sometimes the Asvins free the cows.

In the case of Aditi, scholars know that later Hindus associated her with the sun, because the *Ayin-i-Akbara* lists her as the goddess of Sunday. (This work was a statistical and geographical account of the Mogul empire in India, during the reign of Jelaleddin Mohammed Akbar.) This work also says that fire and fiery bodies originate in Aditilogue, the region the sun passes through (Durdin-Robertson, 1990).

The linkage of fire and sun with the female principle is common to all the Indo-Europeans in this book. The common themes of sun and moon marriage, sun maiden and twins, and the solar mare all appear in Indian mythology, confirming that they are part of a shared spiritual heritage.

Iran

The other half of the Indo-Iranian branch does not have its own chapter in this book, for several reasons. First, they do not appear to have a sun goddess, or very many goddesses of any kind. The basic mythology of the Iranians was overlaid early by the tenets of Zoroastrianism, which made demons of many gods resembling those of Vedic India, and promoted its own. Mithra, the god of contracts, took over the solar symbolism of the local equivalent of Surya and the rest. The sun god, Hvar, survives in one hymn which describes him as 'he who possesses swift horses'. In Persian he is called Xursed, and the eleventh day of each month (*xur*) was set aside for his worship (Williams, 1928). He conforms to the Indo-European image of a sun deity.

Another hymn in the same series praises the moon god Mah, who resembles the Indian Mas. Soma has his counterpart in Haoma, who had a similar ceremony until it fell out of favour with those who objected to ritual drunkenness. There is a similarity also in the myth of the divine twins Haurvtat and Amrtat, who in borrowed myths chased a young woman who was raised into the sky as Venus (called Zohra or Anahid). Anahita is a goddess of waters who was important as a transfunctional goddess, but there is a hint here of the courting of Suryaa by the Asvins. Ushas the dawn seems to have fallen out of favour, since Puhvel (1987) points out that her counterpart was the goddess of sloth, who lured people into sleeping late and putting things off. The cult of fire and water, similar to that of the Armenians, was important to Iranian religion. The fire god Atar and the water god Apas were both given libations in rituals: Atar got dry fuel, incense and fat, while Apas got milk, water and the juice of two plants (Eliade, 1987).

One can also find other parallels, but essentially the Iranians went their own way, while the Indians preserved their tradition by writing and reciting, so that it still exists for the modern scholar.

Mazes

THE SUN MAIDEN and her rescue from the forces of darkness and winter are part of several European mythologies, and hinted at in some others. The myth is overt among the Balts and Greeks, and in the Vedic hymns. This myth also explains the spring rituals surrounding the labyrinths in Scandinavia and Germany, as a re-enactment of the original event that gave rise to the belief.

SUN MAIDEN

The Baltic Saules meita, the Vedic Suryaa, and the Grecian Helen are three examples of the Proto-Indo-European sun maiden. Her function is to represent the spring sun, as the days grow longer and warmth returns. As the sun's daughter, she shares in her solar nature. She represents the sun of spring and dawn, and sometimes the morning star as well.

Saules meita is the daughter of the sun, which is the meaning of her name. She (or they – sometimes there's more than one) is the other side of Saule's character, the 'little sun'. This makes her the goddess of the spring, dawn and morning star complex associated with sun maidens. The dawn goddess is called Auszrine, and her sister the twilight is called Wakerine. Like Helen, she may have been born of an egg; there is an Estonian myth about Salme, who was hatched from a goose egg, and courted by the sun, the moon, and the eldest son of the stars, the latter being a successful suitor. This Salme is thought to be a version of Saules meita (West, 1975).

The Vedic sun maiden Suryaa is the daughter of the sun god Surya (her name is the feminine form). The longest reference to her in the *Rig Veda* is the wedding hymn *Surya-sakta*, which tells of her marriage to the moon god Soma. However, in other places she is married to the Asvins, and passages in the Vedas hint at a rescue myth. She is the 'third wheel' of their chariot, and when she mounted it, 'birds of blue hue were round you [the twins], and burning splendours were round you' (Griffith, 1991).

The story of Helen and the Trojan War is familiar to most people. However, behind the story is the sun maiden of older legend. Helen's name can be read as 'shining' or 'divine splendour', and in some traditions she is the daughter of Helios, the personified sun god of the Greeks. Her name means 'torch', which connects her again to the dawn goddess who lights up the sky so the sun can follow. Her brothers are the twin sons of the sky god Zeus, the Dioscouroi. There are a number of myths of Helen's abduction, including one where Theseus snatches her and she is rescued from his mother's care by the twins.

Heavenly twins

The heavenly twins who accomplish this rescue are equally consistent across the Indo-European spectrum. In all the mythologies in this book, they are the horse-riding or sailing twin warriors and protectors of travellers. They are usually the sons of the sky god, although the Asvins are his grandsons. All of them also have associations with fertility, especially the Dieva deli, who look after the sky-farm, and the Asvins, who make the old young and virile.

The twin suitors of the Baltic sun maiden are the Dieva deli, 'sons of God', and their father is god of the sky. Many folksongs emphasize their relationship with the maiden. They are the steeds of both sun and moon, which befits the morning and evening stars. This relation to horses is common among the twins of Indo-European myth. They are also associated with sailing, and are said in some songs to go out boating with the sun maiden.

In the *Rig Veda* there are several hymns addressed to the *Divó napala*, sons of God. Their [grand]father is Dyaus, 'the sky', and one of their names is Asvins, which means 'having horses'. The horses are essential to them; they travel the sky in their chariot in the morning, along with the dawn goddess Ushas. They are healers, who can make the old young and fertile. They are the suitors or husbands of Suryaa, an honour they share with the moon god Soma. They are the ruddy gods of morning.

The Dioscouroi ('sons of God') were the twin sons of Zeus, who, in the form of a swan, visited their mother Leda. Castor was mortal and Polydeuces wasn't, so they asked Zeus to let them daily alternate between being in Olympus and the underworld of the dead. This is the reason given by those who see them as the morning and evening stars, although they were also the constellation Gemini (the twins). They were also patrons of mariners, and prayed to for rescues at sea. Twin St Elmo's Fires were their symbol, while one such flame stood for their sister Helen. The twins are her brothers, one a boxer and one a horse-tamer. One of their titles is *leuko polos* Dios ('white colts of Zeus'), which fits with the horse motif of the divine twins (Puhvel, 1987).

Celtic and Germanic variants

The Celtic and German myths show traces of such myths of a sun maiden and twins, although one has to search a little more for them. The Germanic Svanhild, who one of the early sagas says is the daughter of the sun and day, seems a good candidate. Her husband kills her by having horses trample her, because he has been misled into thinking she is unfaithful. The horses won't trample her because of her radiant beauty and burning glance, but the king has her head covered so that the horses won't shy. Her two brothers come from across the sea, kill almost all the king's warhost, and then die after exacting their revenge. The two brothers certainly correspond to the twins. They come to avenge her at the urging of their mother in some sagas, who has become the warlike Gudrun. Even in the sagas where Gudrun is the mother, she describes her daughter as sunlike.

The two brothers may be the same as the sons of day saluted by Sigrdrifa in the saga that bears her name. A hero wakes her from an enchanted sleep, and she immediately says:

> Hail to thee, day! Hail, ye day's sons!
> Hail, night and daughter of night!

This seems to indicate the day god Dag, who is sometimes Svanhild's father. He seems to have sons, who would then be the divine twins, since the sky god is the god of the day, as opposed to night. (This would make Tyr and Dag the same god.) These sons would then be Svanhild' s brothers. Other candidates for the position of Dag's sons include Heingst and Horsa, who had a sister named Swana who appears in a variant on the Svanhild tale. Since they are sometimes associated with horses, they are often identified with horsy pairs like Heingst and Horsa, the putative invaders of England, who may have been mythical (like Arthur or Roland). They may also be linked to the two horses that pull Sól's chariot (Davidson and Gelling, 1969). Another pair of obscure deities are the Germanic Alcis, compared by Tacitus to Castor and Pollux. They may also be divine twins; some relate their name to words for horses.

As for the Celts, it has been suggested that the similar stories of Rhiannon and Macha could provide the basis of a twins and sun-maiden legend. Rhiannon has a son who is born on the same night as a foal, and the horse connection is vital to the twins. Among the Gauls there was a god called Uintios ('windy one'), who was compared by the Romans to Pollux (MacCrossan, 1993). It would be interesting to know if he had a twin, as his Roman counterpart did. Anne Ross mentions portrayals of the Dioscouroi (sons of God/Zeus) and a horse on several Gallo-Roman monuments (Ross, 1992). There was also a pagan altar at Notre-Dame in Paris with a dedication to several deities including the heavenly twins (Hastings, 1980).

The rescue

The myth of the sun maiden's rescue is a very simple one. She is captured by the moon god, who hands her over to another, older female figure. This woman humiliates her and sets her difficult tasks. The twins then come to her rescue, take revenge on the older woman, and return the goddess to her home (Ward, 1967, 1968; Dexter-Robbins, 1984). The male abductor does not seem to receive any punishment from them (although in the Baltic myth the moon is punished by the sun for stealing her daughter).

That the twins are the suitors of the sun maiden, or at least closely associated with her, is established. The capture is less obvious. Helen is taken by Theseus as she dances in Artemis's temple, when she is young. Later there is the more famous abduction to Troy. The songs of the Balts (Ward, 1968) hint at a capture:

> Today the Sun is moving
> More warmly than other days;
> Today someone has taken the Sun Maiden
> From the Daugava to Germany.

They are similarly explicit (Ward, 1967) about the rescuers' identity:

> The Sun maiden was wading in the sea,
> Only her crown was visible.
> Row your boat, O Sons of God,
> Rescue the Sun's soul [var. life].

In the Vedic myths the Asvins are said to mount their chariot 'for Suryaa's sake', and bring her home. In a folktale from Motinala a daughter of the sun called Suraj is stolen from her home by a rival who wishes to marry her. (Suraj would be the same as Suryaa, and is similarly rescued by twins.) Cader (1976) suggests that the twins rescue the sun from night each evening, one going after it as it descends, and the other leading it back in the morning (which corresponds to their appearance as the morning and evening stars).

In the case of the Baltic and Vedic mythologies the moon has stolen the maiden. The song quoted on page 39, and above, describes how the sun maiden was taken by the moon, which angered the other gods. The Vedic Suryaa sometimes marries the moon, which presumably disappoints the twins, who are usually her suitors. In the Greek stories this seems to have been lost from the story, since there is nothing inherently lunar about Theseus or Paris (although one scholar sees Helen's husband Menelaos as an echo of the moon god [Dexter-Robbins, 1984]).

The older woman who holds the maiden does appear in the Greek stories. Theseus's mother, Aethra, was entrusted with Helen because he had to go somewhere. The same element appears in the *Iliad*, where Helen has to be guarded by women because of the Trojan War. It also appears in versions of the Svanhild saga, in which she is turned over to the care of the kidnapper's mother, who makes her wash clothes. The same element is present also in Baltic folksongs about young married women.

Then of course the twins ride to the rescue, or else arrive by boat. The German versions have them either avenging her death or being tipped off by the maiden herself, so that they can find her and rescue her. (This happens in the story of Culhwch and Olwen, a Welsh myth in which Olwen is locked in a castle and must be freed.) She does this by casting the clothes she has been washing into the water. The Grecian Dioscouroi find Helen with Theseus's mother, and reverse roles by taking the old woman to be a servant. The Dieva deli retrieve their sister from drowning as she washes her linen.

Smith God

One variant of this tradition is found in an account by Jerome of Prague, which says that he found the Balts worshipping a giant hammer because it had liberated the sun from a high fortress where an evil king had imprisoned it in a tower. The rescuers were the 'stars of the zodiac', whom Ward (1968) identifies as the twin star sons of the sky god Dievas. The hammer belonged to the smith god Kalvatis or Teljavel, who made the sun and moon. Sometimes Perkunas is a smith, and then the twin rescuers are called 'the workmen of Perkun.' A variant form is found in the Finnish *Kalevala*, where the smith god Ilmarnien forges a replacement for the sun when a witch steals the other one. Ward suggests that Ilmarnien and Vainonmen are twins who rescue the sun maiden.

Labyrinths

The myth can be connected to the labyrinths of northern Europe, which often feature a vestigial sun-goddess connection. Many of the northern European mazes called Troytowns (Old High German *draja*, Celtic *troian*: 'turn, twist'[Gitlin-Emmer, 1993]) have a motif of this kind attached to them. They can be found in Germany, Sweden, Finland, Norway, Denmark and England. By folk etymology they have been connected to the famous city of Troy, which is reputed to have had a mazelike pattern of walls, to confuse invaders.

Finnish mazes are sometimes called Jungfrudanser (Virgin's Dances). An account published in Helsinki in 1874 by A.O. Freudenthal says that in the ceremony a virgin would stand in the centre and young men dance in to her, following the twists of the maze. A variant was one young man running the maze and dancing with the woman in the middle, as at Malax in western Finland.

Many of the stone mazes of Scandinavia seem to have some such purpose attached. (A stone maze is laid out on the ground with stones to mark the paths.) It is common to find them by the sea. Swedish peasants living in Finland would build them, and young men would race through the turns to a young woman in the centre (Bord, 1976). A large example of this type was seen in Wisby, Gotland, which was 20 yards across (Matthews, 1922). There was a similar custom at Saffron Walden in Essex, where a young woman stood in the middle and a young man tried to get to her as fast as possible without stumbling (Pennick, 1990). Another type of maze had two entrances, and two young men raced through them to the young woman in the middle. A maze of this type, called Jungfruringen (Virgin's Ring), is located in Köpmanholm in Sweden.

It was also customary in Sweden to erect ice and snow labyrinths in winter so that people could ski along them in imitation of Grimborg, a hero who had rescued a king's daughter he wished to marry by breaking through fences of iron and steel. The people sang a song called 'The Song of Grimborg' and a man skied through up to the final turn before the centre, where another man had been set as guard (Pennick, 1990). The connection to the sun-maiden myth, where the winter is overcome by the forces of spring, is obvious.

In the Baltic version the sun is kept by an evil king. The 'mother' seems to be absent. However, the earth goddess was the keeper of the dead, and in some versions of the sun's journey her daughters have to rescue her from the bowels of the earth every morning. It could be that the actual labyrinth symbolizes these 'bowels' and the sun disappears into them in winter; when it grows weaker and the days colder, a rescue must be effected. (The 'king' would then be the moon, keeping the maiden with the collusion of the earth goddess.)

In the Rig Veda there are hints of a contest similar to the maze-running races. The Asvins win Suryaa through a race, after which she mounts their chariot with the approval of the gods. The idea of the two men racing to the maiden was preserved in the labyrinths of northern Europe. The Theseus connection is relevant here as well, since he was paired with Ariadne of the Maze, and with Helen of Troy (which would enter folklore as a labyrinth). Put this beside the northern European mazes where two men would 'rescue' a young woman symbolizing the sun maiden, and there seems to be a definite pattern of labyrinths in sun-goddess worship.

The excavations have shown that the Trojans built their city with the walls overlapping, to make it easier to defend the gate, which may have formed the basis of the idea of the Trojan maze, helped along by folk etymology. An Etruscan vase that shows warriors on horses next to a maze called 'TRVIA' proves that the idea of Troy as a maze was an ancient one (Pennick, 1990). Troy is associated with labyrinths in many engravings, and a reference to a Trojan labyrinth appears on an Etruscan wine-jug (Matthews, 1922). Virgil mentions Ludus Trojae in the Aeneid, as a game that Aeneas's son Iulus takes part in, and which involves a processional parade/dance with some of the men on horseback. (Did they represent the Dioscouroi?) Pliny also mentions mazes on the open fields in Italy (Hamkens, 1982).

Another possible version of a primitive labyrinth existed in Helen's native Sparta. The Plane Grove in Sparta was part of the male initiation ceremonies. It was a ring of plane trees near a temple of Helen where contests took place. Inside the ring was a moat, with two bridges spanning it. It is not certain, but it may have been a double-entrance labyrinth (Lindsay, 1974). Some labyrinths in Europe have trees in the middle, which may reflect Helen's connection to the plane tree (just as the Baltic tradition connects Saule to the *axis mundi*). The sun-goddess labyrinth may not have originated in the north after all.

The makers of labyrinths are also connected to the sun-goddess myth. In Scandinavia and the Baltic countries smith gods like Völund/Wayland are the builders of the mazes, while in the south Daedalus built the famous Labyrinth. Monaghan (1994) suggests that the hostility between Sunna and the dwarves is because the tiny artificers built the stone labyrinths that trap her each winter. These same builders, however, often provide the tools with which to free the goddess, as when Teljavel gives the twins a giant hammer to smash the tower that holds Saules meita captive, or Ilmarnien forges a mock sun to fool Lonhi into returning the real one. The place of the smith god in this myth is an ambiguous one.

Presumably the goddess is captured in the maze, held there for a period (winter) and then released by the young twins, with their connections to fertility and youth. This is why the mazes are so often connected to two youths who free a maiden, by running a double-entrance maze. When the goddess is freed, spring comes, which is when the rituals are enacted. Dumézil's (Mallory, 1991) comment that the twins and sun maiden are connected with the third function, fertility, becomes more appropriate than ever, for they bring with them light and new life as they are reunited after winter.

The European labyrinths and the Vedic material together illuminate an area of mythology that was obscure. The rescue of Helen, Suryaa or Saules meita is another facet of the rich mythology of the sun goddess.

Moon God

IN THE CHAPTER on the Indo-Europeans (page 9), I quoted Varenne (1991) as saying that the identity of the moon deity was still a problem for scholars. As he pointed out, this problem is connected to the related question about the solar deity. The main part of this book explores the mythology of the sun goddess as an answer to his question. Now we are going to survey the moon in these cultures to see what his relations to the sun are, and what functions he has.

Although many occultists assume that the true moon deity is a triplicate goddess, most of the peoples mentioned in this book worship a lunar male. The triple goddess of the moon is a late classical idea, and so can hardly be assumed as a common pattern throughout Europe and the east. Despite this, authors will try to fit together three goddesses to make what they feel is a 'proper' moon goddess. It hardly needs pointing out that these goddesses often have little in common and cannot be shown to have any relation to each other. Sometimes mere triplicity is the basis for making a goddess the moon; Brigit is often misidentified this way. (Besides, if this were all that was required, what of Odin or Lugh, who have triple form? Or indeed of the sun goddesses Saule and Solntse with their two daughters?)

The moon god is not a 'northern peculiarity'. He and his spouse/sister are often dismissed in this way, but what of Thoth (Egypt), Amm (southern Arabia) and Bahloo (Australia)? Surely there can be few gods further from the cold that is supposed to produce these irregularities? The authors seem to feel they must apologize for the inferior quality of deity they are reporting. The moon as male seems to satisfy his worshippers. He regulates time, makes women and plants fertile, and gives health. These are hardly unimportant functions.

The seducer god

The Balts called the moon Menuo (Lithuanian) or Meness (Latvian). Both of them are married to the sun and seduce her daughter the sun maiden or morning star. Menuo wore a starry robe and travelled the sky in a chariot drawn by grey horses (Savill, 1977). Because he lit up the night, he is the patron of travellers (Eliade, 1987). He is often at Saule's silver gates courting her daughters (Gimbutas, 1963). He is the same as the Latvian Meness, although there are some differences in their myths. In the Latvian

119

version there is more tension between the sun and moon, and in one version it is the sun who is the adulterer, having taken up with the thunder god behind Menesis's back.

Before the split between the moon and sun, they used to ride side by side through the sky, but now they are divorced and avoid each other. Their associations are completely opposite on every point. Saule stands for summer and peace, while Menuo is patron of winter and war (Jouet, 1989):

> There where Saule runs in the summer,
> That's where Menesis runs in the winter.
> There where the girls lead cattle,
> That's where the boys go to the guard.

While she looks after women, he takes care of men. She is goddess of marriage; he seduces women without respect for bonds.

The sun and moon divorced because the sun maiden was betrothed to the god of the morning star, Auseklis, but the moon god seduced her before the marriage. When Saule learned of it, she slashed at the moon god with her sword. In the Lithuanian version, the daughter was the morning star, and the thunder god Perkunas cut the moon in half as punishment. Menesis finally married the weaver of the star canopy. As a result of this incident, he is considered dangerous to young women, whom he may kidnap (McCrickard, 1990). Folktales relate how he took an orphan girl who prayed to him, and another who boasted that her body was brighter than the moon (Leach, 1975).

Another version of this story is that the moon decided to marry the sun's daughter, and went to ask for her hand. The sun refused him, saying: 'Shine for someone else. Don't bother my daughter.' The moon wept, and his tears became the stars. This is interesting because of the close connection between the moon and stars. They are often portrayed as his army, or else he is counting them to see that they are all there.

In both countries the moon is the war god, and is responsible for healing and the growth of plants. In his character as a warrior he is invoked at the start of military campaigns and for the consecration of the army's standard (Lurker, 1994). The stars are his troops, and he protects military expeditions (Jouet, 1989):

> Where are you running to, Menesis,
> With that bouquet of stars?
> I'm going to the war, I run to the war,
> To help the young men.

He had a sword with six blades, a bit of mythological hyperbole, which befits his role as the light that travels the dangerous night sky.

GENDER CONFUSION

Pears says, of the Slavic moon god Myesyats (Russian for 'month'), that although the name is masculine, s/he is 'usually' the wife of Dazgbog, whom the authors describe as a Russian sun god (Savill, 1977). In the Ukraine, however, he is husband to the sun goddess, and may have originally been male in Russia as well, as the folksongs show (see pages 44–53). All the prayers to the moon address him as Myesyats, and in masculine terms.

The Slavs saw him as a young man who grew old and died each month. His power to renew himself made him a healing deity. Although he lives with the sun, they do not like each other and so avoid each other. Myesyats seduces the sun's daughter Dennitsa, the morning star, just like his Baltic counterpart. The southern Slavs call a groom 'Mr Moonshine', and a Russian wedding song describes the groom and his potential sons as the moon and stars, and the bride and hoped-for daughters as the sun and her swans (McCrickard, 1990).

Since the moon gave health, he was prayed to for health in children and greeted with round dances. During eclipses, people would weep and wail in sympathy with the moon, who was being devoured by monsters. Russian, Bulgarian and Serbo-Croatian songs call the moon a father or grandfather. At Risan, in the former Yugoslavia, it was said that when a baby was four months old it had four 'grandfathers'. Bulgarians taught their children to call the moon Dedo Bozhe, Dedo Gospod ('Uncle God, Uncle Lord'), and the Ukrainian peasants averred that the moon god was their deity, and no other would be as effective. (This must have been an answer to evangelists.) Two Greater Russian prayers call the moon god Adam, which would make him the father of humanity, a typical role for the moon god (Gasparini).

The sun's brother

While anyone who reads the *Eddas* can see that there is a moon god about, it is amazing how many try to ignore this in favour of their triple moon goddess. It is difficult to see why people do this since there are no triple goddesses among the Norse to correspond to the young–middle–old pattern required. There is no crone figure among the Norse. There are goddesses specific to women who are unmarried, married or sexually active outside marriage (Gefjon, Frigg, Freya) but no figure of the older, cast-off woman (Gundarsson, 1993). Generally these authors link three goddesses who really have very little to do with each other, or to the late-classical pattern the authors have in mind.

Scholars know very little about Mani, the Norse and German moon god. Only a few stories about him remain, including the Huiki and Bil legend. Although the sun has a daughter who survives Ragnarok, the moon isn't mentioned after the wolf eats him. In general, we know little about him, which may be due to his being worshipped mainly by peasants rather than by the aristocracy that gave Sturluson his material, and which favoured Odin and company. Several of these shifts occur over the course of history, as Tyr, then Odin, then Thor became the most popular god. The sun and moon worship may have been a more primitive cult that the more cultured types left behind as their life became more sophisticated.

One thing that is known is what the *skalds* (poets) called him, because the 'Lay of Alvis' gives the poetic terms for the moon (Hollander, 1990):

> 'Tis hight 'Moon' among men,   but 'Sunlight' among gods
> call the wights in Hel it 'Wheel'
> the etins 'Speeder',   the dwarfs 'Splendor'
> and the alfs 'Teller-of-time'.

The Norse made use of the moon's cycle as a calendar, just as most ancient peoples did. The *Poetic Edda* says that the gods made the moon's phases so that humans could tell time. Even now words like 'fortnight' reflect this way of counting.

The creation myth (Sturluson, 1987) states that:

> Moon guides the course of the moon and controls its waxing and waning. He took two children from the earth called Bil and Huiki as they were leaving a well called Byrgir, carrying between them on their shoulders a tub called Saeg; their carrying-pole was called Simul. Their father's name is Vidfinn. These children go with the moon, as can be seen from earth.

The two children are thought to represent the waxing (Huiki) and waning (Bil) moon, as they are smaller than the full moon, and their names can be interpreted as meaning 'increasing' and 'decreasing'. (This story is thought to be the origin of Jack and Jill.) Swedish folklore preserves the idea that the spots on the moon are two people carrying a pole (MacCulloch, 1925).

The Norse distinguished between the moon and sun and the deities in charge of them: the word for moon in Old Norse is *tungl* (Anglo-Saxon *tungol*, Gothic *tuggls*: 'star'), while the god of the moon is always referred to as Mani (Hastings, 1980). This is obvious also in the myth of how the sun and moon were made. Odin and his brothers Villi and Vé made the two lights, and put the deities in charge of moving them across the sky.

In modern German folklore, Mani is Herr Mond ('Mr Moon'), the man who lives in the moon after God cursed him and his wife for doing work on Christmas Eve. God offered them the choice of living either in heaven and hell, or in the sun and moon. They chose the luminaries, and the man can be seen in the moon with his bundle of wood, while his wife sits in the sun and spins (Ranke, 1966).

Celtic possibilities

The Celtic peoples seem to have believed in a female sun and moon, to judge by their words for the moon (Irish *gelach*, *ré* and Welsh *lleuad*, *lloer*), and some of the charms recorded in the *Carmina Gadelica*. There is, however, some variance. One of the words for moon in Irish is *luan*, which is a masculine word. It also describes the hero light that appeared around a man's head when he was in battle. A Scottish saint, Maol Rubha, seems to have assimilated an ancient moon deity, possibly called Mourie. People sacrificed bulls to the saint or for health. One man killed a bull on St Mourie's Island to ensure his daughter's recovery from illness. This may be connected to the small bull's heads found in ancient graves there. The fact that many people take earth from the St Maol Rubha's grave to protect them when travelling also indicates that he was a moon god, because many lunar deities protect travellers, especially at night (NcNeill, 1989).

Selene/Luna

Both Selene and Luna are goddesses of the moon, sisters of the sun gods of the classical Greek and Roman pantheons. They have some features in common but are not identical. Selene means 'light, radiance' and she was also known as Mene, 'moon'. She wore a radiate crown and was winged. Like her brother she drove across the heavens, in a chariot with two horses or oxen. She had a lover, Endymion, who slept perpetually as the price of eternal life. Pan was also her lover, although it would be more accurate to refer to him as a rapist, and one story has it that she married Zeus, and bore him Pandia ('the entirely shining') (Kerényi, 1951). She was the tutelary deity of magicians and sorcerers. In the cosmology of the Greeks, she didn't appear until just before the war of gods and Titans, so that the Arcadians born before her suffered the violence of men and wolves at night (Carlier, 1991). Luna was the Roman goddess of the moon, and had a temple on the Aventine hill. She protected charioteers just like her brother Sol. Her worship was apparently introduced in the time of Romulus, and she only had a small temple on the Via Sacra for a long time. She was more popular with the early Romans than her brother because they calculated their time by the moon (Bell, 1991).

Men

Men of Phrygia was associated with rain and water, and rejoiced in the epithet 'The Saviour' (Briffault, 1927). His cult arose in Anatolia after the collapse of the Hittite empire, based on the many moon gods around that area. He was also called 'Bull-faced', in association with Dionysus (Briffault, 1927). Inscriptions found in Athens suggest that he was a god of water and rain, and others connect him to rivers. Most of his images show him wearing a chiton and tight pants, a Phrygian (conical) bonnet, holding a sceptre in one hand and a pine cone or offering plate in the other. He rides a horse in Asia Minor, but also is shown in an open chariot drawn by a bull.

He appeared beside Cybele in an Anatolian temple, which is fitting since they were both native deities. That and his pine cone have led some scholars to associate him with Attis. He often appears with Hecate in her aspect of saviour, and Artemis Anaitis. Childbearing women invoked him as the Deliverer, along with Artemis or Hecate. Children were dedicated to the two of them (Munro, 1870). One inscription records a priestess of Men and a priestess of Artemis Anaitis in Lydia (Lane, 1971). He was also a healer, for stelae erected to him show legs, eyes and especially breasts praying for healing. He received sacrifices from the first to the fifteenth day of the lunar month only, and that could be a bull or a bloodless offering of fruit or cakes. On the seventh day of the month, at the moon's first quarter, he was given a special sacrifice. The bull seems to have been his particular symbol, since coins show him with a bull on the obverse, and statues show him with his foot on a bull's head.

AMINS

In Armenia the brother of the retiring sun goddess is Amins or Lusin. Lusin is probably cognate to Luna, while Amins now means month, and corresponds to the Latin *mens*, 'month'. The moon is reborn every month, and when he wanes he is pining for love of his sister. The Virgin Mary is his mother, replacing an earlier goddess. It was said that sorcerers could milk the moon like a cow, which suggests that it was full of some substance, perhaps semen (Ananikan, 1925).

In Georgia, the patron saint of the country was confused with the moon god, with the effect of making him a lunar deity, called Tetri Giorgi ('White George') (Lang, 1980). Strabo described a temple of the moon on the borders of Iberia where the hierodules prophesied while possessed by the god. The one most strongly possessed was well treated for a year, then sacrificed to the god along with other victims. As part of a special ceremony he was killed with a spear, and the way he fell was interpreted by the priests. Then his body would be taken to a special place where those needing to be purified would tread on it. The custom survives, as part of the cult of St George. Now the victim voluntarily lies in the doorway of the church, with all who enter treading on her (the victim's gender appears to have changed along the way) (Charachidzé, 1991a).

Kushukh

The Hurrian moon god Kushukh, corresponding to the Hattian Kashku, had the sacred number 30, the number of the lunar month (close enough: 29½ days). The Luwians knew him as Arma (Leick, 1991). In one myth a storm knocked him out of heaven, and the raging of the weather god kept him from returning, but the goddess of healing comes to his aid so that he can return. (This sounds like the enmity of Menuo and Perkunas in Baltic myth.) In another version he falls (or is blown) from the sky, and the thunder god sends rain after him, gives him a talking-to, and essentially frightens him into returning.

Soma/Mahs/Chandra-mas

Mahs or Chandra-mas is the moon god of the Vedas, opposite the sun god Surya. The churning of the ocean to make soma produced Chandra, and he became the moon god. He was assimilated to Soma, perhaps because of his origin.

The image of the moon as Soma was a chalice full of semen or soma-juice, an intoxicating liquid central to the Vedic priesthood. It was the juice of a plant that the priests pressed, but no one agrees on what the plant was. It was sacrificed to the gods, or drunk ceremonially to achieve holy ecstasy. When the chalice is full, the moon is full, but, since the gods require soma to maintain their immortality, they drink a finger of soma each day until the moon is quite empty. As a god, Soma rules water and the tides of the sea, and his sphere is the reservoir of rainwater. As the god of the moon, the milky soma-juice and semen, he is milky white in pictures.

Soma also brought health, and was described as 'medicine'. He was said to make the blind see and the lame walk (Jayne, 1925). In India it was lucky to be born during the full moon (Knappert, 1991). He was the giver of rain in some parts of India. Mas fertilized women through rain/semen, combining two of the moon god's functions. There were many cults of the moon and water in the Indus region in prehistoric times, and by the time of the Vedas sorcerers knew that the moon influenced tides (Joshi, 1989).

Another explanation for the shrinking of the moon is that Soma seduced one of the twenty-eight star daughters of a giant. He married the rest of them, but the giant wished to spare his last daughter. Nevertheless, she loved the moon god, and they hid away and made love. To punish him the giant cursed him with leprosy, but mitigated his curse so that Soma recovers each month, as he visits his wives in each part of heaven. Despite this, people invoked him for healing all diseases, as the guardian of bodies, who gives long life, makes the blind see and makes the lame walk (Jayne, 1925).

Soma also ran off with another woman, in typical moon-god fashion.

He eloped with Tara, the wife of the god of the planet Jupiter. This caused great anger among the gods, and they fought with him. Finally Brahma the supreme god ordered Soma to return her, which he did. Tara had become pregnant during her time with the moon god, which caused consternation. However, Siva had slashed Soma's face with his trident during the fight, and this was punishment enough. There are two interesting aspects to this story: one, the hint of the idea that the moon god impregnates all women; and two, the similarity to the story in Baltic mythology about Perkunas attacking Menuo to punish his infidelity.

Siva and the moon god are somewhat alike, since both are connected with the north quarter; intoxication was part of both cults, both are related to mountains, and Siva was often shown with the crescent on his head (Bhattacharji, 1970). This complex and popular deity was also a storm god, whose trident represented lightning bolts. His bull totem (Ions, 1967) corresponds to both storm and moon god, and both are connected to moisture and fertility. He is a phallic god, and his wife Parvati and he are the main deities of Tantra.

Patterns

The moon god has several purposes. One is to ensure the fertility of women, as the moon god is the cause of menstruation and pregnancy. Another is the measurement of time. He also takes his place in the mythologies we have looked at as the husband or brother of the sun, and often as the seducer of her daughter.

The moon's phases were accounted for in one of several ways. It could be because it was full of some substance that was gradually depleted and then refilled. This substance was often an elixir of either intoxication or immortality, like the Hindu soma. The Slavic and Hindu moons fill up with souls, which they return to earth during the waning phase. The other possibility was that the moon had been cut into pieces, probably by one of the other deities. Another is that the moon shrinks or hides away from fear and shame, or else pines for his sister like the Armenian moon god.

The primitive moon god is often seen as the real fertilizer of women. The link between menstruation and the timing of the lunar month gave rise to the idea that the moon 'caused' menstruation in women, usually by intercourse with them. It may be from this idea that the notion of renewable virginity in goddesses came, as women bled every month instead of just once, and so seemed to be deflowered many times. A further example of this idea is the Hindu god Mahs or Chandra-mas, who was the real husband of women, since he caused their first period, presumably by deflowering them.

The moon as the repository of souls can be linked to this idea. As the lover of women, the god made them fruitful like he did with plants. The Hindu Mahs sent souls back to earth to be reborn by means of rain.

Among the Slavs it was believed that souls went to the moon to be reborn. Men was associated with graves and the underworld for the same reason. Arrival of new lives makes the moon wax, and loss of them to rebirth makes it wane. This seems to deny the theory that ancient peoples were unaware of the male role in procreation, since it is a male god who impregnates women.

The moon was the first calendar, as it disappears and reappears every month. The word for 'month' comes from 'moon', and that in turn comes from the Indo-European root *me- ('measure'). The god Mani determined the waxing and waning of the moon. One of his titles was 'year-counter', and another was 'time- teller'. The Norse and Anglo-Saxons had two kinds of month, a properly lunar month of 29½ days and a common law month of 28 days (Pennick, 1989). Caesar remarks that the Germans would not fight before they saw the new moon, as that was against the gods' will (MacCulloch, 1993). Some scholars suggest that Anglo-Saxons called the sixth and seventh months 'moon', if Litha can be translated that way (Branston, 1993). The Celts also told time by the moon, and made efforts to correlate the solar and lunar time in the Coligny calendar.

The moon also has a connection to crops through sympathetic magic. People sowed their seed when the moon was waxing so that their crops would likewise grow large. There is a vast amount of lore connected to the moon and crops, concerned with both planting and harvesting. The Balts believed that flowers must be planted at new or full moon. They thought that prayers to the new moon were especially efficacious (Gimbutas, 1963). Early Baltic settlers honoured the moon by worshipping its different phases at certain stages in the farming calendar (Hastings, 1980). The *Carmina Gadelica* says that the Irish would not cut things or slaughter animals at the waning moon, as they considered them thin and poor then. They also engaged in many kinds of worship of the moon (whom they saw as female) (Carmichael, 1992).

People also prayed to the new moon for good health and blessings generally. The cult of Men, a saviour who cured all ills, is typical of the moon god. A Lithuanian prayer (Gimbutas, 1958) goes:

Moon, moon, little moon,
Bright god of the sky!
Give him orb, give me health;
Give him completion, and unto me the kingdom of Perkunas!

Another prayer (Gimbutas, 1958) requests more widespread benefits:

Young moon, our prince, always you shine, always cheer us, always you bring
us wealth and happiness. Give him, O God, completion, and unto me the king-
dom of Perkunas.

They thought that the moon god brought health because he renewed himself every month and so could give this resilience to his petitioners.

One of the symbols of the moon god was the bull. Soma was a bull among his cows, and Men had the bull as a totem. In Scotland the bull's curved horns represented the moon on prehistoric grave carvings. This symbolism continued in the cult of St Maol Rubha, whose feast (25 August) was celebrated by sacrificing bulls (McNeill, 1989). People married during the waxing moon to secure the moon bull's gift of fertility.

The moon god granted health and fertility, while ruling the night sky as its light. These qualities made him a fitting companion for the sun, his sister or wife. His periodic renewal was a counterpoint to her yearly cycle, and affirmed his position as the true lover of women.

Thunder God

VERY FEW SCHOLARS will disagree with the statement that the thunder/storm god is an important part of Indo-European mythology. Where I think some of them go wrong is in identifying him with the sun, since he is the god of storms and so opposed to her. This may be due to syncretizing influences on classical mythology which identified everything important with the sun, including the head thunder gods Jupiter and Zeus. Later writers tried to force other gods into this pattern. Another problem is the confusion caused by the fact that both the thunder and sun deities live in the sky. Sometimes it is assumed that any sky god is the sun, rather than admit to a sun goddess.

The thunder god can be found in all the mythologies in this book, although in one case he is also a she (Russia). In some cases he is paired with the sun goddess, in others with an earth goddess of some kind. In the Hittite tradition he is the sun's consort, while in Baltic myths he is often her rival, so there is a great deal of variation in his relationship with the sun.

The Storm God

In the Baltic and Slavic tradition, the thunder god's name and attributes are quite consistent. He is called Perkunas (Lithuanian), Perkons (Latvian), Perkonis (Prussian), Perun (Czech) or Pyerun (Russian). (Strangely enough, Perun and Pyerun, despite seeming almost the same, are not etymologically related to the other names. This oddity is increased by the resemblance in their descriptions.)

The Baltic Perkunas/Perkons was depicted as a red-bearded man who drives a chariot drawn by a billy goat. He carried an axe. His home was a castle at the hill-top of the sky, since the sky was a large hill. (This explained why the sun seems higher at noon and 'sinks' at night.) He was the agent of justice and struck evil doers with his thunderbolt (Savill, 1977). The first thunderbolt in spring purified the earth, and encouraged growth. The Baltic Perkunas brought fire to the world with one of his thunderbolts, an alternative to the myth which credits Saule with this benefit (Gimbutas, 1963). In Prussia, his temple featured an eternal flame tended by 'vestal' virgins, who were punished severely if the fire went out (Puhvel, 1987). He was also a smith, who forged jewellery in the sky, and a mighty warrior.

The rumbling of his chariot wheels caused the thunder, and he smote evil spirits with his copper axe or whipped them with lightning. His nature put a strain on his relationship with his wife Saule, for the sun goddess was opposed to dark clouds and rain. During rainstorms children sang (McCrickard, 1990):

> Mother Sun, to us here, to us here!
> Father Cloud, to Prussia, to Prussia!

Since Perkunas controlled the rain, he is important to farmers. They set aside a special place for him at their tables, especially at harvest time (Biezais):

> What do we give to Perkons
> For his scolding of summer?
> A ton of rye, a ton of barley,
> A half quintal of hops.

In folksongs those seeking revenge called on him to strike down their enemies. In contrast to the benign influence of Saule and Dievas, who fixed things for the sufferer, Perkunas blasted the oppressor with his bolt. In one song a wife asked for her drunken and abusive husband to be struck by lightning. In another a girl turned into a cuckoo is shot by a boy who knows she is really human; she prayed as she died for the 'Thunder' to avenge her, and the boy is duly killed by a thunderbolt (Balys, 1954).

Among the Slavs the thunderer was known as Perun ('striker'), and his cult still continues under the auspices of St Ilya (Elijah) and St George. This can even be a conscious transition, as in the Serbian song that states that 'The Thunder' began to give gifts: 'To God it gave the heavenly heights, to St Peter the summer heats, to John the ice and snow, to Nicholas power over the waters, and to Ilya the lightning and thunderbolt' (quoted in Ralston, 1977).

His role as the Lord of the Harvest has been transferred to St Ilya, whose festival on 20 July marks the beginning of harvest and is celebrated as such. On this day peasants set out rye and oats on their gates, and a special service asks for Ilya's blessing on the crops. In some places they roast a beast after the service and share it out among everyone. In old Novgorod there were two churches, one for Ilya the Wet and one for Ilya the Dry, with processions to one or the other depending on what sort of weather was desired. Ilya is also invoked against disease, since the thunder god smites demons and pestilence (Ralston, 1977). Another method of rain-making was considerably less amenable to assimilation. A chaste girl, naked and draped in flowers, would whirl ecstatically in a ring, while Perun was invoked (Cotterell, 1979). In the spring, Perun would ride out and strike at demons with his blazing darts, which made them bleed. This presumably brought on rain.

Red-bearded God

Thor is god of thunder and lightning, defence and strength. From this comes his Germanic name, Donar ('thunder'). Early statues show him with his hammer or else clutching a lightning bolt (Gundarsson, 1993). He was the god of the common people, especially those who worked in the fields or forges. He had a powerful hammer, Mjöllnir, a belt of power, iron gauntlets and a magic oath ring. Sif the golden-haired was his wife, a swan goddess who ruled the bright fertile period of summer (Pennick, 1992). Monaghan (1990) suggests that her hair represented the sheaves of wheat at harvest.

Thor drove his chariot drawn by goats over the stormclouds, throwing his bolts as he went. The noise of thunder was made by his chariot wheels rumbling over the sky. The male goat and bear were sacred to him. Places named after Thor/Thunor are plentiful in Essex and the west of England, although there are others throughout England. He was also extremely popular in Norway. People in trouble invoked his red beard, and his hammer was also part of conversation: 'Hammer strike you!' was a common oath (Grimm, 1880).

Many images show him with an axe or mallet, and sometimes there is a nail in his forehead. These were used to strike flints on to start or maintain the perpetual fires in his shrines. Out of this custom came a just-so story in the Eddas, about how Thor got a whetstone stuck in his head during one of his many battles with giants. A witch chanted over him to remove the stone, but she was distracted by the stories Thor told her to keep his mind off the pain, and so one piece was left embedded in his head. Striking the flintstone against the nail would produce sparks (lightning) and reproduce an ancient event (Davidson, 1964).

Taranis: God of the Wheel

In the Celtic tradition there is Taranis, of the British and continental Gauls. Taranis is the thunder god; his name (Welsh *taran*, Irish *torann*) and iconography point to his identity. Statues of him depict a man with a wheel and lightning bolt. (In Welsh the thunderbolt was *mellt*, from *meldos*, which is from the same root as *mjöllnir* [MacCrossan, 1993]). It has been suggested that the wheel is the sun, which would seem an odd thing for a storm god to carry, but it may also signify something specific to the Gauls. R.J. Stewart (1990) suggests that it may be the wheel of the seasons or stars. It may also be that the wheel is a chariot wheel, as with other storm gods whose chariot wheels make the rumbling of thunder, especially since the god often holds a lightning bolt in his other hand.

Taranis does not seem to have an Irish equivalent, but the British island had Leucetius, god of lightning, and Taranuctus, a thunder god.

TARANIS, WITH LIGHTNING BOLT AND THUNDER-MAKING CHARIOT WHEEL.

Some of the Gaulish statues have Taranis depicted as Jupiter, with oak and eagle, and toga (Ross, 1967). This could be dismissed as mere syncretism except for the evidence of the myth of the Welsh god Lleu. He was slain by his wife's lover and lived as an eagle in an oak tree until rescued by his uncle. The cult of the oak did not originate with Roman influence; the Druids venerated it and worshipped in oak groves. The oak is associated with the thunder god's cult in many places, so it would seem that Lleu and Taranis somehow got tangled in myth. The eagle may also have been part of the indigenous myth, by the same reasoning.

The Russian Goddess

An anomaly to this thunder-god and sky-god pattern is the Russian thunder goddess Perperuna. She lived with the sun in her palace and bathed her at night when she returned from riding across the sky. There was a Lithuanian equivalent, Percuna tete, 'mother of the thunder'. The god and goddess may have been twin deities, or perhaps she was the mother of Perun/Perkunas (McCrickard, 1990). The Russian thunder mother was assimilated to the Christians as Mary, and often paired with Ilya or Elias, who were stand-ins for the thunder god. Grimm says that the Lithuanian rain goddess was called *dievaite sventa*, 'holy goddess', and she was probably the same as Percuna tete (Grimm, 1880). A song from Latvia (Katzenelenbogen, 1935) suggests that this is the case there as well:

Five little brothers of Perkons,
What is your mother doing?
She is weaving a sieve
To sift the light rain.

Percuna tete may be the origin of the myth that there were nine Perkunases, of whom the last was female. Each ruled a year, and the ninth, the woman, was the stormiest (Katzenelenbogen, 1935).

Another possible thunder mother may be Fjörgyn, who was Thor's mother. While she is described as an earth goddess, another god with the same name is called a thunderer. In reality nothing is known of any cult they may have had. However, when scholars began reconstructing names, they noticed that her name is the same as that of other thunder gods, unlike Thor's (Mallory, 1992). It is similar to Parjanya and Perkunas, and possibly Perun. Since she literally was Thor's mother, this suggests that she was a goddess like the Baltic and Slavic mother of thunder.

Zeus/Jupiter

The leading sky god of the Greeks and Romans was also the thunderer, with a cult similar to that of other storm gods. A sort of levelling resulted in the thunder god being raised to the level of sky god, while the war god (Ares, Mars) was given responsibility for fertility among his other duties. This is another example of why the Greeks in particular are not very productive for Indo-European scholars. Whether the Romans imitated the Greeks or just had a similar shift is unknown.

The Greek god Zeus was mainly the god of the sky, who ruled the Olympians. However, he also was the thunder god, which gave him the name *Keraunos* ('lightning') (Lurker, 1994). Showery Zeus had altars on Mount Hymettus and other places, as well as altars to Rainy Zeus. Athenians would pray to him during droughts. Places struck by lightning were especially holy, and often fenced in. Mount Lycaeus was supposedly Zeus's birthplace, and a special spring that flowed there was a focus of ceremonies in times of drought (Frazer, 1926). His symbol was the eagle, and the oak tree was his oracle, as his voice was heard in the rustling of the leaves in the oak grove at Dodona. His many liaisons suggest the fertilizing function of the thunder god.

Jupiter of the Romans had two names in his thundering capacity: Fulgar caused lightning, and Tonans made the thunder boom (Lurker, 1994). His weather function was the most important thing about him early on, when most Romans were farmers. He was known as Rainy and also Serene, depending on the sky's condition. The Campus Martius had a temple of Lightning Jupiter, and the Capitol Thundering Jupiter (Frazer, 1926). His oldest guise appeared in the Capitoline temple: Jupiter Ferritus, 'the Smiter'.

Teshub

The chief god of the Hittite pantheon was the storm god Iskur, known to the native Hurrians as Teshub. His symbols were the double-headed axe and the cluster of lightning bolts, and he rode a chariot drawn by two bulls called Seri and Hurri ('Day' and 'Night'). The bull was his symbol because of its bellowing voice and its fertility. Many tablets invoked him along with the sun goddess of Arinna, and they were often housed together in temples. He is often shown standing on or beside mountain gods, and his image and that of Hebat were often set up on mountain tops.

As the king's patron, he judged kings and princes, and let the one he favoured win battles. The weather god of Nerik (a city) was appealed to by King Hattusilis when he had to fight his uncle, and the weather god and sun goddess are the main deities on treaties (Pettazoni, 1956). Like Zeus, he got his throne after struggles among the gods. First Alalu ruled, then he was deposed by his cupbearer, Anu, who was in turn pushed out by Kumarbi, who unwisely bit off his genitals. Anu cursed him to bear his successor, and Kumarbi bore a number of gods, including Teshub, who took over heaven (Eliade, 1987).

Vahagn

Vahagn was the national god of Armenia. He personified lightning and fire, so he was a storm god. His special name was Vishapaχ alλ, 'dragon slayer', since he fought many of them. He is said to be a son of the sea, earth and heaven. He also has a fiery aspect, which links him to Agni the Hindu fire god, who was identified with the fiery lightning bolt of Indra. Another minor storm god is Dsovean/Dsovinar, a deity of ambiguous gender.

The Georgians worshipped Ko'p'ala, the lightning god. He was also a warrior, who killed demons. He was armed with a mace, and an iron bow made for him by the celestial blacksmith P'irkusha. He drove off demons who invaded shamans and possessed them, which made him a useful god. He had other shamanic functions such as curing soul sickness and rescuing the souls of those who died violently so that demons couldn't get them. Ko'p'ala possessed women, contrary to the usual practice that gods possess men and goddesses women. Once a year there was a nocturnal vigil in his honour, during which young couples were expected to sleep together, or risk the god's wrath. (The couples were divided according to the sibling–spouse pattern that the deities follow – a mark of the sacred nature of the ritual.)

The Ossets, a Caucasian people who are descendants of the Scythians, worshipped a version of St Elias as their thunder god. (They shared this god with the plains Georgians.) If Watsilla sent lightning at a man and the man survived, he had to offer the god a lamb and a kid, the heads placed on two young trees that should be planted on the spot that had been struck. The trees were replaced yearly. If the man died from the lightning, he was buried where he was struck. Watsilla was also important in agriculture, and the Ossets sacrificed a fattened bull to him before the haying. They ate the head, feet and entrails, and skewered the rest for the god.

Indra/Parjanya

Indra took over the Vedic pantheon as the chief god, as Dyaus the sky god began to fade from prominence. He wielded the thunderbolt, and brought rain. After he made rain for the first time, he killed his father Dyaus to show his power. His main exploits were the killing of various demons. He lived on a mountain, which is typical for a thunderer. He was gold or reddish in colour, with long arms that reached across the skies. He was the god of life-giving rain, opposed to the drought of Vritra. The demonic Asuras and Daityas were his enemies.

Parjanya was an old Indian rain god who appeared as a bull. His name is linguistically similar to Perkunas, Perun and Fjörgyn, Thor's mother (Mallory, 1992).

Patterns

One common theme of the thunder god is his struggle against a monster of some kind. Thor fought the serpent Jardtharmegin, or the world serpent. Perkunas 'smites the winter spirits with his axe' (McCrickard, 1990). Zeus fought off the monster Typhon, who was half-human and half-snake, before he could claim his kingship. Indra defeated the demonic Asuras and various other monsters. Branston (1993) suggests that these combats are a form of the defeat of winter, which was very important to northern Europeans. This conflict could have explained the generally stormy weather of spring. Another idea makes a connection between the serpent and the dragon or serpent power of geomancy to suggest that Thor and other thunder gods tamed the destructive powers of earth so that they could be useful to humanity (Gundarsson, 1993). It has been suggested that a common root (which means 'to beat') links these gods' names and those of Zeus and Parjanya. The thunder god was often charged with driving off the forces of evil and infertility, so the word may connect to this function.

A related theme is that of the 'Rider God and Serpent-footed Monster' group in Gaul. Several of the riders carried the wheel of Taranis and bore a weapon or sometimes the lightning bolt. The mounted figure rode down a serpent-footed monster (Ross, 1967). This could be a remnant of some myth of the defeat of the monster by Taranis, which was not recorded, like many Celtic myths which are now lost.

The association of thunder and mountains can be seen in many of the gods discussed here. The Hittite weather god was often shown standing on mountain gods, and many of his shrines are on mountains. Thor and Perkunas had temples on mountains as well. Indra lived on a mountain, and we can assume he was worshipped there as well. Jupiter's oldest temple was on the Capitol, and many of Zeus's shrines were on hills. Another recurrent idea is the sacredness of the oak to the thunder god. (Oaks tend to attract lightning, which may explain this idea.) Lithuanian men sacrificed to the oak for fertility of crops. A perpetual fire was kept in honour of Perkunas, of oak only, and if it was extinguished it could only be relit by rubbing oak sticks together (Arburrow, 1994). An oak in which Thor was believed to reside was felled by Boniface in Geismer in Hesse (Branston, 1993) during the conversion of the Germans. Oaks figured in many representations of Taranis, which is not surprising as the oak was venerated by the druids. Oak is reputed to protect against lightning, which may be because by carrying it you attract the favour of the god concerned.

The rowan tree is also associated with the god, especially among the northern peoples. Thor was supposedly saved from drowning by a rowan he grabbed hold of, which explained its significance for him. The gods of the nearby Finns and Lapps were married to a rowan goddess who was sometimes also the goddess of lightning. In all cases, she was thought of as childless, unlike Thor's wife Sif. Sif may have been identified with the berries of the rowan as well as the wheatsheaf; both are harvested at around the same time. Rowan was also said to protect against lightning, since it was thought never to be struck by it.

Two birds appear to be connected with the thunderer. One is the eagle (Armstrong, 1958), the other the woodpecker. The eagle is associated with Zeus and Indra, two thunder gods, as well as Lleu and possibly Taranis. The woodpecker is a rain-forecaster, and often dwells in oak trees, which may account for the association. A green bird that brings rain is very likely to be connected to the fertility-bringing storm deity (Armstrong, 1958). As for animals, the goat is associated with the god, as it pulled his chariot, as well as the bull, because of its habit of roaring, and its association with fertility.

The axe or hammer appears to be the favoured implement of the thunder god. Perkunas carried his hammer to throw at evil-doers, as did most of his namesakes. Amber amulets of the axe were popular in the late

Stone Age, known among the Teutons as 'Thor's axelets' (Gimbutas, 1958). Among the petroglyphs in Sweden and eastern Europe are men with axes, who can be assumed to be the thunder god. Taranis is never shown with an axe or hammer, although his lightning bolt should be sufficient clue to his identity. It seems that as technology progressed the god transferred from the axe of the Bronze Age to the hammer of the Iron Age (Gundarsson, 1993) (as with Thor, who took up the hammer and left the axe to Forsite, the justice god). Sometimes it shaded over into being the bolt itself, as Thor threw his hammer to strike the earth.

The hammer or axe was sometimes worshipped as a symbol of the god. Perkunas's hammer was revered for its part in freeing the sun, and defeating the spirits of evil. The Balts used axes to keep houses, barns and fields free of malign forces. Before Christianity, it was common among the Norse to make the sign of the hammer over things to sanctify them, just as with the cross later. The hammer also had magical uses, such as being placed under the bed to ease childbirth, in a field to keep off hail and during sowing, on the threshold to be stepped over by the new spouses, and in a barn to keep the cows' milk flowing (Gimbutas, 1958).

While the thunder god was a beneficial force, there seems to have been an enmity between him and the sun, as the rivalry between Indra and Surya and Perkunas and Saule shows. The fierce red-bearded god with his violent ways would exist uncomfortably beside the benign, calm sun.

Sky God

IN MANY INDO-EUROPEAN CULTURES the sky was personified as a god, whose functions were to rule over the other gods, fertilize the earth (often his wife), and represent the forces of light. The names of many of the sky gods came from a common root: *dyew*: 'to shine'. From this we get Dyaus (Vedic), ᴅSius (Hittite), Dievas (Baltic), Tyr/Tiwaz (Norse/German), Zeus (Greek), Jupiter (Roman) and Nuada (Celtic). Since the god of the sky had to fit into the culture he inhabited, many of them have picked up secondary functions along the way. (In Norse society, Tyr took over the war-god function, for example.)

Because the sky god sits in the heavens and is of a brilliant nature, he is often misidentified with the sun. Even among Indo-European scholars, Tyr is sometimes said to have 'solar' qualities (Boyer, 1991). Part of this problem is that many people do not seem to be aware of what it is that a sky god actually does. This chapter is intended to explain his functions, and show that these do not include being the sun.

King of the sky-hill

The Baltic Dievas/Dievs was depicted as an Iron Age king in a silver robe, wearing a cap and belt and sword. He lived beyond the hill-top of the sky, in an estate with three gates of silver. Inside was his house, sauna bath, farms, garden and surrounding forest. Each day he drove down the hill in a chariot/sled of copper, being careful not to disturb the earth or its dew, because he was responsible for the earth's fertility. He trampled weeds and stimulated the corn's growth. He was first among equals, more a chieftain than king of the gods (Savill, 1977). He also ruled mountains, as he did the hill of the sky.

A rivalry seemed to exist between Dievas and Perkunas. *Dainas* such as (Jouet, 1989):

> God crossed the bridge of stones
> On a spotted horse
> Strike, Perkons, the bridge of stones
> Menace God's horse

certainly suggest a hostility of some kind. His sons also quarrelled with Perkunas's steward over the management of the heavenly farms. The root of the conflict lay in their functions, since Dievas was the preserving kind, while the thunderer stirred things up and destroyed that which had grown old and stale.

Dievas also warred on the devil, or underworld god. This was a motif shared with the Finno-Ugrian civilizations of the far north, although it appeared in some Indo-European civilizations as well. In one song he hung the son of Velns (Christianized as the devil) from the top of an oak, while another time (Jouet, 1989):

> God met with the Devil
> In the middle of the sea, on a stone;
> The furs hummed,
> The swords clinked.

This is a cosmological myth, common to the Indo-Europeans, that posits a dual sky god, one of day and one of night. Velns was the night god, who was one-eyed, prophetic, treacherous, and led the hordes of *velns* (spirits) across the night sky (Puhvel, 1987). As with the god of thunder, the myths showed them as fundamentally opposed.

Dievas and Laima divided up the future of humans between them. Laima was present at births and governed the destiny of women, while Dievas decided the destiny of men. Laima was more connected with destiny in the *dainas*, while Dievas was connected with justice. He is asked to chastise enemies of a peasant in one *daina*, and another uses a star as a symbol of conscience. Orphans also appealed to him for aid: one song tells how a young woman asked him to release her dead father so he could come to her wedding, but Dievas said he would come himself instead (Balys, 1954).

As Dievas was the heavenly farmer, he also visited the farmers on earth, to inspect fields and advise on planting. When the horses were led out for the first night watch, he would visit for a feast, and stayed the night, tending the fire and protecting the horses. He left at dawn, forgetting his mitts (since it's spring, maybe he doesn't need them) (Eliade, 1987).

Mars Thingsus

Tyr seemed to get on much better with Thor than their Baltic equivalents. Tyr was once the supreme sky father, who was fertilizer of the earth mother (Branston, 1993). Places named after him in England are listed in *The Lost Gods of England*, all derived from his Anglo-Saxon title, Tiw. (Both he and Thor are still remembered in the days of the week, Thursday and Tuesday.) He derived from the old sky god Tiwaz. Pennick (1989) suggests that he was originally paired with the goddess Ziza under the name Ziu. (He was known as Zio to the Germans [MacCulloch, 1993].) However, he later declined in importance besides Odin.

He continued to share with Thor the attribute of oath-enforcer and administer of justice. He was the god of the Thing, the assembly of judgement that was customary in Germanic countries. The reputation of Tyr as god of fairness may stem from his encounter with the Fenris Wolf. When the gods were binding this animal, the wolf demanded that one of them place their hand in its mouth as a pledge. Only Tyr would do so, so that the wolf was bound, and the world saved for a while.

By the time of the Romans he had become a war god primarily, as Tacitus shows by identifying him with Mars (and Odin with Mercury, interestingly). Tyr was especially popular among the Danes, who believed he could influence the outcome of battles. According to the *Gylfaginning*, an extraordinarily brave man was tyr-valiant.

The seventeenth rune of the Elder Futhark is called 'tyr', and is shaped like a spear-point. It symbolizes victory. In *The Lay of Sigrdrifa*, the heroine tells Sigurth (Hollander, 1990):

> *Learn victory runes,   if thou victory wantest,*
> *and have them on thy sword's hilt —*
> *on thy sword's hilt some   on thy sword's guard some,*
> *and call twice on Tyr.*

The later Anglo-Saxon Futhark calls it 'tiw', meaning 'glory'. In this connection the rune-poem suggests that the nail star or north star is meant, which appears to be the one the other stars revolve around. Tyr was therefore identified both with the order of the heavens and with victory.

One extremely interesting by-name of Tiw was Irmin (Carlyon, 1981), which could be related to Irminsul. This was a pillar symbolic of the world-tree, which was worshipped by the Saxons. They believed that the pillar held up the sky, a sort of *axis mundi* (see page 15). This tied in well with Tyr as the nail star, that held the heavens in place. This pillar was so important to their worship that when Charlemagne defeated them he had coins made of himself standing on a broken pillar (see page 00). It could very well have been seen as a symbol of the marriage of earth and sky, just as maypoles were.

There are some other minor gods who could equally well have been the sky god, or they may have once been aspects of Tyr himself. Sól was married to Glen/Glaur, a rather mysterious character whose name means 'glow'. Rydberg (1889) says that she was married to Dag, the day god, by whom she had her daughter, which was at least poetically valid, since day and the sun would produce dawn. Dag and Glen could have been the same person, since the glow could come from the sky, which seems to have a light of its own. If Tyr was originally the sky god, then the day and glow names may have been by-names, like the many that Odin went under.

One-handed

A Celtic god with marked similarities to Tyr was Nuada, the king of the Irish Tuatha de Danann. Like Tyr he lost a hand in the defence of his people, in this case against the race of giants whom every group of settlers in the mythological history of Ireland had to defeat. The efforts of Nuada and the other gods ensured the end of the giants, but Tyr just managed to delay things. Another hint that they may both be sky fathers originally is that both were married to earth goddesses, Tyr/Ziu to Ziza, and Nuada to Macha in her role as goddess of sovereignty. Both were rather shadowy figures, although Tyr was better defined than Nuada, who had little mythology. (One of his descendants was Finn, the hero who married Gráinne.)

Nuada's main weapon was the sword of light from the magical land of Gorias. He kept it with him through both the battles against the Fomorians, an older group of gods. In the first battle he lost his hand and the healer god gave him another of silver. He had a Welsh counterpart named Nudd or Llud, who appeared in an Arthurian tale as Llud Llaw Ereint (Llud Silver-hand). This tale was yet another cosmological battle, perhaps a memory of the Battle of Magh Tuireadh. He also appeared in a temple in Gloucestershire under the name Nodens. Lugh became king after him and eclipsed him the way Odin did Tyr.

Zeus, Jupiter

While Zeus was the name of the Indo-European sky god, it is his grandfather Ouranus who bears the name 'sky'. Ouranus's primal marriage to the earth goddess Gaea brought about creation, and the first group of gods, the Titans. (From the Titans came Helios, Selene, Eos and other gods such as Hecate.) Gaea eventually incited her son Cronos to rebel, and he castrated his father. (Aphrodite, a possible dawn goddess, was born from the foam his genitals made on the ocean.)

Of course, Cronos in his turn is removed from kingship, this time by his son Zeus. Cronos knew this would happen, and so ate his children. The goddess Rhea managed to save Zeus, and when he grew up he released the rest of the twelve Olympians from Cronos's belly, hurled his father into Tartaros (the underworld) and began his career as chief of the gods. Zeus then defeated the Titans and Typhon, and became king of Olympus. In this capacity he was head of the gods.

Zeus was a giver of human characteristics in the *Iliad*, which said he had two jars with bad and good traits, which he dipped into when he made people's characters. He could also grant boons, as long as it was within the bounds the Fates had decreed. He was a protector of guests, and guaranteed oaths and contracts (Grimal, 1965). As Zeus Panhellenios, he was the guardian of law and justice. He saw all from Olympus, and would blast any who were false. The storm was a manifestation of his anger. It is apt that the statue of Zeus of the Oaths held a thunderbolt in each hand (Pettazoni, 1956).

Jupiter of the Romans derives his name from two words: sky (Ju) and father (piter). He fits into the Indo-European category of sky god of light. His main festival was on the Ides of each month, when the full moon was shining, giving light day and night (Lurker, 1994). His oldest temple in Rome held the *lapides silices*, the thunderstone. He was the guardian of public morality, oaths, alliances, treaties and wars. His dedication day was 13 September, when the new consuls took office (Grimal, 1965). Oaths were taken in his main temple, under the hole in the roof, to let the sky see, and on the thunderstone, so that Jupiter would blast whoever broke their word. The Romans had a separate god of contracts, treaties and oaths as well, called Semo Sancus Dius Fidus. The Sancus part is Sabine for sky, and it would seem that he was their god as well as the Romans'. Oaths to him were of course sworn under the open sky, or under the hole in the roof of his temple (Pettazoni, 1956).

Aramazd (Armenian)

A peaceful and wise deity, Aramazd was the sky god of the Armenians. He was concerned with the prosperity and abundance of the land, and sent rain. The New Year festival, which was once in spring but later moved to 11 August, was in his honour. He was featured in a triad with Anahit the water goddess and Vahagn the war god (Ananikan, 1925).

Morige was the supreme deity of the Georgians. He created everything, mostly in response to challenges by his sister, the first demon. When he made something, she found its weak spot and he would be forced to make something else to fix it. Although his name means 'the ordainer', he did not directly run the world. He sat on his golden throne in the highest heaven and made sure that things continued to run along the lines he decided in the beginning. He mostly worked through intermediaries (Charachidzé, 1991a). The Ossetic Khutsauty Khutsau ('god of gods') was also a sky god who worked through intermediaries.

DSius (Hittite)

DSius of the Hittites was a sun and sky god. His name in Hittite, *siwaz* ('day'), is cognate to the word for 'deity', *Siwat*. These words correspond to the name of the sun god of the heavens, who, unlike the state deity, the sun goddess of Arinna, was concerned with the transcendent realm and justice (Haudry, 1987). She was invoked for kingly matters which suggests that she was a more practical deity and closer to humans.

As the sky and sun god, he saw and heard all. He was said to have three sets of eyes, which was probably related to his three aspects of sky, earth, and sea (Pettazoni, 1956):

The eyes of the sun are three pairs, one to govern . . . one to make mild . . . one to give direction.

A prayer to him by the king praised him for seeing into people's hearts and knowing whether they were sinning or not. ^DSius is called the shepherd of men, who judges all conflicts, of humans and beasts alike.

Dyaus

The pre-eminent sky god of the Vedas seemed to fade away as more active gods came on the scene. He was slain by his son Indra, wielder of the thunderbolt, rather like the Greek myth of succession. His wife was the earth goddess Privithi, and their symbols were the cow and bull. Their mating was their primary function, as joining heaven and earth. The sky was all-knowing (O'Flaherty, 1981):

Sky and earth, the all-knowing father and mother who achieve wondrous works — let them swell up with food to nourish us.

Their children were Ushas, Agni and Indra. His name as a noun indicated 'the place where the gods shine'. The plenitude of secondary names gives an idea of his function; two of them are 'Abode-of-the-Clouds' (Meghavesman) and 'The Covering' (Vyoman) (Daniélou, 1963).

Patterns

One obvious thing about all these gods is that they were the head of their pantheons, or at least, like Dievas, the first among equals. Zeus was undisputed head of the Olympians; when they revolted, he told them he could hold out against them all. Nuada was the king of the Tuatha de Danann, this was explicit in the stories. The sky god's sons, who tend to be twins, were also important. Dievas had his sons the Dieva deli. Zeus fathered the Dioscouroi in the shape of a swan. Dyaus may be the father of the Asvins, although their father was often said to be Surya, in which case he was their grandfather.

The sky god was closely involved with fertility. Dievas visited farmers, and sent rain. When he drove he was careful not to hurt plants, although he trampled weeds. He even had his own farm. Since Dyaus was identified with clouds he may have originally been thought to fertilize the earth with rain. He was married to the goddess of earth, so that their relationship took on the aspect of a sacred marriage. Dyaus was another fertilizing god, whose wife was the earth, along with Tyr.

The sky god was also involved with the operations of fate. Zeus was said to give blessings where he could. Dievas and Laima share the responsibility of deciding people's fates (Jouet, 1989):

> For God passed the day
> Talking with Laima,
> Who would have to die, who live,
> In this white sun.

Justice was a principal concern of the god. Both Jupiter and Zeus were protectors of oaths and contracts. Tyr was the god of the Thing, an assembly where justice was meted out by the tribal leaders. This was not in conflict with his role as war god, since single combat often settled the matter; the winner was chosen by the gods. Dievas, like Saule, ensured that the unfortunate were not oppressed, and was generally merciful and just.

Dumézil (1988) makes an interesting point in his study of trifunctionality among gods in the Indo-European civilizations when he observes that many of the ruler gods are missing a hand or an eye. The sky gods of the Norse and Celts were obvious examples. Their 'other halves' Odin and Lugh were both notable for oddness about the eyes; Odin having lost one, and Lugh's two becoming one in his battle frenzy. (Lugh and Odin were similar in other ways: Lugh probably derives from Gaulish loûgos, 'raven' [Puhvel, 1987].) Mitra and Varuna were also examples. The whole group seems to reflect a cosmic version of the good-cop/bad-cop routine, with the light god as the nice one, and the dark god as the enforcer. Other gods who can be fitted into the pattern include Dius Fidus and Jupiter, since one ruled in the daytime and one at night.

The sky god, as ruler of the celestials, was naturally connected to the sun goddess. Both lived in heaven and embodied the principle of light. Their children acted out a myth of returning spring. More than that, they both personified the calm, beneficent principle contrasted to the violent storm god or the dark vengeance of the Varuna/Odin-type god.

Overview

A NUMBER OF THEMES recur throughout the myths of the sun goddesses. Some of these are clear from the stories and images of the goddesses in the previous chapters. Others have to be reconstructed from bits and pieces that were scattered from an Indo-European myth.

One recurrent pattern is that of the transformation or rescue of the sun goddess in spring. She is transformed from an old hag into a young woman, as a representation of the arrival of spring. One version of this myth is the transformation of the Calliech into Brigit (see page 61). This transformation occurs at Imbolc, halfway between Samhain, when winter begins, and Beltane, marking the beginning of summer. Some of the rituals surrounding the arrival of spring in Germany seem to suggest a similar transformation. The winter hag Hel would turn into the solar virgin Sól (Pennick, 1989). The burning of effigies of the hag then take place at the spring equinox. (The Germans would have celebrated on the equinox rather than at Imbolc.) Many folktales also survive where the hag locks the sun maiden in a tower for the winter (Gitlin-Emmer, 1993).

The sun maiden is a multi-layered deity. At first glance it seems there is confusion between her and her mother in spring rituals, but actually they are like Demeter and Persephone, who are really two halves of the one myth-complex. The maiden is the dawn, and also the sun of spring and sometimes the morning star as well. The common thread is that all of these are markers of a time when the sun strengthens in the sky, be it daytime or spring. There are some obvious sun maidens, such as Auszrine and Dennitsa. Others include the young women in the Irish stories mentioned earlier, such as Giolla Gréine, the daughter of the sunbeam. Another is Dér Gréine whose mother is imprisoned, and who marries her mother's rescuer. The Heliades and other daughters of Helios, along with Arevhat and Suryaa, qualify as sun maidens.

The dawn goddesses also have certain characteristics in common. Both Ushas and Eos often seduce men. They are red or rosy, bathe in or emerge from water in the morning, wear gold, and display their bodies (especially Ushas). In the love line, both Auszrine and Suryaa are multiply married, while Ushas and Eos take mortal lovers. If Aphrodite was originally a dawn goddess, then in her the amorous character of this deity is taken to its extreme. Both the word and the goddess can be found all across the Indo-European spectrum. From the proposed root *aswos linguists derive Greek *eos*, Latin *aurora*, Baltic *ausra*, *ausrine*, *auseklis*, Iranian

145

usait ('to brighten'), German *osten, easterne, austron*, Irish *fair*, and Russian *útro* (Friedrich, 1978).

The theme of regeneration runs through the myths of the sun maiden. Obviously she personifies the young sun newly born every spring, but she also presides over rebirths of various kinds. Medea springs to mind, as she made Jason's father young again by letting out his blood and putting in a herbal infusion, and cut up and boiled a ram that came out a lamb. Auszrine also has a similar myth: a king wished to marry her, and bathed in the boiling milk of a magical cow. However, only those who were sufficiently heroic were rejuvenated by the milk, so he died. The actual hero found her, bathed safely, and married her (Jouet, 1989). Soslan the Ossetic hero has to visit the underworld and return safely before he can marry the sun maiden, which is an attenuated version of the myth.

Another form of rebirth is the connection between the returning sun and midwifery. Lucina of the Romans was a birth goddess, presumably after she had birthed herself anew on the solstice. A more minor Roman goddess, Candelifera, was also associated with birth, and carried candles into the delivery room. Both Kolyada and the Virgin Mary, in her aspect as the Christianized sun goddess, were thought to assist at births. Many other light goddesses were associated with birth, on the basis that they brought the child into the light of day from the darkness of the womb.

Part of the festivity associated with the sun's return in spring was the custom of getting up at dawn to watch it dance. The Celts, the Norse and Germans, the Balts and the Slavs all share this belief. The date of the dance varies, although Easter is a popular date. The Irish and Scots would rise early on Easter morning to see the sun give three joyful leaps as it rose, to celebrate the birth of Christ (just as it was supposed to have darkened on the day of his crucifixion). They would also catch its reflection in a pan of water and shake it so that the sun danced in the house (Danaher, 1972). Sir John Suckling immortalized this English belief in his 'A Ballad Upon a Wedding':

> But oh! She dances such a way,
> No sun upon an Easter Day,
> Is half so fine a sight.

In Germany and Sweden also the sun was supposed to dance on Easter morning. There is even a reference to this in the *Poetic Edda*, in the 'Lay of Grimnir', where Odin says that the sun dances in the stream outside Valhalla.

In Denmark it danced on Pinse morning, 50 days after Easter. The Balts thought it danced on midsummer morning, and waited up all night to see it. On the same morning the Slavs likewise expected the sun to dance and emit sparks and whirl about (this phenomenon seems to have survived into the practices surrounding some Catholic shrines, where the sun is supposed to spin, change colour and emit sparks; the pilgrims watch it closely for such behaviour).

The sun's dance can also be seen in the way the sun's reflection is scattered on the waves, and as part of festivals of the dancing sun people would bathe in streams or wash in dew, showing that water touched by sun had special properties. In all the traditions of northern Europe, the water so touched is curative, as well as bestowing other blessings, such as beauty, marriageability and prosperity. This is the meaning behind the association of quartz and wells. The stone stands for the sunlight giving power to the water. The same idea of curative water occurs in Armenia and India.

Another tradition is that of the sun's visit to the hearth. In some myths she was the one who had brought fire to earth, sometimes by means of a swallow or robin. Saule's daughter was said to visit people's hearths six times a year. The Celtic traditions linking Brigit and the hearth have been discussed on pages 56–62. The Scots laid her image near the fire, while on the Isle of Man they looked for her footstep in the ashes the next morning.

The connection between the sun and fire brings out the sun-hearth link. The hearth fire was the sun brought to earth, adapted to human use, just as the fire in the temple stood in for the sun. The Vedic fire god Agni stood for fire, the sun and thunder, all forms of heat. (He was sometimes said to be a form of Surya.) In the same way Brigit was both a hearth goddess and solar. Both of them show strong similarities to the fire and hearth goddesses Hestia and Vesta, in their myths and rites.

The fire of the sun works in other ways as well, especially when she is married to the moon god, who is generally thought of as watery. This pairing brings to mind the archetypal fire and water of our ancestors, and suggests rituals of sacred marriage. I suspect that the hints of this idea that can be found in Hindu tantra are fragments of an ancient pattern in which the solar female was an active force, and the man was perceived as passive and lunar. The ice and fire of the Norse tradition and the Baltic association of the moon with winter and the sun with summer, along with the Vedic belief in the fiery nature of menses, suggest the way that the sexual magic would have worked.

The fire–water pairing is not without its conflicts, however. In the Vedas, Indra battles both Ushas and Surya, who are both solar powers. He drives Ushas from the sky, and steals Surya's chariot wheel. Saule and her second husband Perkunas have frequent rows over the weather, which she wins. One *daina* has him attacking her daughter for no apparent reason, other than their mythological opposition. The frequent pairing of sun and storm, despite the basic conflict of their functions, suggests that the two were seen as complementary or compatible at some deeper level. The weather god and sun goddess of Anatolia were the divine royal couple, uniting the two principles.

The goddess of the sun is often set off by the brilliant otherworld she inhabits. She usually lives in a golden palace, or at least a fairy world so pleasant that none who arrives there wants to leave. Sometimes she is said to shine in the underworld to give light to the dead. The Celtic under- and otherworlds described by Markale (1986) fit this pattern, such as the one that Dér Gréine lives in with her husband. The Norse goddess goes to the underworld to sleep on her golden bed. There are sometimes hints that Hel was once a pleasant place, and the word in Old High German for elysium is *sunna-felt* (Grimm, 1880). Saule is sometimes said to go into the land of the dead at night, so that her daughters have to get the keys and let her out again. The sun goddess of Arinna is also the sun goddess of the underworld, who visits the dead. The Hesperides' and Circe's dwellings on the edge of the underworld continue the same theme.

The tree and the stone are also connected to the sun goddess. These are often in the centre of the world or else in the west. Saule sits in her tree in the west every evening, and Zorya sits on a stone under a tree with healing powers. Saule also dances on a stone in the middle of the sea sometimes, probably the grey stone near the world-tree. The Swedish goddess sits on a stone and spins before sunrise. Her father is the god of the world-mill, which turns all the worlds on its axis. Likewise, the Hesperides dwell among the apple trees on their land in the far west, and sing by the spring there.

The sun goddess is the dispenser of justice. She was the all-seeing eye, so that it was impossible to hide evil done by day from her. For this rea- son oaths were often taken while facing the sun, or invoking her as wit- ness, so that she would punish those who didn't keep their word. The Germans and Norse did this, as did the Lapps. Among the Slavs it was customary to invoke the sun's punishment if the oath was broken. The Baltic Saule is described in the *dainas* as taking pity on orphans and the oppressed, her daylight reducing the likelihood of crime (this character- istic is shared with many other sun gods and goddesses throughout the world). The Hittite sun goddess was said to be 'unwearying in the place of judgement'. The Grecian Helios was invoked along with Zeus and Gaea in oaths, since they saw all that happened.

The main pattern I perceive, which I have as yet only touched on, involves the sun goddess and the deities who share in her myths. She is often represented as a mare who gives birth to twins, and who has a num- ber of husbands. She has a daughter who is a junior version of herself, represented by the glow of dawn or the waxing sun of spring.

That there is a goddess represented by a mare is easily proved, since Macha, Saule, Áine and Solntse have equine imagery associated with them. Of these, Macha gives birth to the twins that name the place she dies in. The mother of the Dieva deli is not named, but since Saule is married to the sky god, it seems reasonable to surmise that she is their mother. Their close connection in the rest of the myths justifies this assumption. If the parallel between Baltic and Vedic myth holds, this is certainly true. The twin Asvins are the sons of a mare that is both the wife and daughter of the sun (in Vedic myth the sun is male, but his name is cognate to Saule's; and there is evidence that the mare is sometimes solar in Indian myth [O'Flaherty, 1980]). Solntse is often shown with two men on horses, the symbol of the twins throughout Indo-European myth, in folk art. This would suggest that she is their mother/lover like Saule.

The goddess represented by the mare and the sun is noted for her free sexuality. Macha selects her own husband, Áine has many lovers, Saule has several husbands, and the Indian mare is closely connected to Tantra and is considered primarily sexual (O'Flaherty, 1980). Even sun goddesses not obviously equine are often polyandrous; Sól has two husbands, Glen and Dag, the latter her daughter's father (Rydberg, 1889). The sun maiden Suryaa is married to either the Asvins, Soma or the traveller's god, Pusan.

The pattern of the duality of the sun is also apparent. She is usually a mother–daughter dyad, one of whom represents the dawn and spring, the other the matured sun. Often this daughter is espoused to the twins who are her brothers, in the incestuous fashion of deities. Once again the Balts are the paradigm, but the Vedas show a similar pattern, with Surya and his daughter. The Greek god Helios has many daughters, including the very typical sun maiden Helen. Sól has a daughter who eventually will take over her job, called Svanhild Gold-feather. Ward (1968) has shown that she appears in legends as the type of the sun maiden, with twins lurking in the background. The sun goddess of Arinna has two daughters, Hulla and Mezulla, while her husband has twin sons.

These patterns, of marriage and duality, of the horse form and twin births, hint at a much larger and earlier body of myth. What the Indo-Europeans and the peoples they mixed with believed about the sun we can only guess. That they believed in her and created myths about her is beyond doubt. We can only piece together the fragments that have survived, using clues and hints to produce a reconstructed mythology.

Sun Symbols

PART OF RESEARCHING THE GODDESSES OF THE SUN is determining their attributes. In some cases it is all the evidence available, so it becomes very important to determine what symbols and emblems are typical of the solar deity.

Circles

The first appearance of the circle as sun symbol is in the petroglyphs of northern Europe. The circle and its companion, the disc, are the most obvious sun emblems. After all, it is a representation of what we see in the sky. This may explain why it is a common sign for Sól, the Norse goddess. Of course, not every circle in the world is a sun, but in the context of other solar emblems it is a basic representation. It may have been the earliest symbol, being easy to make, while the rayed and spoked versions evolved from it. (Another goddess who may have been associated with the circle as sun symbol was Circe, daughter of Helios, whose name means 'circle'.)

Rayed circle

The rayed circle is one sun image recognized by everyone. It features prominently in kindergarten art. Sól is represented in runes as a circle with a ray coming out of it, as the light of the sun. Saule is often compared to a rayed circle, or shown as one in folk art. The design often features as a decoration on Irish passage graves (Green, 1991). A variant of the rayed circle shows up on an altar at Nîmes, where it appears to have slanting external rays or flames, like a Catherine wheel (Green, 1991). It may correspond to the festivals where burning wheels are rolled downhill, as at midsummer and on St Catherine's Day in November.

Discs

In the petroglyphs we often see sun-discs. Sometimes they appear beside a sword or axe, and sometimes they are carried by tiny figures or are mounted on ships or carts. The disc-with-weapon scenes may represent a sacred marriage, as discussed on page 29. The tiny figures who hold the sun may not even be men, since what are assumed to be their penises tend to stick out of the bottom of their backs, rather like tails. They may be priests or priestesses in vestments, carrying the symbol of the goddess about (Kühn, 1966). The boats or carts would have fulfilled the same purpose of carrying the sun symbol to the people.

PETROGLYPH FROM ZEALAND SHOWING A PRIEST OR PRIESTESS OF THE SUN.

Wheels

Like many other deities of the Norse and Balts, the sun was seen as riding through the sky. As a substitution of part for whole, the wheel may stand in for the goddess and her chariot. The Baltic goddess Saule is often shown as a wheel, and her main festival is called Ligo, 'rolling'. This concept also appears in the name 'Fair Wheel' given to Sól in the *Edda*. The solar disc is sometimes carried on a wheel by tiny men in the petroglyphs. This is perhaps the forerunner of the carrying of fires on poles at midsummer so common across Europe. The summer customs of rolling burning wheels down hills or through fields were both to bless the areas with the sun's power and as sympathetic magic to encourage the sun. Grimm connects the Gothic letter Hv, Hveol, which both resembles and means wheel, with the fiery wheel of the sun (Grimm, 1880). The temple of Surya at Konarak has twenty wheels on the two long sides, which along with the horses on the front led Watts (1971) to decide that the temple symbolized the sun god's chariot. The modern symbol of the Armenian sun goddess is a giant wheel, like a water-wheel (Ananikan, 1925).

Spinning wheel

The Gothic rune Hveol, which means wheel, also relates to a spinning wheel, and the sun goddess spinning her rays every morning. People sometimes saw the Light Alfs spinning in spring. In Finnish and Lapp myth, Paivatar was spinning when she met Ilmarnien, and Beiwe was offered a spinning wheel and flax on her altar. Saule governed spinning as a feminine activity, as did Brigit. Circe spun and wove on her island. It may be that the constantly turning wheel, together with its feminine associations, made people link it with the sun.

Rosettes

Saule is sometimes represented as a rosette. In Celtic symbolism there are many of these symbols on tombstones in Alsace (Green, 1991). A clay figure was found in northern France holding wheel/flower symbols, who also has a sun-burst on her back and other solar designs in her hair (Green, 1991). The southern Ukrainians used the rosette as a sun symbol, as well as red roses (McCrickard, 1990). Sól's association with 'Auntie Rose' of the hopscotch chant suggests that she too was represented by a rose. The designs suggest the ever-renewing strength of the sun, and its connection with growth and vegetation.

Eyes

Eyes resemble the sun, both as a rayed circle (eye and lashes) and also a set of concentric circles (pupil, iris, white). The sun deity is often associated with retribution because s/he can see everything from his/her position in the sky. Sul is a goddess whose name has both solar and eye connotations, which may explain the curses offered to her, which ask her to wreak vengeance upon whoever wronged the petitioner. Both she and Brigit are associated with the eye in its connection to healing and wells. The association probably arose from the fact that both reflect light.

The sun was thought to see all that happened on earth, and both eyes and sun radiated light. In most Indo-European languages eyes can stand for the sun, and in Old Irish the word for eye (*suil*) can be traced back to the word for sun (Lincoln, 1986). An ancient Greek prayer refers to the goddess Theia in terms of the sun (McCrickard, 1990):

Thou beam of the sun
Far-seeing mother of the eyes . . .

St Lucia is another example of a goddess whose eyes are significant to her cult, as they became one of her main emblems.

Spirals/labyrinths

The spiral turns up in a context often associated with the sun at the New Grange barrow. A triple spiral is so placed on the wall that on midwinter at dawn a shaft of light strikes it. The pipe-clay figures from Gaul of goddesses have spirals and other solar symbols on them. On the non-gilded side of the sun-disc from Trudholm are spirals, the side that may represent the dark sun, as suggested earlier (Green, 1991). Spirals may be connected to the swan motif found on some Iron Age artefacts, as the swan's neck is often in the shape of an 'S'. The ship drawn by birds (swans) is discussed more fully on page 42. It may symbolize the sun's passage through the sea at night, which strengthens the tie between spirals and the sun at night.

The labyrinth as a sun-related motif is more complicated. It has been suggested that the sun's passage through the sky during the year makes the path of the labyrinth, its crossings and recrossings making the turns. The other connection is the maze dances celebrating the rescue of the sun from winter. The labyrinth may have grown out of the spiral.

Swastika

Brigit's crosses, made from rushes, are often in the shape of swastikas. These modified crosses turn up in designs all across Eurasia, in connection with solar animals (horse, swan). The swastika is often associated with horses in ancient art (Armstrong, 1958). Iron Age motifs frequently associate the two, as in coins and brooches showing swastikas with horse-head ends (Green, 1991). Like the wheel, the idea seems to be to suggest movement as the sun passes through the sky, and the four arms can represent the solstices and equinoxes. The Hindu sun god Surya is often shown with swastikas.

Crosses

Celtic crosses, one form of the Brigit's cross, are frequently identified as solar symbols. The encircled, equal-armed form is suggestive of the sun, with the fourfold shape symbolizing the seasons, or the four directions. This particular form is also frequently seen on the northern European petroglyphs, often raised on a pillar or over a boat, signs of sacredness. In that case the symbol probably represents Sól.

Horses

Macha, Áine, Grian and Saule are all represented as horses. The Celtic goddesses are part of a pattern of equine solar deities, and Saule is part of a group of deities who are symbolized by them. While these four are indeed solar goddesses, their relation to horses is part of a larger argument over whether horses are inevitably related to the sun. The frequent combination in early art of sun-wheels and horses suggests that the two were paired, although this need not exhaust the associations of the horse, which is also often associated with male fertility (stallions). It is striking, however, how many solar deities in the Indo-European cultural group are associated with horses, either as a symbol or as a means of conveyance.

In the case of the Celtic deities, there is ample proof that Macha, Áine and Grian were connected to both horses and the sun. Ross (1992) states that this sun connection is often made with deities who represent healing. All these goddesses have some therapeutic power, as discussed earlier. The three are also connected by a thread of horse symbolism. Saule's identification with the horse can be traced to the early association of the horse and sun in northern and eastern Europe. There are depictions of a horse (or two) and chariot drawing the sun among the petroglyphs, which suggest a link to both her and Sól, who are drawn across the sky. We know that horses were sacrificed by the Scandinavians, which suggests a ritual importance (Davidson and Gelling, 1969).

Reindeer

In the Slavic countries and sometimes among the Scandinavians, the stag or reindeer replaces the horse as the sun animal. The two horses of Sól are sometimes replaced by a reindeer driven by twins (Ward, 1967). Among the petroglyphs at Bohuslän are representations of stags pulling chariots with sun-wheels, or the wheels themselves. Gelling suggests they were a substitute for horses (Green, 1991).

Rooster

In Norse mythology, the rooster Goldcomb crows every morning to hail Sól's rising. The cock was also one of the symbols of the sun appropriated by the Scythian great goddess when she came to the Slavic lands and took over the sun worship there. Its crowing at sunrise made it a natural symbol of the goddess. The firebird, which resembles an elongated cockerel, is a variation of the same idea.

Swans

This concept is derived from a Slavic bridal song (McCrickard, 1990):

The red sun with its rays
Is Anna with her daughters
Dear Ivanova with her swans.

On page 42 I discussed how the sun's chariot was sometimes drawn by swans in Bronze Age art. Swans are frequently associated with the sun all across Europe, and from prehistoric times they turn up on pottery along with more obvious sun symbols.' [M]etal-using, horse-riding and sun worshipping peoples incorporated swan-beliefs into their cults' (Armstrong, 1958). This could be any Indo-European people.

The boat of the sun, pulled by swans, is a common feature of sun myth. Saule and Solntse are both transported in this way (Saule at night). The Greek god Apollo had a golden chariot drawn by swans, unlike his alter ego Phoebus who was drawn by golden horses. The Celtic goddess Graínne was also drawn by swans (McCrickard, 1990). This goes back to Bronze Age ideas that the sun was sometimes pulled by swans, so that it could go both in the sky and on the water, as it could be seen to do as it rose and set. The swan became an extremely popular motif for art of that period (Davidson and Gelling, 1969). One such engraving on rock was found in Russia at Besouvnos (Kühn, 1966).

The other connection is the swan maiden, who is thought by some to be a solar emblem, or at least the memory of the connection of sun goddess and swans. Other swan maidens include the Valkyries and Brunhild of Norse mythology. In both cases they flew to earth and removed their plumage to bathe. Brunhild, who was captured by Odin along with her eight companions, was held in a tower that was surrounded by a ring of flame, and which shone with incredible brightness – possibly solar imagery.

Cow

Solntse is a cow in one riddle told by the Slavs that compares the moon to a bull and the stars to calves. Another solar cow is Pasïphae, who mated with the Bull from the Sea. The cows of light in Vedic mythology are also images of the goddess. They are stolen by the demons and rescued by the Asvins, or Indra. The primal goddess Aditi was often symbolized by a cow.

Gold

This metal seems to be the solar metal *par excellence*, although its colour varies, since gold can be red among the Celts and Germans. (All through *The Niebelungenlied* things are said to be 'as red as gold'.) Surya is described as being all gold, and Helios sails in a golden goblet, which seems to have been yellow. Saule is often described as golden, or her crown, rings, belt or threads in her dresses are golden. Sometimes she herself, or at least the sun-disc, is metallic, since Latvian legend has it that she was forged at the beginning of time.

Colour

White, yellow and red seem to be the colours associated with the sun. Solntse is called the red sun in folksongs, and the Balts associate red specifically with the sun's daughter. Saule herself is white, the colour of honesty and goodness.

Ships

The ships seem to be part of some sort of cult, as many scenes take place on them. The sun-disc is shown as if mounted on a ship, which is explained as the journey of the sun at night, across the water to the east. This may have been believed in places where the sun appeared to set into the water, and so had to get back to the east by sailing across the water. The sun may be intended to stand up in the ship the way it does in the famous chariot.

BRONZE AGE RAZOR DECORATED WITH SUN-BOAT FOUND IN A TOMB.

Feet

Another image of the sun is the feet found in some petroglyphs. (The foot pattern also turns up on a pot alternating with sun-discs as a border [Davidson and Gelling, 1969].) It is suggested that the 'sandal' pattern is the basis for the four-spoked wheel that sometimes appears and is thought to be a sun-disc. The feet presumably are the footprints of the sun as she moves across the land during the day. They may also relate to the sun's dance, which would burn footprints into the earth as she dances near the horizon, so it would seem that it danced on the earth. Other ideas about the sun and feet are the myth that daffodils sprang up in the sun goddess's footsteps as she returned in spring, and the footprint Brigit leaves in the hearth ashes of houses she visits at Imbolc. A bridge near Knockaine has Áine's footsteps on it. In all cases the print is the visible sign of the goddess, a token of her presence and her power which although celestial is nevertheless deeply connected to the earth.

The wealth of symbolism associated with the sun goddess proves that she is not just an accident of mythology or a marginal figure. Her imagery is that of a goddess with a rich and influential cult, since so much of it survived for researchers to find.

Practice

SO FAR, THIS BOOK HAS STUDIED SUN GODDESSES from a theoretical point of view. This chapter is devoted to various practices aimed at a personal, immediate knowledge of these deities. If the reawakening of the sun goddesses is to have any meaning, we must be ready to contact them and work with them.

To do this, the knowledge that we have of past practices must be interpreted in the light of today. A totally purist revival is impossible. The best that can be done is to stay as true as possible to the spirit of the ancient worship while adapting to the forms of today. One example of this synthesis is Wicca, whose circles have called many ancient deities with a blend of old pagan and new ceremonial worship. However, all neo-pagan movements are aiming for the same end, a religion that is both rooted in the past and meaningful today.

Some basic skills will be needed for the practices in this part of the book. Meditation and visualization skills are essential, as these are the foundations on which all else is laid. There are rituals in the next chapter, but this chapter consists of guided visualizations. The other skill, meditation, is essentially just good practice for anyone on a spiritual path. A calm mind and relaxed body will promote contact with the more ethereal levels, which makes invoking and visualization easier.

To do exercises like guided pathworking requires that you have a powerful imagination. This can seem difficult at first. It is essential that you work on this until you can 'see' yourself in the scene and are not just watching it like a movie. A book by Peter Jennings (1993) called *Pathworking* is very useful for beginners. The secret seems to be to create a scene with vivid details and spend time imagining it until you can see it as a real scene. It will be difficult at first but really you see everything in the same way – your eyes bring in data which your brain interprets into a picture. This time the data comes from a different source, that's all.

Try it right now. First memorize the visualization. Then, close your eyes, get comfortable, and begin. Imagine a small grove of oaks with a well in the middle. It is noon, and the sun slants down through the trees. The well is of stone, a circular structure with a pulley and bucket. Hanging on the side of the well is a small tin dipper. On one side of the well is a small heap of quartz stones. Drop one into the well and hear it splash on the water far below. Sit quietly there and absorb the atmosphere. When you are ready, put down the bucket and take a drink of water with the dipper.

Thank the well spirit and wake up. When you open your eyes take a moment to readjust to your surroundings. Be sure to do this last step, or you will feel spacy and disconnected, which can cause problems. Write down any feelings or ideas that occurred to you if you like.

As part of this book I have created a set of visualizations that can be used to gain a more personal vision of the sun goddesses. The technique is just the same as for the exercise above. These visualizations are designed to help you contact the goddesses in the workings. Good luck, and keep practising!

Visualizations

Áine on her hill in procession

Imagine yourself standing near a grassy hill. It is twilight, and the evening star hangs low in the sky. Young women in white are gathering around a bonfire and you join them. They pick up torches and light them in the fire. As you light your torch you join the line snaking around the hill, slowly winding its way in a spiral towards the top. When the women reach the top of the hill, they circle around a large fire, singing softly. Suddenly you notice a woman who seems larger than the rest, with masses of red hair streaming behind her as she dances. She wears a white dress with red patterns embroidered on it. As you gaze into her eyes you hear a message that she has for you. Thank her for her wisdom. When you are ready, wake up and return to now.

Grian in the gríanan

You are sitting in a round room made of pure quartz. It is semi-translucent and glows from the rays of the sun. Around you are women sitting on benches cut into the stone, working or talking quietly. Apart from them sits a woman wearing a black cloak with a hood that shadows her face. The cloak is fringed with silver braid, which catches the light. You approach her, and sit near her feet. When she notices you, she looks up. Now you can see beneath the cloak and the woman is dressed in a bright yellow dress trimmed in green, and her hair is blonde and shining. You may offer her worship or ask her what you feel you need to know about her. When you have done thank her and wake up.

Lucia coming across the ice

You are dressed warmly and standing on the edge of an iced-over lake. The sky is of velvety black, and the *aurora borealis* is playing across it. It is quite bright, but begins to fade, and a glow appears on the horizon, faint as yet. As it grows brighter, you begin to see the figure of a woman in white skating towards you. She comes closer and closer, and you notice her crown of white candles and her hair streaming behind her. She seems quite young. Finally you are face to face, and she gives you the gift she held in her hands. Accept it and thank her, before she moves on. Open it, and consider its significance. Now you can wake up.

Saule on Midsummer

You are standing on a hill with many other people in the twilight of early dawn. A bonfire crackles nearby. As you wait you see the sun's glow as it begins to rise above the horizon. The people around you cheer, and a mood of anticipation takes you all. As the sun comes over the horizon, it seems to whirl in the sky, and sparks fly from it, just as they do from the fire nearby. As you look more closely, you see, within the outlines of the sun, a woman dressed in gold and white, dancing. The sun continues to rise, almost seeming to touch the hill as it comes up in the sky. Once the moment is over, you go to the edge of the hill and see burnt into the rock a footprint. Touch the footprint and then wake up.

Meeting with Weiss Frauen

You are walking up a path that winds around a steep hill. As you turn a corner you meet a white-clad woman with long blonde hair. Something about her dazzles your eyes, and you stop short. She comes towards you smiling, and points to the sky. Above you blazes the noonday sun, at its highest station in the sky. Then she gives you what looks like a lump of black stone. However, you thank her politely and continue on your way. Once you reach the top of the hill, you sit down, and see that the lump has turned to solid gold. Contemplate the meaning of this, then wake up.

Maiden and twins

Before you is a doorway made of clearest crystal, with two powerful young men, obviously twins, guarding it. You approach them and tell them you wish to have speech with their sister. They let you pass, and the door swings open to reveal a bower of crystal, but with flowers everywhere. A young woman dressed in the colours of dawn sits on one bench; you go to her and tell her you need to know how to escape your imprisonment as she did hers. She will tell you what binds you, and how to free yourself. When you have finished, thank her and leave. Pass by the brothers, and wake up.

Barbale and her wheel

You are alone in a temple, facing an altar bright with candles. You raise your arms and reach out with your mind to the sun. After a minute, a woman in a long dress appears before you. In her hand she holds a blazing wheel, which dazzles you with its brightness. The wheel begins to spin in her hands, and the light spirals out from it towards you. A ray shoots out from the centre of the wheel and touches you on the chest. You feel an incredible rush of energy racing through your body, until your aura is almost as bright as that of the goddess. After a while the light vanishes, and you thank the goddess. She vanishes, leaving you in the temple, feeling renewed.

Basic ritual format

Another reason for learning to meditate is that you will need to be able to achieve the states of consciousness that it produces for the rituals in the next chapter. Even if you don't plan to perform any of them, they are an interesting way of seeing what a living sun-goddess religion might look like.

Before you can perform these rituals, you will need to know how to set up both physically and mentally. This section takes you through the basic format, as well as the beginning and ending of rituals so that you can set the stage for the main action you will perform during your ritual.

You will want to prepare an altar for these rituals. It gives a focus, as well as a place to lay things. A small table, or even a box, will do. Cover it with a cloth, which can be black or white, or you can vary it to suit the ritual if you have lots of them. A few candles on the altar are handy for reading the ritual, and the colours provide mood (if you're really short of money, white candles can serve all purposes). If you have ritual equipment such as a knife or wand you lay it on the altar.

Once you've got the altar set up, you may want to have a ritual bath (or shower if this isn't possible) to purify yourself symbolically. Now you can begin by meditating on the purpose of your ritual, and generally calming yourself. When you are ready, stand in your space, and draw an imaginary circle around the area where your ritual will take place. Do this by pointing a finger or a ceremonial knife, if you have one, and imagine that it makes a line of bluish fire as you point it. This circle will contain power you raise and protect you from any unfriendly influences about.

Now you will invoke the elements. The basic magical elements are air, fire, water and earth. By calling them into your circle you make it the world in miniature, and align yourself with the forces of the cosmos.

Face east and concentrate on what the element of air means to you. Try to feel wind on your face, and the breath in your lungs. Now evoke the element of air by pointing your knife or raising your hand in salute and saying:

I summon the spirits of air, powers of strong winds and freshest dawn. May your presence lend power to my ritual!

Turn south, concentrate on the heat of fire, the noonday sun, and the electrical impulses of your nerves. Now raise your hand and say:

I summon the spirits of fire, powers of noon heat and blazing fire. May your presence lend power to my ritual!

Turn west and think about water, the sea, twilight, and the blood pulsing through your veins. Now raise your hand and say:

I summon the spirits of water, powers of salt sea and purple twilight. May your presence lend power to my ritual!

Turn north, feel your bones and muscles supporting you, the solidity of the floor or ground, the firmness of earth. Now raise your hand and say:

I summon the spirits of earth, powers of midnight and black soil. May your presence lend power to my ritual!

Proceed with the ritual.

At the end of the working, you must close down the circle that you have opened, so that the forces can return to earth. Not doing this would cause you to be still carrying this energy in you, and a headache or feelings of dizziness or spaciness would result. First thank the elementals for being at your ritual.

Start in the north, and salute the elementals:

Spirits of earth, I thank you for your attendance. May there be peace between us always. Hail and farewell!

Continue around the circle, finishing in the east. Then turn again to the north, and erase your circle in the same way that you drew it, imagining that the light is disappearing into the ground, so that the power can return to the earth which provided it. Do the same with any power you felt inside yourself during the ritual. Imagine it draining out into the ground. Do not try to hold it. It was only yours on loan, so to speak. To finish the ritual, take your offerings outside if your ritual was indoors, and leave them under a bush or tree.

Rituals

MUCH OF THE PAGAN WAY involves celebrating the cycle of the seasons. Along with the wheel of the year there are also the cycles of days and months. The sun goes through its daily round, and the moon waxes and wanes each month, and these should have their celebrations as well. In this chapter, I have tried to suggest ways of doing this which range from simple things anyone can do through to full rituals for those who wish to do them.

Daily sun rituals

It was customary to greet the sun at dawn with a sign of respect, such as lifting one's hat or bowing. To attune oneself to the passage of the day, it would be suitable to come up with some form for saluting the sun at the four points of a day: dawn, noon, sunset and midnight. A simple formula accompanied with a gesture is sufficient; save the robes and full ritual implements for the more complicated ceremonies.

One way of doing this is to get up just before dawn, and greet the rising sun by holding out your hands, palms up, and greeting it with words such as:

> O blessed mother of light, goddess of the sun, may your bright light shed blessings on this day, that it be fruitful for me and all your light shines on.

If you wish you may greet dawn as the daughter of the sun, the harbinger of newness.

> Beautiful daughter of the sun, may the warm glow of dawn always remind me of renewal and hope, and fresh possibilities.

You may improvise your own prayers, around the themes of the various times of day. At noon the sun is at the height of its power:

> Mother Sun, we see you now at the height of your strength. As you grow full, so may all my plans and projects.

The sun goes to rest at sunset, a time of stillness and reflection on the day:

As you go to your home in the west, and sink down to repose, so do I rest and reflect on the course of my day. May my works also be fruitful.

At midnight the sun is at its nadir, hidden from us yet still present:

Mother Sun, you are there, though I do not see your face. May I always have faith to know that in the darkest hour, the sun still shines.

If you wish you may also burn a solar incense such as frankincense, cedar, cinnamon or juniper. You could also visualize the sun goddess as you salute her, using the descriptions in the last chapter or your own image.

Moon Rituals

Rituals to honour the power of the moon can be simple or complicated. They range from showing respect to the crescent moon when it reappears to the full rituals for the full moon performed by Wiccans. Interestingly, the new and full moon are defined by astronomical data, the new being when the moon is in conjunction with the sun, and thus invisible from earth, and the full moon happens when it in opposition to the sun, being 180 degrees away in the sky (Pennick, 1989). (Think of the sky viewed from earth as a circle divided into 360 degrees for observation purposes.) The waxing moon is growing from new to full (first quarter), just as the waning is fading from full to new (last quarter).

Customs involving the new moon include turning over the silver in your pocket at the first sight of it, so as to increase it. It is considered unlucky to see the new moon through glass. Prayers to the god of the young moon for health are common, as he is thought to age and die each month, and so his crescent phase is his youthful and vigorous stage. The full moon is considered a good time to do magic. Being full, the proper things to work for would be abundance, or fertility. The waning moon is a time of purifying, and also to rid yourself of things that have passed their usefulness. The dark moon is a time for meditation.

All of these rituals can be celebrated as simply or elaborately as you wish. If you do not believe in elaborate ceremonies or are in an environment unsympathetic to pagan ritual, you will find these simpler suggestions more useful.

For the waxing moon, go outside when its crescent becomes visible in the sky, and bow to it. (An inclination of the head is sufficient.) Say quietly or to yourself:

Young moon, rising in your strength, give me strength and health, and may you grow in power as the month goes on.

At sunset on the first night of the full moon, or when it becomes visible, simply sit where you can see it and reflect on the abundance of life and the blessings you have received in your life. Let your heart be full with joy for life and its good times, and let that joy flow to the moon in the sky.

When the moon is waning, set aside time in the evening, and say a quiet prayer to the moon that all the bad habits and things that are holding you back shall be rooted out of your life. Put as much emotional sincerity into it as you can. A slightly more elaborate version is to fill a basin with water, and wash your hands in it, visualizing all the negative things being cleansed away just like dirt. Chant (out loud or not):

Wash away the bad,
Make room for the good.

The dark or new moon is generally a good time to think over the month and evaluate what has been done. It is also a good time to rest. Some people find they are more psychic then, and may wish to exercise their abilities. This can be done as simply as by gazing at a candle flame or a bowl of water. Others may find that the full moon is the best time for this.

Waxing moon Ritual

You will need white candles, some light incense (stick or loose), bread or biscuits and a drink of wine or fruit juice, and a place to use as an altar. Light the incense and some candles, but keep one for the main ritual. Try to arrange things so that you can see the new moon, preferably as it first appears in the sky; if that isn't possible, do the ritual while the moon is still a thin crescent in the sky.

Open with the basic ritual, up to the place where it says to proceed with ritual. As the new moon is a time of renewal, we will work with that theme. Having evoked the elementals, now we will invoke the god. Raise your hands to the sky and say:

Young lord of the moon, with your horns showing proudly in the sky! Appear
to us tonight, in your full glory of new strength.

Visualize the moon god, a young strong man with horns growing out of his head (bull-style) and dressed in a grey tunic and with a black cloak covered in stars. He stands before you, with his left hand extended in a blessing gesture.

Now you light a white candle, and ask a blessing for any plans you have which are in their beginning stages. Say:

As the moon grows to fullness, so may these plans grow, and as you make women
and crops fertile, so will these be fruitful. So mote it be! [This is an archaic way
of saying, so shall it be.]

Now take up your food and drink. Bless them and the earth which produced them, then put a little bit in a bowl to offer to the god. (Or if you're
outdoors lay them on the earth.) Say: 'To the gods!' Eat and be aware of
how the earth sustains us. When you have finished, leaving a little bit to
the gods again, stand up and say:

> Lord of the moon, of increase and growth, I thank you for your blessing. May
> your blessing be on me always.

Imagine the god fading away. Now go to the basic ritual for the rest of the
banishing.

Full Moon Ritual

For this ritual you will need flowers to decorate the altar, purple and silver candles, and a lunar incense such as mugwort, jasmine, lotus or camphor. You will also need the bread and drink, along with a nice cup of
some kind to offer the drink in.

Open with the basic ritual.

Now, to invoke the god of the moon, raise your arms in the shape of
a 'U', and face the full moon. Say:

> Moon, companion of Night, who leads the way across the sky. You guide the light
> of the night, the whirling wheel. We see you now in your fullness, the lord of fer-
> tility and brother of the sun. Your light shines through all the worlds, may it also
> shine on us.

Now raise your cup to the moon. Try to position it so that the moon's orb
is just over the rim. Think of all the things that you have to be thankful
for and imagine them filling the cup, keep going, coming up with things
both personal and any bit of news that struck you as a good sign, until
you feel that the cup is filled. Say:

> God of the moon, you ride the sky in the fullness of your strength. In this cup
> are the good things of life. I offer them to you now. May you enhance all these
> things, so that good may grow and take root on earth.

Tip the cup and spill some of the liquid on the earth, or into a bowl. Then
drink the rest, and say:

> I take into myself good, that good may grow in me. May blessings from this good
> pour out onto the world.

Save a tiny bit to pour out as an offering to the earth, and acknowledge
the goodness of her bounty. Eat your bread, giving the first and last bits

to the moon and earth. Thank the moon god for appearing at your ritual:

Moon, I am grateful for your presence. May your light shine in my path always.

Finish with the closing from the basic ritual.

Waning moon ritual

For this ritual you will need a grey candle, and something to write on the candle with. A sharp knife is traditional, but an old pen is probably the easiest to work with. Candles and altar cloth should be of dark colours. A strongly scented incense is good for this part of the moon's cycle, such as myrrh, poppy, camphor or eucalyptus.

Start with the opening from the basic ritual. Then call on the god of the moon:

Lord of the moon, as you grow thin in the sky, I call on you to be with me as I cleanse my life before you vanish in darkness. As you renew, so shall I.

Take up the grey candle, and write on it things that you wish to banish from your life. Try to keep it short, and focus on things like bad habits, rather than people, which comes too close to cursing. When you are done, put the candle in a holder and light it, cupping your hands around it and chanting:

Candle burn, with fire bright,
Purify me with your light.

Concentrate all your efforts into sending all the things you want gone into the candle. When you feel them gone, relax, and know they are being destroyed. Sit for a few minutes. Now thank the god:

Lord, thank you for your aid in my ritual. May your blessing be upon me. Hail and farewell.

Close as in basic ritual.

New moon

During the new moon it is not customary to perform any kind of magic or ritual. It can be a time of fruitful meditation, and women especially may find it a time of intense psychic activity. This is particularly true if they have their periods then. They may wish to perform divination. Everyone will find that a session looking over the month and evaluating their activities is time well spent.

Women's Mysteries

Another contact with the moon can be made by women at the times of menstruation and ovulation. While some would argue that rituals or meditations for these things should be done at the full and new moon, the best time for the individual woman to do these would be the appropriate points in her own cycle. In *The Wise Wound* (Redgrove and Shuttle, 1986) it is suggested that the menstrual period is accompanied by fantasies and dreams of a dark man who is a lover, because he won't cause pregnancy. This dark man is probably the moon god, since he 'causes' the period.

For the woman who wishes to be pregnant, the time to do a ritual is just before she ovulates, or, if she doesn't know, count 14 days from the last period. On the night, bathe in water to which has been added some rose, myrtle and geranium oil. Then go to a place where you can see the moon (through a window if you can't go outside). Put your hands on your belly, and say:

Moon, father of children, give me a child.

Chant this over and over while visualizing yourself with a baby. When you feel you have raised power, raise your hands to the moon and feel the link between you. Afterwards be sure to ground, and you may find it useful to carry a moonstone, and a rose or blue stone depending on the gender you desire for your child.

To become more attuned to your menstrual time, you may perform the following ritual. Anoint your forehead with a lunar oil (jasmine, lemon, gardenia or coconut). Smear the oil on a red candle and light it. Prepare a drink of some red liquid – wine or grape juice. Raise your hands towards the moon (if you can see it; if not just raise them). Silently concentrate on the image of the moon god, seeing him as if he were before you. Now take up the drink before you and hold it in both hands, meditating on the similarity of cup and womb. Focus on your wish to be more attuned with this mystery. Drink the red liquid, saving a small amount to give the god. Thank him, and ground yourself.

Sun Rituals

Yule (20–21 December)

This festival is dedicated to the reborn sun. As the winter solstice, it is the time of shortest days and longest nights, the darkness that precedes the light. Many Christmas customs can be traced to this mythology.

To decorate for the Yule ritual, use lots of candles, since this is a feast of light. Christmas greenery such as holly, rosemary, bay, pine and cedar would be appropriate for trimmings, as well as any Yule decorations you desire. The tree-top figures of white-clad women would be good images of the goddess. Incenses can be any of the above plants, or frankincense and myrrh. The usual cake and drink will also be needed.

Begin shortly after midnight on the night of the winter solstice. Follow the basic ritual for opening, then light all the candles. Say:

The sun is reborn! The goddess of light is among us once more, the light-bearer returns to the darkened land. At the time of greatest darkness is the seed of light sown. In the birth is the promise of spring to come, warmth and hope. We rejoice in the revitalizing of the sun.

Reflect on times when all has seemed dark around you, and yet you survived to enjoy better times. If things are dark for you now, offer an intention that they will get better, and that you will not lose heart. Say:

Like the goddess of light who must wait to be freed to travel the skies again, so shall I not lose heart, but continue to hope and work for better days. When I lit these candles I affirmed the place of hope in the universe. May all who suffer be likewise inspired by hope, and be freed from their chains of physical or spiritual darkness.

Now offer some of your drink and cake. Then drink some for yourself, after making whatever New Year's resolutions you planned. Ask the goddess for her blessing on your intentions. When you are ready, thank the goddess for her attendance:

Lucia, goddess of returning light, may your rebirth be also a rebirth in my heart. Thank you for gracing my ritual. Hail and farewell!

Finish with closing from basic ritual.

Imbolc (2 February)

This festival is best known as the festival of St Brigit, but more generally the return of the sun maiden from the prison of the hag of winter. Many of the festivals surrounding this time celebrate the waxing light, such as the Irish Catholic practice of blessing candles.

For the Imbolc ritual you will need one white and one black candle. At the beginning of the ritual the black candle should be burning but not the white one. You will also need some sort of serpent effigy, even if only a clay model. Place it next to the black candle. Some snowdrops, or other very early flowers, would be a good symbol of spring's first stirrings. The incense should be floral. Food and drink as usual.

Begin with the opening from the basic ritual, and then face the altar. Say (Carmichael, 1992):

This is the morn of Bride
The queen will come from the mound.
I will not touch the queen
Nor will the queen touch me.

Now blow out the black candle and light the white one. Strike the serpent effigy once and say:

Now is the reign of winter over. The hag of winter is defeated and the goddess of spring victorious. Now the sun may shine and the frozen earth begin to quicken under her warm rays. Blessed be the goddess of the sun!

Offer some food to the goddess, and then feast to celebrate the return of spring. When you are done, thank the goddess and close with the ending from the basic ritual.

SPRING (20–21 MARCH)

The spring and dawn goddess is the focus of this celebration. Having defeated the hag, she brings warmth and fertility to the land.

For the spring ritual you will need candles in spring colours, flowers (preferably daffodils) and eggs that you have dyed red. If you can, buy or make the traditional Ukrainian eggs. This is a ritual best started at dawn at the equinox.

Open with the beginning of the basic ritual. Then stand facing the east, and say:

Beautiful daughter of the sun, we welcome you back from your winter prison. Show your rosy self to us now, as you return trailing flowers in your wake. Gild the sky with your own spring colours. Bring to us fertility again, and the warmth of spring that inspires love.

Make the sign of the quartered circle over the basket of eggs. Say:

With spring comes the egg, symbol of new life, and of wholeness. Life quickens, and the darkness recedes. The forces of life gain in power.

Hold your hands over the eggs, and send the power of fertility into them. See the plants growing, and new litters of animals, the hens laying eggs, the cows suckling their calves. Continue until you feel that you have built up power, feel it tingling in your hands, then send it into the eggs. Rest for a minute after you have done, then stand and say:

Maiden goddess, I thank you. May your powers be manifest everywhere. Blessed be!

To finish, do the closing from the basic ritual, then take the eggs outside and bury them in the earth. If you feel a special need for fertility of mind or body, you should eat one.

Beltane (1 May)

Although it is a fertility festival, Beltane has its solar characteristics, especially among the Balts and Celts. The sun dances at this time in some cultures.

For the Beltane ritual you will need a pan with water in it, and a clear view of the sun. Set up an altar if you wish, or light candles and incense around the pan on the floor. (Be careful not to tip the candles, especially if you're wearing robes.)

Open with the beginning of the basic ritual. Then place your hands around the pan or basin. Say:

On this day of Beltane, the sun rises triumphant in the sky. We salute the sun and its powers of cleansing and healing. This is the day of the sun's dance, when her beauty and colour are shown in all their glory.

As the sun reflects off the water, give the pan a little shake so that the light glimmers across the ceiling and walls of your home.

The goddess is among us! May her radiant presence bring us happiness and prosperity.

Splash the water on your face and hands. If you have any physical ailments, feel them ebbing away. Let the sun-blessed water revitalize you. Stand and offer a little bit of the water to the four quarters, by flicking a drop off your fingers.

Sun, mother of all, bless me on this holy day. As your chariot mounts the skies may my heart rise with you, may I be filled with new strength and hope. Thank you, hail and farewell!

Finish now with closing from the basic ritual. Keep the water in a bottle to use as holy water for saining. You can also cleanse your quartz points with it.

Litha (20–21 June)

The summer solstice is the celebration of the sun at its zenith. Bonfires, rolling burning barrels, and all-night vigils mark the feast of the sun at its strongest.

For the Litha ritual you will need a small crescent to symbolize the moon, and a circle to be the sun, a gold or yellow candle and a silver or white one. Use a summery incense such as rose.

Begin with the opening ritual and then light the gold candle and say:

Lady Sun, you rise over the hills in your chariot drawn by golden horses, shedding your rays over all the worlds. All creation rejoices, you are glad, as you go forth to meet your husband.

Light the silver candle and say:

Lord Moon, you light the darkness to protect your love. Now she comes to meet you, and the sky is lit by your love.

Hold up the crescent and circle.

And now the two grow near, and the marriage of sun and moon commences.

Now hold them so that the circle sits in the crescent.

The sun and moon have joined. All the stars and the fair earth will be their children. Hallowed be their marriage!

Lay down the figures, so that they stay together, on the altar. Now take up your drink and salute the sun and moon, and their children to come. Do the same with your bread or cakes. Put a bit of each into a container or on the ground. Sit and feast the mating of sun and moon. When you have done, reserving the last for the gods, stand and say:

God and goddess, I thank you for your gracious presence at my ritual. May peace and prosperity follow in your wake! Hail and farewell.

Finish with the closing from the basic ritual, then leave the offerings under a bush outside, if it was an indoor ritual.

Lammas (1 August)

This is mainly an agricultural festival, but it marks the beginning of the sun's decline. You will need a loaf of bread, a red candle and a small bowl of rainwater. Open with the beginning from the basic ritual. Then raise your hands to heaven and say:

Gracious Sunna, bless our harvest
The warmth of your loving rays
Called forth the fruit of the earth
And made the harvest good.

Pass your hand over the red candle. Raise your hands again and say:

> Mighty thunderer, maker of rain
> The earth grew fecund in your embrace
> Now see the fulfilment of your love,
> The rain you sent has brought forth the harvest.

Touch the bowl of rainwater. Lower your hands to point at the ground, and say:

> Good mother earth,
> Your golden hair waves in the wind,
> And will feed us through the winter.

Break three pieces off the loaf and put them in the offering bowl, then say:

> One for sun, one for rain, one for grain in store.

Eat some of the bread, and thank the earth and the sky gods for your nourishment. When you are ready thank the gods in your own words, mentioning anything you have to be grateful for in this harvest season. Then close with the form in the basic ritual.

Autumn/Fall (20–21 September)

The autumn/fall equinox sees the day and night equal in length, and the beginning of the moon's half of the year.

For autumn/fall ritual you will need a gold candle and a silver one. Use the opening from basic ritual. Have the gold candle lit. Now say:

> The time of the sun goddess draws to an end. She leaves us as winter begins,
> but will return. Now I celebrate her power for the last time this year.

Close your eyes and reflect on the harvest from this year, and the illuminations or inspirations you have received. When you are ready, blow out the gold candle and light the silver one. Say:

> During the season of darkness, the moon will ride the skies. He is the warrior
> who sails the dark waters, and protects us through the night of winter. May he
> be praised!

Make an offering to the moon god and the power he represents, choosing something you feel to be appropriate. Finish with ending in basic ritual.

Samhain (1 November)

At this time of the year the hag is victorious, and has captured the sun, who remains imprisoned until spring.

For the Samhain ritual, you will need a black candle and a white one, dark cloth for the altar, a serpent effigy and a flameproof container (cauldron, clay bowl). Light the white candle, then do the opening from the basic ritual. Then raise the effigy of the serpent and say:

Once it was the bride of spring who ruled the day. But now winter is nigh and the blue hag of winter is queen over all. The sun shrinks and the raven croaks in the sky and on bare fields.

Blow out the white candle and light the black one.

In the time of the hag it is right that things die. Thus do I show my part in the cycle of life. I lay down these things as sacrifice, since I need them no longer.

Write down things that you wish to be rid of – bad habits, world evils etc. Tear the paper into strips, with one item on each strip. Light them from the black candle and drop them into the flameproof bowl. Watch them burn, and meditate on the changes you are bringing about. Then if you wish you may feast, leaving some for the goddess. When you are ready, hold your hands out and say:

Darksome goddess of wintertime, may you take these things I have destroyed and use them for good. I thank you for your appearance at this ritual, and bid you hail and farewell.

Finish as in the basic ritual.

Special saints' days

Many of the old pagan holidays were attached to saints' days as Christianity made inroads into European life. While the population might have been quite devout, no one ever misses an opportunity to have a party. Also, it may have seemed prudent to keep the old ones happy, even if one wasn't sure they existed. The saints listed below have feasts near or on older holidays. Some of them are even the Christian versions of deities too popular to die.

Brigit

Her day and Imbolc are virtually the same. If you wish to do a ritual honouring her specifically, see page 61 for ideas and traditional practices.

John the Baptist

His festival has taken over many of the old midsummer celebrations. The lighting of bonfires seems to have been the most lasting part of the customary festivities.

Sunniva

Her festival is 8 July, and may be a sun-goddess holy day that survived Christianity. She was buried in a cave when villagers attacked her, a myth of the sun goddess's retreat in winter.

Catherine

Her festival is on 6 November, and involves rolling blazing wheels down hills. This could very well be a form of the retiring of the sun, going down the sky-hill into the darkness of winter. Her chapels are often located on hills that overlook the sea or major highways, making them natural spots for beacons or lighthouses (Hole, 1965).

Nicholas

The feast of this saint (6 December) is also a celebration of Thor in his winter aspect. He rides on a goat, and gives gifts in exchange for fodder and carrots left out for his mount on the eve of his feast.

Lucia

A variant on the celebration described on page 25 would be a good way to celebrate this goddess's day, 13 December.

Thomas

His day is the actual winter solstice, 21 December, and is celebrated by giving alms to the poor; also by saining holy buildings, and dream divination.

Other rituals

Alfblot

It was traditional among the Teutonic peoples to honour the little people during harvest season, to ensure that they would continue to be friendly. In this ritual those connected to the sun, the Alfs, are given offerings. Note that this is a two-person ritual but it can be adapted for one.

For this ritual you will need some milk and honey for offerings, and the decorations should be in white. Begin with the opening from the basic ritual. The priestess raises the god symbol and says:

Great god Freyr, we call you to our rite, ruler of Alfheim, giver of sunlight and fertility, lord of earth.

The priest raises the goddess symbol and says:

Gracious Sunna, glory of elves, warmer of earth and light of the sky, we call you to our rite.

They both say:

Milk and honey we offer to the elves, who are fair and shining helpers of humans. As we harvest the bounty of the earth, and the fruits of our labours, may there be peace between us always.

The priestess pours honey and the priest milk into the offering bowl or pit if the rite is held outside. Now finish with closing from the basic ritual and leave the offerings where they won't be disturbed, or leave the area where the pit is after tidying up.

Healing Ritual

In former times people invoked the moon god for healing of mind and body. This ritual is designed for when you are feeling under the weather or actually ill, and should be used in conjunction with medical care. You will need a bathroom, and some lunar herbs or oils (lemon balm, sandalwood, lemon peel, eucalyptus, willow, calamus) to put in your bath, along with a white candle if you like.

This ritual should be done during a waxing moon, and try to do it in a place where you can see the moon. However, the bath is the important part, as long as the moon is up when you start. Run your bath, add the herbs or oils, and get into it. Have a small healing stone handy.

Face the moon and raise your arms to it. Say:

I call the god of the moon, who renews himself monthly, who is lord of all healing, and ask him to heal me.

Lie back in the water, and visualize your illness washing away. If you're feeling energetic, sit up and slough water off your body to symbolize your intention. When you feel that you have cleansed yourself of negative energy, let the water go. Stand up and chant:

As the moon grows round, so my body is sound.

Keep chanting until you feel sure of what you are saying, because this will make it real. Then thank the moon god for his help, and you're done.

If you are not feeling up to a bath, you can fill a jar of water with the appropriate herbs or oils and leave it in the moonlight. The next night, sprinkle yourself with the water while imagining it healing you.

Appendix

Table 1. Roles of deities in this book

Sun	Dawn	Moon	Twins	Sky	Thunder	Fire
Saule	Auszrine	Menuo	Dieva deli	Dievas	Perkunas	Ugunsmate
Grian	Dér Gréine	Manannan	Emain Macha	Nuada	Taranis	Áine
Sól	Svanhild	Mani	Alcis	Tyr	Thor	Loki
Solnste	Zorya	Myesyats	Cosmas and Damien	Svarog	Perun	Istie
Helios/a	Helen	Men/e	Dioscouroi	Zeus	Zeus	Hestia
Arinitti	Hulla and Mezulla	Kushukh	Sheri and Hurri	ᴅSius	Teshub	?
Arev	Arevhat	Amins	?	Aramazd	Vagahn	Sister Fire
Surya	Suryaa	Soma	Asvins	Dyaus	Paranja	Agni

Table 2. Some suggested correspondences for the deities who appear in the rituals

Deities	Herbs	Colours	Runes	Trees
Sun	juniper	red	sigel	bay
Moon	mugwort	white	lagu	willow
Sky	basil	blue	tyr	ash
Twins	vervain	orange	ehwaz	hazel
Thunder	leek	brown	thorn	oak
Maiden	mint	rose	gyfu	plane
Earth	crocus	green	odal	linden

Table 3. The relations of sun and moon

Sun	Moon
red	white
female	male
hot	cold
blood	semen
fire	water
summer	winter

Ͳhe family of Helios (mothers in brackets)

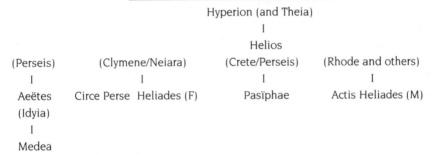

Hyperion (and Theia)
|
Helios

(Perseis)	(Clymene/Neiara)	(Crete/Perseis)	(Rhode and others)
Aeëtes	Circe Perse Heliades (F)	Pasïphae	Actis Heliades (M)
(Idyia)			
Medea			

Glossary

*aswos The PIE word for dawn, found in most names of dawn goddesses.

*dghom The PIE word for earth.

*don-u The PIE word for river.

*dyeus The PIE name for the sky god.

*dyew The PIE word for sky.

functions In Dumézil's (1973) theory of mythology, various deities have certain roles to play within a structure that is consistent across the Indo-European spectrum. These roles correspond to classes in the society that created the deities.

> First function: kingly and priestly.
> Second function: warriors and heroes.
> Third function: producers, farmers, craftspeople.

Indo-Europeans A group of people linked by similarities of language and culture. They spread from India to Ireland, but once shared a common homeland.

Indo-Iranians The original people who became the Indians, Iranians and Scythians.

*me- The PIE root for words like measure, time, month and moon. It can be found in the names of many moon gods.

PIE Proto-Indo-European, the reconstructed language which the first Indo-Europeans presumably spoke before they began to migrate away from each other. An asterisk in front of a word means that it has been reconstructed and appears in no one language.

*sawel The PIE root for words connected to the sun and sun deities.

syncretism The blending together of different myths or deities to make a third thing with qualities of both the originals.

Trifunctional Describing a deity, usually a goddess, who in some way relates to all three *functions*.

Bibliography

Ananikan, M. 1925: Armenian mythology. In *Mythology of All Races*, 1925.

Ann, M. and Imel, D.M. 1993: *Goddesses in World Mythology*. Oxford: Oxford University Press.

Anthony, D.W. 1991: The archaeology of Indo-European origins. *Journal of Indo-European Studies*, vol. XIX.

Anwyl, E. 1906: *Celtic Religion*. London: Constable and Co.

Arans, O.R. and Shea, C.R. 1994: The fall of Elepnor: Homeric Kirke and the folklore of the Caucasus. *Journal of Indo-European Studies*, vol. XXII, nos. 3 and 4.

Arburrow, Y. 1994: *The Enchanted Forest*. Chieveley, Berkshire: Capall Bann Publishing.

Armstrong, E.A. 1958: The *Folklore of Birds*. London: Collins.

Aswynn, F. 1990: *The Leaves of Yggdrasil*. St Paul, Minnesota: Llewellyn.

Balys, J. 1954: *Lithuanian Narrative Folksongs*. Chicago: Draugas Press.

———— 1975: Lithuanian mythology. Latvian mythology. In Leach, 1975.

Bell, R.E. 1991: *Women of Classical Mythology*. Oxford: Oxford University Press.

Benet, S. 1951: *Song, Dance and Customs of Peasant Poland*. London: Dennis.

Beresford Ellis, P. 1992: A *Dictionary of Celtic Mythology*. London: Constable.

Bhattacharji, S. 1970: *The Indian Theogony*. Cambridge: Cambridge University Press.

Bhattacharyya, S. 1953: Religious practices of the Hindus. In Morgan, K. (editor) *The Religions of the Hindus*, New York: The Ronald Press Co.

Biezais, H.: Baltic religion. *Encyclopaedia Britannica Macropaedia*, vol. 18.

Boardman, J. (editor) 1981: *Lexicon Iconographicum Mythologiae Classicae*. Zurich: Artemis Verlag.

Boer, C. 1980: *The Homeric Hymns*. Irving, Texas: Spring Publications.

Bonnefoy, Y. 1991: *Mythologies*. English edition directed by W. Doniger. Chicago and London: University of Chicago Press.

Bord, J. 1976: *Mazes and Labyrinths of the World*. London: Latimer New Dimensions Ltd.

Bord, J. and Bord, C. 1985: *Sacred Waters*. London: Granada Publishing.

Borlase, W.C. 1897: *The Dolmens of Ireland*. London: Chapman Hall.

Boyer, R. 1991 (translated by J. Leavitt): Elements of the sacred among the Germanic and Norse peoples. In Bonnefoy, 1991.

Branston, B. 1993: *The Lost Gods of England*. London: Constable and Co. Ltd.

Bray, O. 1908: *The Elder Edda*. London: Viking Club.

Brewester, H. 1993: *Classical Anatolia*. London: I.B. Taurus Co.

Briffault, R. 1927: *The Mothers*. Woking: George Allen and Unwin.

Burney, C. and Lang, D.M. 1971: *The History of Georgia*. London: The Trinity Press.

Cader, L.L., 1976: *Helen*. Leiden, Netherlands: E.J. Brill.

Caldecott, M. 1988: *Women in Celtic Myth*. Rochester, USA: Destiny Books.

Campbell, J. 1862: *Popular Tales of the West Highlands*. Edinburgh: Edmonston and Douglas.

Carlier, J. 1991 (translated by D. Beauvais): Helios-Selene-Endymion. In Bonnefoy, 1991.

Carlyon, R. 1981: A *Guide to the Gods*. London: Heinemann.

Carmichael, A. 1992: *Carmina Gadelica*. Edinburgh: Floris Books.

Chandler, R. 1979: *The Magic Ring*. London: Faber and Faber.

Charachidzé, G. 1968: *La Système Religieux de la Georgie Païenne*. Paris: François Maspero.

———— 1987: *La mémoire Indo-Européen du Caucase*. Paris: Hachette.

———— 1991a: The religions and myths of the Georgians of the mountains. In Bonnefoy, 1991.

———— 1991b: Near eastern mythology. In Bonnefoy, 1991.

Clarke, D. and Roberts, A. 1996: *Twilight of the Celtic Gods*. London: Blandford.

Clarke, R. 1991: *The Great Queens*. Gerrards Cross: Colin Smythe.

Cohane, J.P. 1973: *The Key*. London: Turnstone Books.

Condren, M. 1989: *The Serpent and the Goddess*. San Francisco: HarperCollins.

Conway, D.J. 1993: *The Ancient and Shining Ones*. St Paul, Minnesota: Llewellyn.

Cook, A.B. 1914: *Zeus, a Study in Ancient Religion*, vol. I. Cambridge: Cambridge University Press.

Cooper, J.C. 1979: *An Illustrated Dictionary of Traditional Symbols*. London: Thames and Hudson.

Cottrell, A. 1979: *Dictionary of World Mythology*. Oxford: Oxford University Press.

Cox, G.W. 1969: *Mythology of the Aryan Nations*, vol. I. Washington: Port.

Coxwell Fillingham, C. 1925: *Siberian and Other Folktales from the Land of the Tsars*. London: C.W. Daniel and Co.

Crossley-Holland, K. 1993: *The Penguin Book of Norse Myths*. London: Penguin.

Crowley, V. 1994: *Phoenix from the Flame*. London: Aquarian.

Dames, M. 1992: *Mythical Ireland*. London: Thames and Hudson.

Danaher, M. 1972: *The Year in Ireland*. Cork: The Mercian Press.

Daniélou, A. 1963: *Hindu Polytheism*. London: Routledge and Kegan Paul.

Dass, A.C. 1984: *Sun-Worship in Indo-Aryan Religion and Mythology*. Delhi: Indian Book Gallery.

Davidson, H.R.E. 1964: *Scandinavian Mythology*. New York: Hamlyn Books.

Davidson, H.R.E. and Gelling, P. 1969: *The Sun Chariot*. New York: Praeger.

Dawkins, R.M. 1953: *Modern Greek Folktales*. Oxford: Clarendon Press.

De Vries, J. 1977 (translated by L. Jospin): *Les Dieux des Celts*. Paris: Payothèque.

Deighton, H.J. 1982: *The 'Weather God' in Hittite Anatolia*. Oxford: BAR International Series.

Dexter-Robbins, M. 1980: The assimilation of pre-Indo-European goddesses into Indo-European society. *Journal of Indo-European Studies*, vol. VIII.

———— 1984: Proto-Indo-European sun maidens and gods of the moon. *Mankind Quarterly*, vol. 25, nos. 1 and 2.

Dineen, Rev. P. 1927: *Irish-English Dictionary*. Dublin: Irish Texts Society.

Downing, C. (translator) 1972: *Armenian Folktales and Fables*. London: Oxford University Press.

Dumézil, G. 1965: *Le Livre des Héros*. Paris: Gallimard.

———— 1970: *Archaic Roman Religion*. London: University of Chicago Press.

———— 1973: *Gods of the Ancient Northmen*. London: University of California Press.

———— 1988: *Mitra-Varuna: An Essay on Two Indo-European Representations of Sovereignty*. New York: Zone Books.

Durdin-Robertson, L. 1990: *The Year of the Goddess*. London: Aquarian.

Durham, M.E. 1928. *Some Tribal Origins, Laws and Customs*. London: George Allen and Unwin.

Eck, D. 1984: *Banares, City of Light*. London: Routledge and Kegan Paul.

Eliade, M. 1987: *Encyclopedia of Religion*. New York: Macmillan.

Elliot, R.W.V. 1959: *Runes*. Manchester: Manchester University Press.

Elwin, V. 1942: *The Agaria*. London: Oxford University Press.

Evans-Wentz, W. 1988: *The Fairy-Faith in Celtic Countries*. Gerrards Cross: Colin Smythe.

Farnell, L.R. 1909: *Cults of the Greek States*. Oxford: Clarendon Press.

Farrar, J. and Farrar, S. 1987: *The Witches' Goddess*. Washington: Phoenix.

———— 1991: *A Witches Bible Compleat*. New York: Magickal Childe.

Faure, P. 1991 (translated by D. White): Crete and Mycenae: problems of mythology and religious history. In Bonnefoy, 1991.

Ferguson, J. 1970: *The Religions of the Roman Empire*. London: Thames and Hudson.

Fischer, E.P. 1979: *Saxo Grammaticus, History of the Danes*, vol. I (edited by H.R.E. Davidson). Cambridge: D.S. Brewer.

Forlong, J. 1906: *Faiths of Man*. London: Bernard Quaritch.

Frazer, J.G. 1926: *The Worship of Nature*. London: Macmillan and Co.

Friedrich, P. 1978: *The Meaning of Aphrodite*. Chicago: University of Chicago Press.

Fries, J. 1993: *Helrunar*. Oxford: Mandrake of Oxford.

Gasparini, E.: Slavic religion. *Encyclopaedia Britannica Macropaedia*, vol. 18.

Gerald of Wales 1982 (translated by J. O'Meara): *Travels in Ireland*. London: Penguin.

Ghosh, S. (translator) 1980: *The Original Yoga*. Delhi: Munshiram Mansharlal.

Gimbutas, M. 1958: Ancient symbolism in Lithuanian folk-art. *Memoirs of the American Folklore Society*, vol. 49.

———— 1963: *The Balts*. London: Thames and Hudson.

———— 1971: *The Slavs*. London: Thames and Hudson.

Gitlin-Emmer, S. 1993: *Lady of the Northern Light*. Freedom, California: The Crossing Press.

Goodison, L. 1989: *Death, Women and the Sun*. London: University of London, Classics Department, Bulletin Supplement 53.

———— 1992: *Moving Heaven and Earth: Sexuality, Spirituality and Social Change*. London: HarperCollins.

Gostelow, M. 1977: *Embroidery of All Russia*. London: Mills and Boon.

Graves, R. 1955: *The Greek Myths*. London: Cassell.

———— (editor) 1968: *New Larousse Encyclopaedia of Mythology*. London: Hamlyn.

Green, M. 1991: *The Sun-Gods of Europe*. Somerset: Hippocrene Press.

Gregory, Lady 1985: *The Blessed Trinity of Ireland*. Gerrards Cross: Colin Smythe.

Griffith, R.T.H. 1991: *The Hymns of the Rig Veda*. Delhi: Motilal Banarsidass Publishers.

Grimal, P. (editor) 1965: *Larousse*. London: Hamlyn.

————— 1987 (translated by B. Blackwell): *The Dictionary of Classical Mythology.* Oxford: Basil Blackwell Ltd.

Grimm, J. 1880 (translated by J.S. Stallybrass): *Teutonic Mythology.* London: Swan Sonnenschein and Co.

Guerber, H.A. 1994: *The Norsemen.* London: Senate.

Guirard, F. 1963 (translated by D. Ames): *Greek Mythology.* London: Hamlyn.

Gundarsson, K. 1993: *Teutonic Religion.* St Paul, Minnesota: Llewellyn.

Gurney, O.R. 1990: *The Hittites.* London: Penguin.

Güterbock, H.G. 1916: Hittite mythology. In Kramer, S.N. (editor) *Mythologies of the Ancient World,* New York: Doubleday.

————— 1950: Hittite religion. In Ferm, V. (editor) *Forgotten Religions,* New York: The Philosophical Library.

Gvelesiani, G. and Javakhishvili, A. no date: *Soviet Georgia.* Moscow: Progress Publications.

Hamkens, L. 1982: Troy towns. *Caerdroia,* no. 9, February.

Harris, J.R. 1906: *The Cult of the Heavenly Twins.* Cambridge: Cambridge University Press.

Hastings, J. (editor) 1980: *Encyclopedia of Religion and Ethics.* Edinburgh: T. and T. Clark.

Haudry, J. 1987: *La Religion Cosmique des Indo-Européens.* Paris: Arché.

Hesiod 1966 (translated by M.L. West): *Theogony.* Oxford: Clarendon Press.

Hinnells, J.R. 1984: *Penguin Dictionary of Religions.* London: Penguin.

Hole, C. 1965: *Saints in Folklore.* London: G. Bell and Sons.

Hollander, L.M. (translator) 1990: *The Poetic Edda.* Austin, Texas: University of Austin.

Holmberg, U. 1925: Finno-Ugric mythology. In *Mythology of All Races,* 1925.

Houwink ten Cate, P.H.J. 1969: Hittite royal prayers. *Numen,* vol. XVI.

Howard, M. 1944: *Angels and Goddesses.* Chieveley, Berkshire: Capall Bann Publishing.

Hubbs, J. 1993: *Mother Russia.* Bloomington: University of Indiana Press.

Hurlstone Jackson, K. 1980: *A Celtic Miscellany.* London: Penguin.

Ions, V. 1967: *Indian Mythology.* London: Hamlyn.

Jackson, N.A. 1994: *The Call of the Horned Piper.* Chieveley, Berkshire: Capall Bann Publishing.

James, E.O. 1959: *The Cult of the Mother Goddess.* London: Thames and Hudson.

Jayne, W.A. 1925: *The Healing Gods of Ancient Civilizations.* New Haven: Yale University Press.

Jennings, P. 1993: *Pathworking.* Chieveley, Berkshire: Capall Bann Publishing.

Jones, P. and Pennick, N. 1995: *A History of Pagan Europe.* London: Routledge and Kegan Paul.

Jordan, M. 1992: *Encyclopedia of Gods.* London: Kyle Cathie Ltd.

Joshi, J.R. 1989: *Minor Vedic Deities.* Ganeshkind: University of Poona.

Jouet, P. 1989: *Religion et Mythologie des Baltes.* Paris: Arché.

Katzenelenbogen, U. 1935: *The Daina.* Chicago: Lithuania News Publishing.

Kennedy, G.C. and Smyth, D. 1989: *Irish Mythology: Visiting the Places.* Killala, Co. Mayo: Morrigan Book Co.

Kerényi, K. 1951: *The Greek Gods.* London: Thames and Hudson.

———— 1991 (translated by M. Stein): *Goddesses of Sun and Moon*. Dallas: Spring Publications.

Kinsley, D.R. 1989: *The Goddesses' Mirror: Visions of the Divine from East and West*. Albany: State of New York University Press.

Knappert, J. 1991: *Indian Mythology*. London: Aquarian.

Kraft, J. 1982: The magic labyrinth. *Caerdroia*, no. 19.

Kühn, H. 1966 (translated by A.H. Brodrick): *The Rock Pictures of Europe*. London: Sidgwick and Jackson.

Lane, E.L. 1971: *Corpus Monumentum Religionis Dei Menis*. Leiden, Netherlands: E.J. Brill.

Lang, D. 1966: *The Georgians*. London: Thames and Hudson.

———— 1980: *Armenia, Cradle of Civilization*. London: George Allen and Unwin.

Laroche, E. 1991a (translated by G. Honigsblum): The pantheons of Asia Minor: the organization of Hittite gods. In Bonnefoy, 1991.

———— 1991b (translated by G. Honigsblum): Tesup and Hebat: the great Hurrian god and his consort. In Bonnefoy, 1991.

———— 1991c (translated by G. Honigsblum): Religions of Asia Minor: definitions and problems. In Bonnefoy, 1991.

Leach, M. 1975: *Funk and Wagnalls Standard Dictionary of Folklore, Mythology and Legend*. London: New English Library.

Lehmann, J. 1977 (translated by J.M. Brownjohn): *The Hittites*. New York: Viking.

Leick, G. 1991: *A Dictionary of Near Eastern Mythology*. London: Routledge.

Lincoln, B. 1986: *Myth, Cosmos and Society*. London: Harvard University Press.

Lindsay, J. 1974: *Helen of Troy*. London: Constable.

Linsell, T. 1992: *Anglo-Saxon Runes*. Pinner, Middlesex: Anglo-Saxon Books.

Logan, P. 1980: *The Holy Wells of Ireland*. Gerrards Cross: Colin Smythe.

———— 1981: *The Old Gods*. Belfast: Appletree Press.

Lurker, M. 1994: *Dictionary of Gods and Goddesses, Devils and Demons*. London: Routledge.

MacCana, P. 1983: *Celtic Mythology*. Feltham, Middlesex: Newnes Books.

MacCrossan, T. 1993: *The Sacred Cauldron*. St Paul, Minnesota: Llewellyn.

MacCulloch, J.A. 1911: *The Religion of the Ancient Celts*. Edinburgh: T. and T. Clark.

———— 1925: Eddic mythology. In *Mythology of All Races*, 1925.

———— 1993: *The Celtic and Scandinavian Religions*. London: Constable.

MacDonald, L. and McSkimming, S. 1992: *Gods of the Celts*. Brodick Scotland: Dalriada Celtic Heritage Society.

Machal, J. 1925: Baltic mythology. In *Mythology of All Races*, 1925.

MacKenzie, D.A. 1994: *India*. Myths and Legends series. London: Senate.

MacQueen, J.G. 1959: Hattian mythology and Hittite monarchy. *Anatolian Studies*, no. 9.

———— 1986: *The Hittites*. London: Thames and Hudson.

Mahé, E. 1992: Le soleil et la lune en le mythologie Caucasienne. In Paris, C. (editor) *Caucasologie et Mythologie Comparée*, Paris: Peeters.

Mallory, J.P. 1992: *In Search of the Indo-Europeans*. London: Thames and Hudson.

Markale, J. 1986: *Women of the Celts*. Rochester, USA: Inner Traditions.

Matthews, C. 1989: *Elements of the Celtic Tradition*. Shaftesbury, Dorset: Element Books.

Matthews, W.H. 1922: *Mazes and Labyrinths*. London: Longman, Green and Co.

McBain, A and MacKenzie, W. 1917: *Celtic Mythology and Religion*. New York: E.P. Dutton.

McCrickard, J. 1987: *Brighde*. Glastonbury: Fieldfare Publications.

———— 1990: *The Eclipse of the Sun*. Glastonbury: Gothic Image Publications.

McNeill, M. 1989: *The Silver Bough*, Vol. I. Edinburgh: Cannongate.

Megus, G. (editor) 1970 (translated by H. Colaclides): *Folktales of Greece*. Chicago: University of Chicago Press.

Mercante, A.S. 1988: *Facts on File World Encyclopedia of Myth and Legend*. New York: Facts on File.

Miles, C.A. 1912: *Christmas: In Ritual and Tradition*. London: T. Fisher Unwin.

Mitchell, S. 1993: *Anatolia* (two volumes). Oxford: Clarendon Press.

Monaghan, P. 1990: *The Book of Goddesses and Heroines*. St Paul, Minnesota: Llewellyn.

———— 1994: O *Mother Sun!* Freedom, California: The Crossing Press.

Motz, L. 1988: The sacred marriage – a study in Norse mythology. In Jazaryery, M.A. and Winter, W. (editors) *Language and Culture*, Berlin: Mouton de Gruyter.

Mueller, M. 1879: *Contributions to the Science of Mythology*. London: Longman and Co.

Mugge, M.A. 1916: *Serbian Folk-songs, Fairy-tales and Proverbs*. London: Drane's.

Munro, J.A.R. 1870: Inscriptions from Mysia. *Journal of Hellenic Studies*, vol. XVII. *Mythology of All Races*. Twelve volumes. London: Harrap, 1925.

Nagy, G. 1979: *The Best of the Acheans*. Baltimore: Johns Hopkins University Press.

New Catholic Encyclopedia. London: McGraw-Hill, 1967.

Newall, V. 1971: *An Egg at Easter*. London: Routledge and Kegan Paul.

Ó Catháin, S. 1995: *The Festival of Brigit*. Dublin: DBA Publications.

O'Flaherty, W.D. 1980: *Women, Androgynes and Other Mythical Beasts*. Chicago: University of Chicago Press.

———— 1981: *The Rig Veda*. London: Penguin.

Oldberg, H. 1988 (translated by S.B. Shrottri): *The Religion of the Veda*. Delhi: Motilal Banarsidass.

Olcott, W.T. 1914: *Sun Lore of All Ages*. London: G.P. Putnam and Sons.

O'Rahilly, T.F. 1984: *Early Irish History and Mythology*. Dublin: Dublin Institute for Advanced Studies.

Otten, H. 1969: *The Religion of the Hittites*. Edited by C.J. Bluker and G. Widengren. Leiden, Netherlands: E.J. Brill.

Pandey, D.P. 1989: *Surya: Iconographic Study of the Indian God*. Delhi: Primal Publications.

Parrinder, E.G. 1980: *Sex in the World's Religions*. London: Sheldon.

———— 1981: A *Dictionary of Non-Christian Religions*. Amersham, Buckinghamshire: Hulton Educational Publishers.

Pennick, N. 1989: *Practical Magic in the Northern Tradition*. London: Aquarian.

———— 1990: *Mazes and Labyrinths*. London: Hale.

———— 1992: *Rune Magic*. London: HarperCollins.

Persson, A. 1972: *The Religion of Prehistoric Greece*. Berkeley: University of California Press.

Petrovitch, W.M. 1914: *Hero-tales of the Serbians*. London: Harrap.

Pettazoni, R. 1956 (translated by H.T. Rose): *The All-knowing God*. London:

Methuen.

Pinsent, J. 1969: *Greek Mythology*. London: Hamlyn.

Puhvel, J. 1970: Aspects of equine functionality. In *Myth and Law among the Indo-Europeans*, Berkeley and Los Angeles: University of California Press.

———— 1987: *Comparative Mythology*. Baltimore: Johns Hopkins University Press.

Ralston, W.R.S. 1872: *The Songs of the Russian People*. London: Ellis and Green.

———— 1977: *Russian Folk-tales*. New York: Arno Press.

Ranke, K. (editor) 1966 (translated by L. Baumann): *Folktales of Germany*. London: Routledge and Kegan Paul.

Redgrove, P. and Shuttle, P. 1986: *The Wise Wound*. New York: Bantam.

Reeder, R. 1975: *Russian Folk Lyrics*. Bloomington: University of Indiana.

Rees, A. and Rees, B. 1991: *Celtic Heritage*. London: Thames and Hudson.

Renfrew, C. 1987: *Archaeology and Language*. London: Jonathan Cape.

Rice, T. 1957: *The Scythians*. London: Thames and Hudson.

Rolleston, T.W. 1994: *Celtic Myths and Legends*. London: Senate.

Ross, A. 1992: *Pagan Celtic Britain*. London: Constable. (First published in 1967 by Routledge and Kegan Paul.)

Rustaveli, S. 1912 (translated by M. Scott): *The Man in the Panther's Skin*. London: Royal Asiatic Society.

Rydberg, V. 1889 (translated by R.B. Anderson): *Teutonic Mythology*. London: Swan Sonnenschein and Co.

Salia, K. 1983 (translated by K. Vivian): *History of the Georgian Nation*. Paris: N. Selia.

Sandys, J.E. 1915: *The Odes of Pindar*. London: Heinemann.

Savill, S. 1977: *Pears' Cyclopaedia of Myths and Legends, Book Two: Western and Northern Europe, Central and Southern Africa*. London: Pelham Books.

Sawyer Lord, P. and Foley, D.J. 1971: *Easter the World Over*. Philadelphia: Chilton.

Schilling, R. 1991 (translated by D. Beauvais): Diana. In Bonnefoy, 1991.

Schmitz, L. 1884: Aega. In Smith, W. (editor) *Dictionary of Greek and Roman Mythology*, London: Taylor and Walton.

Schoeps, H.-J. 1967: *The Intelligent Person's Guide to the Religions of the World*. London: Victor Gollancz.

Segal, L. 1994: *Straight Sex: The Politics of Pleasure*. London: Virago Press.

Simek, R. 1993 (translated by A. Hall): *Dictionary of Northern Mythology*. Cambridge: D.S. Brewer.

Singh, M. 1993: *The Sun in Art*. London: Thames and Hudson.

Stewart, R.J. 1981: *The Waters of the Gap*. Bath: Bath City Council.

———— 1990: *Celtic Gods, Celtic Goddesses*. London: Blandford.

Stokes, W. 1895: The prose tales in the Rennes Dindsenchas. *Revue Celtique*, no. 16.

Stone, M. 1979: *The Paradise Papers*. London: Virago Press.

Stoneman, R. 1991: *Greek Mythology*. London: Aquarian.

Sturluson, S. 1987 (translated by A. Faulkes): *Edda*. London: David Campbell Publishers.

Sunflower 1990: The path of the solar priestess. In Matthews, C. (editor) *Voices of the Goddess: A Chorus of Sybils*, London: Aquarian.

Surmelian, L. 1968: *Apples of Immortality*. London: George Allen and Unwin.

Thorpe, B. 1832: *Northern Mythology*. London: Edward Lumely.

Toulson, S. 1981: *The Winter Solstice*. London: Jill Norman and Hobhouse.

Tyrell, W.B. 1984: *Amazons: A Study in Athenian Mythmaking*. London: Johns Hopkins University Press.

Van der Meer, L.B. 1987: *The Bronze Liver of Piacenza*. Amsterdam: J.C. Geiber.

Varenne, J. 1991: The Indo-Europeans. In Bonnefoy, 1991.

Velius, N. 1989 (translated by D. Tekoriene): *The World Outlook of the Ancient Balts*. Vilnius: Minits Publishing.

Vernaleken, T. 1889: *The Land of Marvels*. London: Swan Sonneschein and Co.

Ward, D. 1967: Solar mythology and Baltic folksongs. In Wilgus, D. and Sommer, C. (editors) *Folklore International*, Hatboro: Folklore Association Ltd.

———— 1968: *The Divine Twins: An Indo-European Myth in Germanic Tradition*. Berkeley: University of California Press.

Warner, E. 1985: *Heroes, Monsters, and Other Worlds from Russian Mythology*. London: Peter Lowe.

Watts, A. 1971: *Erotic Spirituality: The Vision at Konarak*. New York: Collier Books.

Webster, G. 1986: *The British Celts and their Gods under Rome*. London: Batsford.

West, M.L. 1975: *Immortal Helen*. Castle Cary, Somerset: Castle Cary Press.

Wilkins, E. 1969: *The Rose-garden Game*. London: Gollancz.

Willets, R.F. 1962: *Cretan Cults and Festivals*. London: Routledge and Kegan Paul.

Williams, A.V.J. 1928: *Zoroastrian Studies*. New York: Columbia University Press.

Znayenko, M. 1980: *The Gods of the Ancient Slavs*. Columbus, Ohio: Slavica.

Index

Page numbers in **bold** refer to the illustrations

DATE DUE

9-22 99			
10/28/99			
AP 15 '08			